The Ultimate ESL Teaching Manual

By Andromeda Jones

Printed in the United Kingdom
www.bilinguanation.com

Publisher's Cataloging-in-Publication data
Jones, Andromeda.
The Ultimate ESL Teaching Manual/ Andromeda Jones.

1. English Language Teaching. 2. Teaching English without text-books. 3. Oral agility.

Contents

Introduction

English is the most studied foreign language in the world. In fact, an article published by the Washington Post in April 2015 estimated that there were more than 1.5 billion learners worldwide. Its surge in popularity is easy to understand; English is the language of the Internet, technology, aviation and international business. Nowadays a country's modernity is not just judged on its government and infrastructure but also on the level of English of its citizens. This has left a quarter of the world clamouring to join the conversation and English language teachers, and better yet, *great* English language teachers have never been in more demand.

Why should you be the best?

So, you're thinking about becoming an English teacher. Maybe this is the beginning of a lifelong vocation or maybe it's a ticket to a few years of travel and adventure. Whatever your reasons, the experience will be more fun and less stressful if you *really* know what you are doing.

Teaching is a hugely rewarding profession; students are putting their present and future careers in your hands and their gratitude for clear, well-researched lessons will leave you with a sense of well-being even after the longest days.

Likewise, students pay a lot for their classes and so teachers who try to 'wing-it' with only a surface knowledge of the grammar are quickly sniffed out, leading to some red-faced situations when you can't answer a question.

Performance related pay

Most language academies in a given area will pay roughly the same. *Good* English teachers, however, are hard to come and so can charge top prices for private lessons. Moreover, in the age of the Internet, language learning sites are popping all the time where teachers set their own rates. How much a teacher charges depends on how highly they are ranked by their students. I've seen highly ranked teachers charge double that of their peers and still be booked for just as many classes. As with anything else, you can charge a high price for quality.

What does it take to be the best?

Here's the secret; you don't need any special equipment, expensive books or piles of worksheets to produce a great class. In fact, often the less you have the *better* the class is.

Why is this?

Imagine you have booked a session with a personal trainer at your gym. The trainer is very helpful and carries the mat and all the weights over when you arrive. When it's time for the step aerobics, he takes the weights from your hands, puts them in the cupboard and brings over the step. The trainer may think he is providing a great service but actually he is impeding your progress. Picking up equipment and putting it back is part of the exercise and his 'help' means that you will walk out of the session weaker than if he had not lifted a finger.

The same is true with language learning. I have seen many well-intentioned but ultimately ineffective teachers spend hours on the net looking for verb tables and vocabulary lists to hand to their class. The students may say thank you but this information will never transfer itself to their brains because the teacher has just done all the heavy lifting for them.

Language learning is hard, requiring hours of dedication and repetition. Information handouts deny the student their first step to really understanding the content by writing it out themselves. You need a verb table? Draw one as a class. Don't volunteer information; make them work for it by answering your questions. If they are wrong, correct them – we learn more from our mistakes than from the things we get right.

In this method the conduit for learning is you, the teacher. Your voice, ideas, knowledge and cleverly directed questions together with their hard work is what is going to make this language stick, which is why the best lessons happen with the sparsest resources.

The tools for teaching English: The benefits of the 'no text book' method

No matter what publishers say, text books are not the best way to teach English. You didn't learn your native language bent over a book, you learned it through speaking. Some academies require teachers to teach from their preferred text books (often earning a sales commission as part of it). Even if this is the case, the text book (typically 120-150 pages long) won't provide enough material for the whole course. Because you care about your students you owe it to them to provide supplementary material to drill in those grammar points and get them talking. This manual provides exactly that.

If you belong to a more enlightened academy, or if you've decided to go it alone, then the only resources you need are this manual, some picture cards that you can find in any good toyshop and some small slips of paper and paperclips. If you're teaching a large class you'll need a black or whiteboard to model the grammar and for private lessons, a notebook and pen.

And that's it.

The picture cards are not for vocabulary, but rather half a dozen grammar games that I will show you in the following chapter. The slips of paper are endlessly useful for things like:

a) Vocabulary lessons: Students understand so much better when they can play, reshuffle and categorise words written on loose pieces of paper (they write the words by the way, not you – make them work for everything). At the end of the session you can also collect them up and reuse for the next class.

b) Situations for simple roleplays.

c) Questions for speaking activities.

d) Games.

The book contains drills and speaking activities to cover all grammar points from complete beginner to upper advanced student level. It also contains lists of words (known as lexical sets) to cover all main vocabulary points. In addition, you will find great ways to ease your students into the lesson (Starters) and end on a high note (Finishers) as well as games, roleplays and homework resources.

What, this book teaches you how to teach *every* grammar point?

Yes, why not? In my years of teaching I have taught all the grammar points covered in a standard ESL (English as a Second Language) syllabus in addition to many more covering the finer details for advanced students who want to know everything the language has to offer. As a result, this book contains drills, activities and speaking practices that you wouldn't find in the range (typically five to six books) of a traditional English text book publisher.

How this book is designed

This book uses the ESL terms Beginner, A1 (slightly better than beginner), A2 (pre-intermediate), B1 (intermediate), B2 (upper-intermediate), C1 (advanced) and C2 (upper-advanced).

The first part provides a step-by-step guide of how to teach beginners up to lower A2 level. I have set the information out in this way as it is important to teach beginners in a certain order or they will get confused.

The second part tackles the grammar from A2 to C2 level but instead of writing in order I have grouped them together in blocks of tenses such as the past, the future, adverbs and modifiers and so on. I have structured it this way to make it easy for the teacher to reference. Obviously the teacher should not teach the past tenses one after another. You must pick and choose, moving from past to future, to modal verbs and back again depending on the level of your class.

The beauty of this method is that once students reach A2 level it is the teacher who decides the topics depending on the needs of their students.

Part three 'The Details' are for students of at least a B1 level who want to learn the finer details of English grammar. Many of the lessons here you will not find in traditional text books, boosting your value as a teacher and your potential earning power.

After the grammar chapters you will find Question Practice, an often overlooked skill in language learning and then the Vocabulary chapter with all the lexical sets you would expect, and more with a special chapter at the end just for business classes.

Finally you will find Starters and Finishers to help you begin and end your lesson as well as games, extra Games and Speaking Activities and Homework resources and at the very back pictures for grammar practice.

What this book is not for

Classroom control: If you have an unruly class there are plenty of resources on the web. It is not covered, however, in this book.

Exams: As each examination body has their own system this book is not for exam preparation (although it can help to drill the grammar and vocabulary, obviously). Each body has resources online.

Young children: While you can use these lessons for teenagers (they work very well) they are not suitable for young children as the drills often require logic beyond their capabilities.

The basics of teaching

Before our first class it is important you know at least a little of the technique of teaching.

The importance of repetition

How long does it take you to learn something new? The answer is longer than you think. When learning words, in my experience, a student needs to see and repeat a word from five to twenty times before it sticks and so teaching a lexical set once and never repeating it is a waste of everyone's time. The same is true for grammar. At the beginning of each lesson spend 10 minutes going through what you did last lesson and test your students on their knowledge. If they did well, then move on. If they didn't do well, spend more time on it. Even if your students seem to know the point well go back to it a few months later to review.

Eliciting

When I did my CELTA (Certificate in English Language Teaching to Adults) my trainer gave me a very valuable piece of advice and that is: never try to 'teach' a language point, instead highlight it and help your students try to make sense of it in their minds through eliciting.

Eliciting basically means, instead of *giving* the information, extract it from your students through questions.

For example you write 'She has eaten an apple today.' With experience you could easily explain the tense and the negative ('she hasn't eaten...') and the question version of this sentence but you would leave no way of knowing:

a) Whether your students understood what you said.
b) If they could produce a similar sentence themselves.

And so, instead of giving information, ask questions such as what is the tense? What is the negative? And the question? Why is there 'an' before 'apple' and not 'a'? Give me another sentence in this tense?

By walking your students through each language point in this way they do the work –meaning they are better able to memorise the content, while you will know whether they understand and can tackle any confusion.

Controlled speaking practice: What is a drill?

As stated before, the conduit for this method is the teacher. A drill is either a question or statement carefully designed to get the student to reproduce the grammar point you are studying. Getting students to repeat the words replicates in a shorter space of time how they learnt their native language when they were children. This is known as 'controlled speaking practice' and it is the best way to drill the language into their minds. The drill can either be asked teacher to student or student to student. Every grammar point contains 12 drills to get you started. Once you understand the content I encourage you to write more.

Freer speaking practice: roleplays and question activities

After drills you must allow your students time to practice the point themselves. The best way to do this is in pairs either through roleplays (simple situations where students act out a part) or question activities (students ask each other questions on the topic). This part of the lesson is known as freer speaking practice rather than free speaking practice because it is very important that your students make sentences with the grammar point they are studying and do not go off on a tangent.

How to produce a fantastic roleplay

I have seen many great roleplays fall flat because again the teacher has given too much information stifling the individual's creativity and freedom. The best roleplays are two lines long; a sparse canvas from which students can create their own mini-play. For this to work, however, you must set the scene. Ask students to brainstorm the vocabulary and grammar they need and write a few prompts, then let them fly.

Pictures

Pictures are a fantastic way to provoke a conversation. At the back of this book you'll find many and more on this book's accompanying www.eslteachermanual.com. However, I encourage you to collect more.

The structure of a great lesson

Great lessons do not come out of thin air, they are planned. Thankfully with the help of this book you don't have to spend too much time on it – but there is a pattern to follow. The best teachers spend about 30% of their time on drills and 30% on freer speaking practices. The final 30% is on activities such as starting and finishing the class, reviewing the last class and homework. In a 1.5 hour lesson I usually cover at least two grammar points or a vocabulary point followed by a grammar point that I can team together to form a great roleplay. Never introduce two vocabulary points in one lesson, this is too much.

A typical lesson looks like this:

5 minutes: Easy Starter activity.

10 minutes: Content of last lesson reviewed (perhaps some drilling).

10 minutes: Introduction of grammar or vocabulary point.

10 minutes: Controlled speaking practice of above grammar or vocabulary point.

15 minutes: Freer speaking practice of above point, including the preparation work before.

5 minutes: Give and hand back homework. Deal with questions.

10 minutes: Introduction of second grammar (easier) point or review of an old grammar point.

5 minutes: Controlled speaking practice of second point.

15 minutes: Freer speaking practice of above point, including the preparation work before.

5 minutes: High energy finishing activity or game.

In addition, you can substitute the second grammar point for a game, debate or other speaking activity.

Classroom layout

It is important that you design a classroom layout that is conducive to speaking. For small to medium sized classes I usually seat students around a large table with any props in the middle. For larger classes I suggest seating students in a large semi-circle and breaking it up to make smaller circles for the speaking practice. Never allow your students to converse shoulder to shoulder, this is completely unnatural. Get them to turn their chairs around to face each other.

Language terminology
Here is a brief guide to some of the terminology.

Noun: This is the name of something like 'cat', 'house' or 'bird'.

Verb: This is the action commonly preceded by 'to' such as 'to run', 'to cry' or 'to grow.'

Adjective: This is a description of something and is always preceded by the verb 'to be' such as 'quiet', 'tall', 'French' and 'green'.

Adverb: These modify a verb, an adjective or another adverb to expresses how, when or where something happens such as 'quickly', 'surprisingly', 'here', 'there', 'often' or 'tomorrow'.

Preposition: A word that goes after the verb and before a noun to provide the necessary details to the sentence. There are over 80 prepositions but common ones include 'in', 'on', 'at', 'between', 'under', 'below', 'above', 'up', 'down' and 'of'.

Subject pronoun: These are: I, you, he, she, it, we, you (plural) and they. They indicate the person or thing that is doing the action in a sentence.

Object pronoun: These are: me, you, him, her, it, our, you (plural) and them. They indicate the person or thing that is receiving the action.

Auxiliary verbs: These make the question and negative in a sentence. The most common are 'do' ('Do you like cats?') 'to be' ('Is she French?') 'can' ('Can they drive?') and 'have' ('Have you spoken to your mother today?').

Modal verbs: This is a type of auxiliary verb that expresses necessity or possibility such as must, should, may, might, would and will.

Question words: Otherwise known as interrogative pronouns these are what, which, who and whose. Under the 'question word' banner I also include when, where, how, how many, how much and how often. Write these words on the board before any speaking activity to give your students ideas for questions.

Part I

1. Beginners to A2

1.1 To be verb

It can be pretty daunting to walk into a room of people with zero knowledge of English. Fortunately, this doesn't happen often – in most cultures English is the primary second language taught in schools meaning that the majority of your students will have had some contact with English in their life, even if at this moment they don't remember it.

Whether they are 'reacquiring' English or starting from scratch I always start the same way – with 'to be' verb.

This may seem strange; it may seem more logical to start with introducing yourself, or days of the week, or countries, but 'to be' is the base block for all of these sentences. For example,

'My name *is* John', 'They *are* Spanish', 'It *is* Tuesday'.

Starting out

Vocabulary: Classroom Objects

To keep everything simple start with 'It is...' Spread out some everyday objects on a table; pens, pencils, cups, books, a bottle of water, a mobile phone and so on. Pick up an object and say slowly and clearly 'It is a pen'. Gesture for your students to repeat what you have said and write it on the board.

Pick up other objects and do the same, each time getting your students to repeat you. Then pick up one of the used objects and either point or smile at a strong student. Shake the object with a look in your eye that says 'What is it?' Your student should understand and say unprompted 'It is a pen.'

Do this a few times with other students and then pick up an object, let's say a pen, and ask 'Is it a cup?' Elicit 'No' from the class and write on the board, 'No, it is not a cup.' Underline 'is not', make a shortening gesture with your hands and say 'contraction'. Rub out the 'is not' and put 'isn't'.

The 'Is not' vs 'isn't' debate

English is a strange and wonderful language, we use contractions when many other languages don't, therefore your students will find 'isn't' complicated. However, I still advocate teaching it early as 'isn't' and 'aren't' are commonly used. Just remind your students that they stand for 'is not' and 'are not'.

Making questions

Already we're on to the big stuff! Learners find making questions one of the hardest things about English. The reason is word order; we reverse the subject pronoun (I, you, he, she, it, we, you, they) and the verb.

Let me give you some examples:

Affirmative	Question
It is a pen	Is **it** a pen?
They are French	Are **they** French?
He can swim	Can **he** swim?
She has eaten a banana	Has **she** eaten a banana?

Whether they find it difficult or not, it is something your students have to learn, and fast, so practice it from your first lesson.

They have already heard the 'Is it a pen?', 'Is it a cup?' question several times during this exercise. Highlight the word order by writing the affirmative sentence and its corresponding question on the board. Underline where the order reverses. Now hold up an object and say to your strongest student 'Is it a pen?' They will answer. Now gesture for them to ask the same question to another student. If they get it wrong, point and cross your hands over one another in a big gesture to indicate word order. Get another student to pick up a different object from the table. Ask them to make a question by underlining the question mark on the board. Go around the class like this.

Practice negative answers also, by picking up objects, let's say a cup, and ask 'Is it a dog?' Smart students will start to do this for you with their own questions.

Going plural

Once students have a good idea of 'it' and the singular, move on to plural. This time pick up two pens and say 'They are pens'. Write the sentence on the board. Continue round the class in the same way as before. Ask students to pick up two of an object and say unprompted, 'They are cups.'

Now move on to negative. Pick up two pencils (let's say) and ask 'Are they books?' Elicit 'No'. And write on the board 'No, they are not books.' Show the contraction: rub out 'are not' and write 'aren't'.

Don't say 'Are *these* pens?' It may sound more natural but 'these' is a whole other grammar point and will get you into a load of trouble at this early stage.

Highlight word order and practice questions in the same way. Get students to pick up objects on the table and ask questions unprompted.

When to use 'a/an': The indefinite article

Introducing plurals means you will now start hearing this mistake 'They are a pens'. You now need to explain about the indefinite article.

The indefinite article is 'a' or 'an'. They are placed before all singular nouns such as a pen, a dog or a house. They are never used before names; you cannot say 'Here is a Sophie', even if she was one of many Sophies in the room.

They are never used before plural nouns. Therefore 'They are a pen' or 'They are a dogs' is impossible and you must drill this mistake out of your students immediately. 'A' precedes nouns which begin with a consonant and 'an' nouns which begin with vowels such as 'an apple', 'an insect', 'an orange'.

The meaning of the indefinite article 'a' and definite article 'the'

'A' refers to one of a group of things, or not one thing in particular. For example, 'Pass me *a* book' refers to one book of many and you really don't care which one. If you wanted a specific book you would say 'pass me *the* book.' 'The' is known as the definite article. It means 'the only one that I am referring to at the moment.' For example, 'Speak to the teacher' means not any teacher but rather the one that I want. 'Speak to a teacher' means speak to one of the group, I don't care which.

But 'a' and 'the' are obvious, right?

Well, no. While most European languages have articles, they are not used in the same way (and Russian doesn't have them at all) and therefore must be taught. In some languages 'a' and 'one' are the same word and so you must highlight the difference. 'One' refers to quantity while 'a' to one of a group.

It would be impossible to explain this in detail to your students at this stage. Write a singular sentence with 'a' before the noun and a big tick to show correct and a plural sentence with a big cross where the 'a' would be to show 'no a'.

Introducing I, you, he, she

Vocabulary: Boy, girl, man, woman, children. Well-known nationalities such as French, German, Spanish, British, American. Common adjectives to describe people: Tall, short, noisy, quiet, relaxed, stressed.

Write on the board:

I	Am
You	Are
She	Is
He	Is

Underline the verbs and write at the bottom 'to be verb.' Now write:

My name is Mark (or whatever is your name)

I am British (or whatever is your nationality)

I am (your emotion or characteristic)

Now ask your students to do the same in their notebooks. When they have finished ask them one by one to tell you what they have written. As Student A is introducing themselves stop them periodically, point to Student B and ask them, 'What is she?' Elicit, 'Is she French?' or 'She is from France,' depending on the question.

Now point back to Student A and say to Student B, 'Tell them.' Elicit, 'You are French,' 'You are from France.' Do this until everyone has practiced I, you, he and she. Do not linger on the name function. Teach them 'my' to introduce themselves but do not go into 'his' and 'her' unless absolutely necessary as this is too complicated at this stage.

1.2 Prepositions of place
Vocabulary: On, in, in front of, behind, next to, under, between and where.

Place a pen <u>on</u> a book and ask the class 'Where is the pen?' Elicit, 'It is <u>on</u> the book.' Now place it <u>in</u> the book and elicit 'It is <u>in</u> the book.' Do this until you have covered all the prepositions. For 'between' place the pen between two books. Now give the pen and book to a student and ask them to go through the same process, asking the class 'Where is the pen?' When a student answers, ask the student holding the pen whether it is correct. Do this activity for five minutes every few lessons for at least six weeks.

1.3 Basic adjectives
Vocabulary: Building, person, tree, house, city, country, dog (and other animals as needed).

Print out some landscape and people scenes and ask your students to describe them. In many cases your students will already know some adjectives, add to their knowledge with the list below:

Big/small, quiet/noisy, fast/slow, tall/short, old/new, stressed/relaxed, dark/light, easy/difficult, hard/soft, cheap/expensive, young/old, new/old, far/near, high/low, good/bad, rich/poor, clean/dirty, hot/cold, wet/dry, ugly/pretty, tired, happy/sad.

Using the answers introduce: 'We', 'you (plural)', 'they' + to be. For example:

Tom: The buildings are tall.

Teacher: And with subject pronoun? (Teacher underlines 'they' on the board)

Tom: They are tall.

Teacher: And the class Tom?

Tom: 'We are tall.'

Next elicit the negative, 'The buildings are not tall' and contraction, 'The buildings aren't tall' and the question, 'Are the buildings tall?'

Freer speaking practice
Pairs' activity 'Describing a photo': Tell your students to ask each other questions about the pictures. Get them also to use more personal pronouns by relating the question to their partner. For example:

Tom: 'The mountain is cold.'

Sarah: 'And you?'

Tom: 'I am not cold.'

Sarah: 'And your family?'

Tom: 'Yes, they are cold.'

This repetition is the best way to practice 'to be' verb.

Adding modifiers
Modifiers change the strength of adjectives. Write the most common in a cline like this:

Very

Quite

Not very

'Really' is also another very popular modifier but for now let's keep it simple as although you can say something is 'not very big' you can't say it is 'not really big' which will cause confusion.

Take an adjective that applies to you, for example 'short' and elicit whether you are 'very short,' 'quite short' or 'not very short'. Use gestures to illustrate your point. Then elicit whether it is 'very hot outside,' 'quite hot' or 'not very hot'.

Controlled speaking practice
Do this until they understand and then in pairs get them to ask each other questions about their family. For example:

Tom: 'Is your father tall?'

Sarah: 'Yes, he is quite tall. And your father?'

Tom: 'No, he is not very tall.'

1.4 Introducing yourself
It may sound strange not to include introducing yourself lessons earlier but that is because it not as easy as it first appears.

a) Possessive adjectives
To introduce someone else requires the word 'his' or 'her'. These are possessive adjectives and something students often struggle to get right. The list is as follows:

Subject pronoun	Possessive adjective
I	My
You	Your
He	His
She	Her
It	Its
We	Our
You	Your
They	Their

Write on the board, 'My name is (and your name),' they will recognise it from previous 'to be' lessons. Elicit the question: 'What is your name?'

Ask your students to introduce themselves also. As they do so, ask other members of the class 'What is *his* name?' and elicit 'His name is...' 'Her name is...' When they are comfortable with this introduce 'Their names are...' by asking Student A to recount the names of two classmates.

b) The alphabet and spelling your name

Here is a good time to introduce the alphabet. Some teachers use phonetic symbols but if your students have never seen these before you'll spend half of the trimester teaching them this instead of English. Instead I use vowel sounds which, if your students speak a European language, they should understand.

Write each letter on the board, pronounce it clearly and write the vowel sound next to it (see below).

A – ai, B – bi, c – si, d – di, e – I, f – ef, g – ge, h – eich, I – ai, j – 'DJ', k – kei, l – el, m – em, n – en, o – on, p – pi, q – kiu, r – ar, s – es, t – ti, u – iu, v – vi, w – double u, x – ex, y – guay, z – zed

Controlled speaking practice: The alphabet game

Divide your students into teams. The teacher says the name of a country and selects a team which must spell back the name of the nationality. The other students must write what Team A say letter by letter. If Team A correctly spells the nationality they receive two points. The other teams who write exactly the letters Team A say receive one point. The winner is the team with the most points. Make sure that everyone in the team gets a chance to spell.

Once your students are comfortable with the alphabet get them to ask each other's names and how to spell them.

c) Age

The next language point is age. Write on the board 'I am (and your age)'. Elicit the question 'How old are you?'

Get your students to ask each other their ages. Periodically stop them to practice more personal pronouns by pointing to a student and asking 'How old is *she or he*?' Elicit the answer with 'she is...' Or 'He is...'

d) Country and origin

Write on the board, 'I am from (and your country)'. Elicit the question 'Where are you from?' Putting the preposition at the end of the question probably won't come easily to your students and so highlight the word order.

Get your students to ask each other where they are from (their countries and towns). If they are all from the same place introduce some celebrities. For example, 'Where is Tom Cruise from?'

Again periodically stop the conversation and ask 'Where is he or she from?' Elicit an answer with 'He or she is from...'

Putting it all together: Name, age and origin

By now everyone will know each other's names, ages and origins and so in the middle of the table place slips of paper with the names, age and nationalities of famous people. In pairs tell your students to ask and answer questions about them including how to spell their names.

1.5 This and that, these and those

Vocabulary: Book, dictionary, scissors, sunglasses, pencil, pen, notebook, mobile, water bottle.

These prepositions are simple to learn but take practice to get right every time.

How to teach it

For this activity your students must be sitting around a table. Place some objects near to different students.

Write on the board: 'this' and 'that', 'these' and 'those'. Explain that the first set of words are for singular objects and the second for plural.

Hold a pencil and say, 'This is a pencil.' Then place it just out of reach and say 'That is a pencil'. Elicit or explain that if you are holding an object or it is close to you (within an arm's reach) it is 'this.' Otherwise it is 'that.' Go around the table, point to the objects at random and elicit what they are. Remember to choose a student that is near to an object and another that is further away to elicit a 'this' and a 'that.'

Now pick up two pencils and elicit 'These are pencils,' then place them just out of reach and say 'Those are pencils.' Explain that 'these' are again for things that you hold or are within reach and 'those' are for things that are further away.

Add a second pen, pencil, dictionary and so on next to the original and then point to them at random and elicit from your student whether they are 'these' or 'those.' Use a pair of sunglasses and scissors to illustrate that a single object can be plural.

Do this activity for five minutes every three to four lessons during the first six weeks.

1.6 Numbers

Teach numbers periodically, twenty at a time until you reach 100. Each time write the number on the board and next to it the pronunciation. Ask your students to repeat them as a class.

To practice zero to ten ask your students to write a ten digit fake telephone number and dictate it to the class. Their classmates must write the numbers they hear and the winner is the student who gets the most correct.

1.7 Time

Once your students know at least zero to 25 you can teach them the time. Begin by writing 6.00am on the board and elicit how to say it using 'o'clock' ('It is six o'clock'). Use the 24 hour clock to avoid confusion. Progress to 6.30 ('It is half past six'), 6.15 ('It is quarter past six'). Next go on to the numbers in the 'past' half of the clock and then onto the 'to' numbers which are more difficult.

Don't teach this all in one go but in two or three 10 minute activities over a couple of classes. Once they have the concept, practice periodically by writing random times on the board. Push them by asking whether it's in the morning, afternoon, evening or at night.

1.8 There is and there are

Vocabulary: House and furniture such as bedroom, bathroom, living room, kitchen, dining room, garage, bed, bath, sofa, coffee table, shelves, wardrobe/closet. Left and right.

We use 'there is' and 'there are,' with nouns. It is a grammar point best taught with furniture vocabulary as it is commonly used to describe rooms.

How to teach it

As a class, brainstorm house vocabulary. Most students will know something, so fill in any gaps.

Next write on the board, 'There is a bed in the bedroom' and elicit or explain its meaning ('there is' is plus singular noun). Elicit the negative, 'There is not a bed in the room' and with contraction, 'There isn't a bed in the room,' and the question, 'Is there a bed in the room?' Like all questions the subject and the verb reverse so make this clear.

Next write 'There are four chairs in the dining room' and elicit the meaning ('there are' is for plural nouns). Elicit the negative, 'There are not chairs in the room' (with contraction, 'there aren't chairs in the room') and the question, 'Are their chairs in the room?'

Really, here you should be using the word 'any' but this will confuse students at this stage.

Now as a class, go through the house picture again and use 'there is and are' plus prepositions of place to describe the furniture. For example, 'There is a coffee table in front of the sofa', or 'There are shelves next to the TV.'

Now place objects or pictures of objects on the table (you can use your picture cards here) and ask your students to describe what they see. Make sure to ask plenty of incorrect questions to elicit the negative. For example:

Teacher: 'Is there a bag under the hat?'

Sarah: 'No there isn't a bag under the hat.'

Teacher: 'Are there pencils next to the book?'

Tom: 'No there aren't pencils next to the book, there are pencils behind the book.'

When they get the hang of this, tell your students to continue by asking each other and prompt some negative questions also.

Note: You can also say 'There is water on the table.' This type of 'there is' is not for a singular noun but rather an uncountable noun. This we will cover in a later lesson.

Freer speaking practice
Pairs' activity 'Draw your favourite room': Student A describes their favourite room to Student B who draws it out and clarifies by asking prepositions of place questions so that they draw all the furniture in the right place. Make sure your students use verbal communication only with no pointing. For example:

Tom: 'Is there a sofa in front of the shelves or next to the shelves?'

Sarah: 'There is a sofa next to the shelves on the right and there is a coffee table in front of the sofa.'

1.9 Have and the auxiliary do
Vocabulary: Family, mother, father, son, daughter, brother, sister, uncle, aunt, cousin.

It is now time to move on to verbs which use the auxiliary 'do' starting with 'have.'

How to teach it

First review the introducing yourself language function by writing information about yourself on the board and eliciting the question. For example:

Teacher: My name is Mark.

Sarah: What is your name?

Teacher: I am 28.

Tom: How old are you?

Continue until you have covered your nationality, where you are from and a personal characteristic to elicit a 'to be' question. Now add, 'I have a brother' (or whatever family you have) and elicit or explain that the question is, 'Do you have a brother?'

Explain that all normal verbs (non-auxiliary and modal verbs) require a form of 'do' for the question and negative.

Elicit the negative of the statement, 'I do not have a brother' and with contraction 'I don't have a brother.'

Now write the statement, 'Lisa has a sister.' Underline 'has' and elicit why the verb changes (for the third person). Elicit the negative, 'She does not have a sister' (with contraction 'She doesn't have a sister') and the question, 'Does she have a sister?' To clarify write the following verb table:

Subject pronoun	Have	Negative	Question
I	Have	Don't have	Do you have...?
You	Have	Don't have	Do you have...?
He	Has	Doesn't have	Does he have...?
She	Has	Doesn't have	Does she have?
It	Has	Doesn't have	Does it have...?
We	Have	Don't have	Do you have...?
You (plural)	Have	Don't have	Do you have...?
They	Have	Don't have	Do you have...?

How many
Now write, 'I have three sisters' and elicit or explain the quantity question, 'How many sisters do you have?' Write, 'Lisa has two brothers' and elicit the question, 'How many brothers does Lisa have?'

Common mistakes

Some students may want to say, 'She doesn't has a sister.' This is a mistake because it is the first verb that makes the person of the verb (whether it is third person or not) and the tense while the second verb is always infinitive (with or without 'to'). This is the case with all European languages.

Have got

Many students would have been taught 'I have got' at school, which is fine – but means that students will often answer a 'do' question with, 'No, I haven't a brother,' or even worse use it in the question with 'Have you a brother?'

This is completely wrong. In the phrase 'have got', 'have' is the auxiliary and 'got' the participle of the verb, making the present perfect tense. In the present perfect 'have' is never used without a participle and so 'Have you a car?' or 'She hasn't a car' is impossible. Eliminate this mistake by telling your students that you will study 'Have got' at a higher level. For now, 'have' is just a normal verb and must be used with 'do' for interrogative and negative.

Freer speaking practice
Pairs' activity 'Tell me about your family': People generally like to talk about their families. Tell your students to ask each other about whether they have siblings, children, cousins, aunts and uncles, and how many. Tell them to ask each other about names with the question, 'What is his name?' and 'What is her name?' Get them also to ask about the family of siblings and cousins to practice the third person. For example, 'Does she have children?' 'How many children does she have?'

1.10 Like, don't like, live and work

Vocabulary: Hobbies and professions (brainstorm vocabulary with your students). Where, what, when, how many.

Extend the concept of 'do' by adding these common verbs. Write a verb table on the board showing the change for third person.

Controlled speaking practice

Now write some statements and elicit the questions and negative. Add questions words, (where, when and so on) to the sentences. For example:

Teacher: 'I live in Hong Kong.'

Tom: 'Where do you live?'

Teacher: 'My sister doesn't like yoga.'

Sarah: 'Does your sister like yoga' or 'What does your sister like?'

Teacher: 'She works five days a week.'

Tom: 'How many days does she work a week?'

And so on, until your students are comfortable with both first and third person, the new verbs and question words.

Adding adverbs

Here is the perfect time to introduce the adverbs 'a lot', 'quite a lot' and 'a little/a bit'. Write, 'My sister likes swimming a lot.' Underline 'a lot' and make an expansive gesture with your hands to indicate that she really likes it. Do this with the other adverbs and ask your students questions until they understand that they describe the degree of liking something. Highlight the word order also. This type of adverb always goes at the end of the sentence.

Freer speaking practice
Pairs' activity 'What do you like to do?': Tell your students to ask each other about their work, hobbies, and living arrangements using the above verbs and adverbs. Make sure they also talk about at least one family member to practice third person.

1.11 The Saxon Genitive
Vocabulary: The family, including grandparents, great-grand parents, and family-in-law.

The Saxon Genitive is the possessive 's'. For example, 'My mother's name is Laura,' or 'His sister's dog is brown.' It may look daunting but introduced in the right way it is not difficult to teach.

How to teach it

Continuing with the idea that most people like to talk about their families, explain to your class that they are each going to draw their family tree, starting with the teacher. Your students will love this as they will no doubt be curious about their teacher's life.

Write your name in the centre of the board, indicate that there are more family members and elicit some questions. For example, 'Do you have brothers or sisters?' 'How many?' Draw some branches to show yes and tell them to ask you their names with the question such as 'What is your sister's name?' Underline the possessive 's' and elicit what it means. From now on insist they use the possessive for all further name questions.

Now move on to cousins and prompt a question like, 'What is your brother's sister's son called?' Of course you can negate this entirely by asking 'What is your aunt's son called?' or even 'What is your cousin called?' However, this way highlights that you can use more than one possessive 's' in a sentence. There is in fact no limit, you could say, 'What is your mother's, mother's, brother's, son's name?' and it would still be grammatically correct.

Plural possessives

Highlight the plural by writing, 'My aunt's name is Jill' and 'My aunts' names are Jill and Louise' and eliciting the difference. In the second example the 's' in 'aunts' refers to both plural (two aunts) and possessive (their two names). To show this the apostrophe goes after the letter. To check understanding, ask your students to give you more examples.

Freer speaking practice
Pairs' activity 'Draw my family tree': Once you've finished your family tree, ask your students to draw their partner's family tree by asking lots of questions. For example, 'How many cousins do you have?' and 'What is your cousin's name?'

Add to the activity by getting them to ask further questions such as 'Where does your cousin live?' and 'What job do they do?' And so on.

1.12 Dates

In English dates use ordinal numbers (first, second, third and so on) making them harder than in other languages.

How to teach it

First teach ordinals from first to thirty-first. This requires lot of repetition. Point to different students in the class and get them to say a number each, forwards and then backwards. Next teach the months and start writing numeric day and month dates on the board and elicit the answer. For example, '23/6' would be spoken 'The twenty-sixth of June' and 15/2, 'The fifteenth of February.'

In a separate lesson teach years. Explain that dates before 1999 are spoken in double digits, (for example, 'nineteen, ninety-nine') while after 2000 you say the entire number, ('two thousand'). From 2010 you can go back to double digits but whether you want to teach this is up to you.

Write complete numeric dates on the board, for example 5/10/2006, and elicit the phrase.

Practice this for five minutes every few classes for six weeks.

1.13 How much and how many

Vocabulary: Food and drink (brainstorm with your students words for popular food in their country).

'How much' is used with uncountable nouns (chocolate, water, fruit and so on) and 'How many' with countable (apple, egg or a glass of water). This topic works well with food.

How to teach it

As a class brainstorm food and drink vocabulary. Now write on the board, 'I eat three apples a week' and elicit the question. In most cases they will answer 'Do you eat apples?' and so you must explain that the question you want is 'How many apples do you eat a week?'

Elicit or explain that 'How many' is the quantity question for countable nouns.

Now write, 'My sister drinks a lot of coffee every week' and elicit the question, 'How much coffee she drink a week?' Elicit or explain that 'How much' is the quantity question for uncountable nouns.

Elicit the structure:
How many + noun + auxiliary + subject pronoun/noun + verb
Example: How many potatoes does she eat a month?

How much + noun + auxiliary + subject pronoun/noun + verb
Example: How much wine do they drink a week?

How do you know when a noun is countable or uncountable?
In most cases it's simple. If you can add an 's' to a word to make it plural, then it is automatically countable. If you can't normally add an 's', then it is uncountable. For example, you cannot normally add an 's' to 'fruit', rendering it uncountable, however, with the word 'vegetable' you can, meaning that it is countable.

In addition, all liquids are uncountable. However, if the liquid is in a container such as a cup it becomes countable. In the case of 'coffee' or 'beer' you can say, 'How much coffee do you drink?' referring to the general liquid but also, 'How many coffees do you drink?' referring to cups. We often omit the container in the sentence but that is what we *mean*.

Pairs' activity 'countable and uncountable foods:' Ask your students to make a table headed 'countable' and 'uncountable' and divide the food vocabulary you brainstormed accordingly.

Modifiers
In this type of sentence modifiers come after the verb and before the noun. For example, 'She eats quite a lot of fish.' They differ slightly depending on whether the noun is countable or uncountable. Write the table below on the board.

Uncountable	Countable
A lot of	A lot of
Quite a lot of	Quite a lot of
A little	A few

> **Freer speaking practice**
> **Pairs' activity 'Tell me about your diet':** Tell your students to ask each other about their eating habits with 'How much' and 'How many.' Tell them also to extend the conversation with questions such as 'When do you eat...?' 'What is your favourite...?' 'What do you eat with your family?' And so on.

1.14 How often and adverbs of frequency

Vocabulary: Food words from previous lesson.

Once your students are using 'How much' and 'How many' comfortably it's time to move onto the frequency question, 'How often.'

How to teach it

Write on the board, 'My sister eats fish twice a week' and elicit or explain the question, 'how often does your sister eat fish?' Elicit or explain that 'how often' means 'how frequently?'

Elicit the structure:

How often + auxiliary + subject + verb + noun

The answer can be expressed in one of two ways. The first is with a time marker at the end of the sentence such as 'once a week', 'twice a month', 'three times a year' and so on.

The second is with an adverb of frequency which goes before the main verb, for example, 'I <u>always</u> eat toast for breakfast.'

Write the common adverbs of frequency in the cline like this:

Always

Often

Quite often

Hardly ever

Never

Once they learn this your students may be tempted to use adverbs in all frequency statements and say things like 'I always eat bread' which without a context sounds totally crazy. Explain that in most cases time markers are more appropriate.

Putting it together: 'How much,' 'how many,' 'how often'

Freer speaking practice
Pairs' activity 'Our eating habits': Tell your students to talk together about what they typically eat and drink in a week and how often. Tell them to extend the conversation using 'How much' and 'How many.' Next ask them to speak about a family member's habits to practice the third person.

1.15 Can
Vocabulary: Sports and hobbies (brainstorm as a class), include common verbs such as go, read, write and do.

'Can' is an auxiliary verb used to express ability. It is a simple grammar point but may cause confusion in later lessons as its infinitive is the very irregular 'to be able to.'

How to teach it

After brainstorming vocabulary, question your students for a moment on what they can do and from that write the statement, 'Sarah can ride a bike' (or whatever applies).

Underline 'can' and elicit or explain the meaning (ability). Can is an auxiliary verb meaning that like 'do' it you can be put together with 'not' to make a negative ('can't') and make a question.

Elicit the negative: 'Sarah cannot ride a bike' and with contraction 'Sarah can't ride a bike,' and the question, 'Can Sarah ride a bike?'

Elicit the structure:

Subject pronoun/noun + can + infinitive

There is no change for third person.

Putting it together: 'Can' and 'How often'

Freer speaking practice
Pairs' activity 'Our exercise and activity habits': Tell your students to talk together about their hobbies and sports and how often they practice them. Tell them to extend the conversation by asking questions such as 'when' 'where' and maybe 'how much does it cost?' Next ask them to speak about a family member's hobbies to practice third person (which doesn't exist with 'can' but does with 'how much.')

1.16 Daily Routine
Vocabulary: Wake up, get up, have breakfast, have lunch, have dinner, go to work, write emails, read the internet, meet friends, speak to my boss, come home, watch TV, listen to music, go to bed.

As your students will discover later present simple is only used for a few things, one of them being the daily routine. For this exercise your students need to be familiar with the time language function.

How to teach it

Write your own daily routine on the board eliciting questions from the statements. For example:

Teacher: I get up at 7.30.

Tom: What time do you get up?

Teacher: I eat three slices of toast for breakfast.

Sarah: How many slices of toast do you eat?

And so on. To ensure that your students understand all the vocabulary you may have to mime.

Who

Now is a great time to teach questions with 'who' which is not so easy as the preposition 'with' falls at the end of the sentence. For example, 'Who do you work with?' Teach it by writing statements such as 'I go running with my friends' and eliciting the question.

Freer speaking practice
Pairs' activity 'What's your routine?': Now tell your students to speak about their own routines and their partner must ask questions. Extend the activity with 'how often?' 'can', 'who' and other question words. Next tell them to speak about a family member to practice the third person.

1.17 There is + uncountable noun, some and any

It's time now to return to 'there' and introduce 'there is' + uncountable noun, for example, 'There is some water on the table.'

This language point is also a good time to introduce the pronouns 'some' and 'any'.

How to teach it

Place some plural and singular objects on the table and elicit sentences using 'there is' and 'there are'. Now introduce an uncountable object such as a liquid, paper or rice and elicit the sentence.

Elicit or explain that uncountable nouns are expressed with 'there is' + 'some' in affirmative and 'any' in negative and interrogative. The same system is used with plural nouns while 'a' or 'an' is used with singular. Illustrate this with the following table:

	Affirmative	Negative	Question
There is: singular	a/an	a/an	a/an
There are: plural	Some	Any	any
There is: uncountable	Some	Any	Any

At this point your students may protest. After all they have already learnt 'there are' without pronouns, so why are you adding them now? Explain that language learning is a process; pronouns would have been too complicated to add before but now they are ready.

Controlled speaking practice
Review what makes a countable and uncountable noun from the 'How much and how many' lesson. Next, practice by making sentences and eliciting the negative and the interrogative, such as 'There is some air in the room,' 'There isn't any air in the room' and 'Is there some air in the room?'

Now as a class study this picture of a kitchen and tell your students to ask each other questions. As the teacher you must direct this activity and prompt them with ideas. For example:

Teacher: Tom, ask Sarah about books.

Tom: Sarah, are there any books in the room?'

Sarah: Yes, there are some books in the room.

Also ask, deliberately wrong questions to elicit the negative. For example:

Teacher: Tom, is there any beer in the room?

Tom: 'No, there isn't any beer in the room.'

Freer speaking practice
Pairs' activity 'Commenting on a photo': Once your students are using 'there' + pronouns comfortably, get them to ask and answer questions using other visual material. This could be about the classroom, this week's newspaper pictures, or photos of famous events.

Getting pronouns right takes time and so go back to this grammar point every few weeks in the first term.

There are + quantifiers

It is important also to highlight the use of 'there are' quantifiers such as 'a lot of,' 'many,' 'quite a lot of,' 'not many,' 'at least, 'more than' and 'less than.'

A fun way of doing this is to spread a map of the city out on the table and ask your students to test each other's knowledge. For example, 'There are at least four large parks in the city, can you name them?' or 'There are quite a lot of swimming pools, but which one is the biggest?'

1.18 Imperatives

Imperatives express an order such as 'Shut the door', 'Do your homework' or even 'Enjoy yourselves!' They are grammatically very easily; remove the subject pronoun and put the verb into infinitive without 'to.'

How to teach it

Write the above examples of imperatives on the board, elicit the meaning and highlight the structure. Now ask your students to give each other (pleasant) orders such as, 'Put on your coat', 'Close your eyes' or 'Pick up your pen.'

1.19 Object pronouns and possessive adjectives and pronouns
Possessives adjectives

These express possession of an object with the structure:

Possessive adjective + noun (object) + to be verb + noun or adjective
Your students have already studied this when introducing themselves with the phrases 'My name is...' 'His name is...' 'Her name is...' and so on.

Object pronouns:

These go after some verbs to substitute the noun with the structure:

Subject + verb + object pronoun
For example, 'Give him the ball' or 'Tell her the story.'

Possessive pronouns

These also express possession but the sentence is reordered with the structure:

Noun (object) + to be + possessive pronoun
For example, 'The white house is mine', 'The small cat is his' 'The two cars are ours.' As the pronoun always ends the sentence, the phrase 'Mine cat is black' is impossible.

How to teach it
Pronouns can often leave students confused even after weeks of practice. To eliminate this it's important to introduce a real world application for them in the classroom. First write the following table on the board.

Subject pronoun	Possessive adjective	Object pronoun
I	My	Me
You	Your	You
He	His	Him
She	Her	Her
It	Its	It
We	Our	Us
You	Your	You
They	Their	Them

The first column shows the pronouns used in all subject sentences and the second your students should recognise from talking about names. The third column, however, will cause confusion.

Write the following examples, 'He gives <u>her</u> the keys', 'They pass <u>him</u> the pencil', 'She tells <u>us</u> the secret,' and elicit the meaning (the pronoun is used in place of the noun – in example one this could be, 'He gives my sister the keys'). All European languages have pronouns like this. To help your students understand it is a good idea to find examples in their language.

The Possessive Card Game

The word 'game' is probably a stretch but it is a good way to apply these otherwise abstract words to a physical 'real world' activity that your class will remember.

First, hand the pack of picture cards to Student A. Tell Student B to ask Student A to distribute the cards among the class using the phrase, 'Give him a card', 'Give her a card' and so on. To use all pronouns, pair two students together to create an opportunity to try saying 'Give them' and place a card in the middle of the table for the class to create a 'Give us'. This activity should be done quickly.

Next direct your students to ask each other about their cards, using as many possessive adjectives as possible. For example:

Teacher: Tom, ask Sarah about José's card.

Tom: 'What is <u>his</u> card?'

Sarah: '<u>His</u> card is a house.'

Teacher: 'Sarah, ask José about the class's card.'

Sarah: 'What is <u>our</u> card?'

José: 'Our card is a hat.'

When they have finished, collect the cards together and pick two more student to redistribute them using 'give him', 'give her' and so on.

This time pick up a student's card and ask 'what is her card?' Elicit 'Her card is a horse' (for example) and write on the board '<u>Her</u> card is a horse' or 'The horse card is <u>hers</u>.'

Underline 'hers' and elicit or explain the meaning; it is the possessive pronoun which substitutes the noun ('The horse card is <u>hers</u>' or 'The horse card is <u>Sarah's</u>'). Elicit or explain the structure and that the possessive pronoun never precedes a noun. Finally, add this final column to your table.

```
Possessive pronouns

Mine

Yours

His

Hers

Its

Ours

Yours

Theirs
```

Direct your students to ask each other about their cards, using the questions, 'What is your, his, her, our and their card?' Get them to answer using both the possessive adjective ('His card is an elephant') and the possessive pronoun ('The elephant card is his.')

Don't expect students to use pronouns perfectly after one lesson. This activity should be repeated several times during the term to practice.

1.20 Whose

Whose is the possessive question. To practice, replay the Possessive Card Game during another lesson, pick up a student's card and write on the board, 'It's his card.' Now, elicit or explain that the question is 'Whose card is it?'

Elicit the structure:

Whose + noun + to be + subject pronoun

During the game ask periodically, 'Whose house card is it?' and elicit an answer, and get them to ask each other also.

1.21 Language function: Directions
Vocabulary: Roundabout, traffic lights, zebra crossing, take a right/left, turn, past, go, towards, keep going straight, crossroad, exit.

In between the grammar it is important to add the occasional vocabulary lesson to allow your students to perform basic language functions. A good place to start with is directions.

How to teach it
As a class brainstorm directions vocabulary and next do the activity below.

Pairs' activity 'Find the destination': First, brainstorm direction vocabulary. Next hand your students an A4 sized print out of a section of their city. Tell Student A to think of a secret destination and, beginning from an agreed starting point, tell them to guide Student B to the destination using only their language skills (no pointing). If your students are sitting opposite each other make sure they agree on what is left and right, first. When they have finished, swap roles.

1.22 Phrasal verbs
Vocabulary: Pick up, put down, put on, put in, take off, take out.

Phrasal verbs are verbs paired with a preposition or adverb which typically have at least two meanings. For example, 'take off' means 'to remove clothing' and the opposite of 'to land.'

In most cases, nouns can be placed either between the verb and preposition or at the end, for example, 'Take <u>the hat</u> off' or 'Take off <u>the hat</u>.' Pronouns, however, must go in the middle to make 'Take <u>it</u> off'. 'Take off <u>it</u>' is impossible.

This works in around 80% of cases. If the phrasal verb has three words, however, both the noun and pronoun go at the end, such as 'I get on with <u>my sister</u>', 'I get on with <u>her</u>.' There are also some awkward verbs where the preposition simply must go at the end such as 'care for' ('I care for <u>her</u>'). For further reading, see the Phrasal Verbs Advanced chapter.

How to teach it

As phrasal verbs are difficult to master, introduce them early with this activity. Put some objects on the table, including some sunglasses, a hat or scarf. Tell one of your students to tell you in imperative form to pick up a pen. Pick it up and follow the routine below.

Teacher: 'What am I doing?'

Tom: 'You are picking up the pen.'

Teacher: 'And with the pronoun 'it'?

Tom: 'You are picking up it.'

Teacher: No, I am picking it up.

Now write on the board: 'I am picking the pen up', 'I am picking up the pen' and 'I am picking it up' to highlight that the pronoun goes in the middle. Now repeat this action for 'Put down the pen', 'Put the pen in the bag', 'Take the pen out the bag', 'Put on the sunglasses' and 'Take off the sunglasses.'

Now get your students to ask each other to do an action practicing both the noun and pronoun.

For example:

Tom: 'Sarah, put on the sunglasses.'

Teacher: 'Sarah, what are you doing?'

Sarah: 'I am putting the sunglasses on.'

Teacher: 'And with pronoun, Tom?'

Tom: 'She is putting them on.'

Continue this activity for at least 10 minutes making sure every student gets to practice. Over the following weeks repeat it several times until everyone is comfortable with pronoun placement.

1.23 Language function: Ordering in restaurants and would like

Vocabulary: Knife, fork, spoon, teaspoon, serviette, dish, meal, menu, set menu, starter, main course, dessert, waiter, waitress, the specials, the dish of the day, the bill, to pay for, salt and pepper, condiments, to order, to complain, to make a complaint.

Ordering food is another important language function for beginners.

How to teach it

As a class, brainstorm vocabulary until you have something like the above. Now write on the board, 'I would like a sandwich.' Explain that English is a very polite language and so when ordering we use the phrase 'would like.' Its structure runs:

Subject pronoun/noun + would + like + infinitive (with 'to')

Example: 'I would like to drink a coffee.'

'Would' is a modal verb and so it makes the negative and question. Elicit or explain the negative 'I would not like a sandwich' and with contraction 'I wouldn't like a sandwich' and the question 'Would you like a sandwich?'

Controlled speaking practice

Practice for a few minutes by getting your students to ask each other what they would like to do that afternoon. Ask some crazy questions to elicit the negative. For example:

Teacher: 'Sarah, ask Tom if he would like to swim with sharks this afternoon.'

Sarah: 'Tom would you like to swim with sharks this afternoon?'

Tom: 'No, I wouldn't like to swim with sharks this afternoon.'

Freer speaking practice

Pairs' roleplay 'In a restaurant': Student A is the customer and Student B is the waiter/waitress. In the centre of the table place some slips of paper with typical restaurant problems such as your dessert hasn't arrived, a dish has arrived cold and there is a fly in your soup. Ask your students to do the normal order routine including asking for the specials and dish of the day. Student A then picks up a problem and makes a complaint. When the meal is concluded, swap roles.

1.24 Someone, something, somewhere

If you want to ask about a person, thing or place you have to use one of the above words, but they are not as easy as they first appear.

How to teach it

Write on the board, 'I know someone who speaks French'. Underline 'someone' and elicit the meaning. Next underline 'who' and elicit why it is there; it is the connector used when referring to people.

Elicit the negative, 'I don't know anyone who speaks French' and the question, 'Do you know anyone who speaks French?' Note that in negative and interrogative 'someone' changes to 'anyone', just as 'some' changes to 'any' when speaking about uncountable or plural nouns.

To highlight this write the following table:

	Affirmative	Negative	Question
People	Someone	Anyone	Anyone
Things	Something	Anything	Anything
Location	Somewhere	Anywhere	Anywhere

The connector for things is 'which' and for location 'where,' for example, 'Somewhere where we can go for coffee'. However, native speakers often omit 'where' to avoid repetition.

Controlled speaking practice

Tell your students to ask each other the below questions. For example:

Teacher: Tom, ask Sarah if she knows anyone who can repair a car.

Tom: Sarah, do you know anyone who can repair a car?

Sarah: Yes, I know someone who can repair a car.

To make the drill less repetitive ask a follow up question such as 'Who do you know who can repair a car?'

Questions

If he/she:

- knows anyone who can repair a car.
- has anything which can help with my cold.
- knows anyone who can install our internet.
- knows anywhere where I can get a good coffee.
- knows anyone who can drive me to Barcelona.
- has anything which can help me learn Spanish.
- knows anyone who can repair my computer.
- has anything which can help you learn English.
- knows anywhere where to buy clothes.
- has anything which I can eat.
- knows anywhere where I can go skiing.
- has anything which I can give my mother as a birthday present.
- knows anyone who can cook me dinner.
- has anything which I can drink.

Freer Speaking Practice

Pairs' activity 'Asking advice': In the centre of the table place slips of paper with simple information requests such as 'Somewhere to celebrate a party', 'Something to help learn English' or 'Someone who can repair a computer.' In pairs tell your students to ask each other whether they know anyone, anywhere or have anything that serves this purpose. Tell them to extend the activity with questions such as 'Where is it?' 'How much does it cost?' and 'How do you know this person or place?'

1.25 Language function: Shopping

Vocabulary: Try on, take back, size, refund, receipt, till, changing rooms, to look for, to pay for, aisle, sales, bargain, customer, shop assistant.

How to teach it

Practice shopping language by brainstorming vocabulary and potential shopping problems. Once you have five or six issues ask your students to act them out in simple roleplays where one is the shop assistant and the other the customer.

1.26 Present continuous

When do we use present simple? Well, really only for three things; routines ('I get up every morning'), the imperative ('Close the door') and future when speaking about timetables ('The plane leaves at 8pm tonight'). English likes to emphasise the action and so when speaking about the 'now' we don't usually use present simple but rather present continuous. For example, 'I am working', 'She is thinking' or 'Are you playing?'

How to teach it

Write on the board 'I am working' and elicit the tense and structure:

Subject pronoun/noun + to be verb + verb in gerund ('ing')

Next to it write 'I work' and elicit the difference in meaning. 'I work' means this happens as part of my routine while 'I am working' means it is happening now.

Emphasise that it we use second form to express the present moment much more then present simple and explain why.

With the above sentence elicit the negative, 'I am not working' and with contraction 'I'm not working' and the question, 'Are you working?'

Elicit versions of this sentence with all persons of the verb such as 'You are working', 'He is working' and so on.

Controlled speaking practice

To practice, tell your students you are going to ask them questions about the pictures on the Continuous activity sheet and they must answer in the continuous form. This activity has a certain technique to it and so practice with a fellow teacher before the lesson. If done right, it should start easy and then get progressively harder.

First ask questions that they can't get wrong. You do this by giving them two options, one of which is ridiculous, for example for picture A, 'Is Mr Smith holding an umbrella or a cat?' Your student will automatically answer 'He is holding a cat.' Do this a few times until they are comfortable with the complete 'He is' or 'She is' answer and then start throwing curve balls. For example:

Teacher: 'Is Mr Smith wearing a hat or a banana?'

Tom: 'He is wearing a hat.'

Teacher: 'And you Tom?'

Instead of blindly repeating what you say the question forces Tom to think and use the grammar himself to form the sentence 'I am wearing...'

To use more persons of the verb, bring in classmates. For example:

Teacher: 'Is Mrs Vincent looking at the buildings or her book?'

Sarah: 'She is looking at the buildings.'

Teacher: 'And Tom and Joe?'

Sarah: 'They are looking at the blackboard.'

Teacher: 'Am I looking at the blackboard?'

Sarah: 'No, you are not looking at the blackboard, you are looking at me.'

Here are some suggested questions for the first two pictures to give you some ideas.

Picture 1: Passengers in an aeroplane

- o   Is the woman in the orange dress sleeping or dancing?
- o   Is she lying back or lying forward?

- Is she wearing pink shoes or yellow shoes?
- What colour shoes are you wearing? And your neighbour?
- Is the man with the red jumper reading or writing?
- What is he reading?
- Are you reading?
- Is he looking at you or the book?
- What is the boy looking at? And you? And the other students?
- What is he listening to? And me? And you?
- What is he wearing? And your friend?
- Is he feeling happy or serious? And me?
- How are you feeling?
- Is he dancing or sitting? And the class?
- Are they flying in an aeroplane or travelling in a train?

Picture 2: The train station

- Is the young man standing or siting? And your neighbour?
- Is he listening or me or listening to music? What are you listening to?
- Is he relaxing or concentrating?
- What is he doing? What are we doing?
- What are you looking at? What is he looking at?
- Is he wearing a sweater or a dress?
- Are you wearing a dress?
- Is the young woman holding a bag or a dog?
- What are you holding?
- Is the train arriving or leaving? Why do you think that?
- What is the young woman looking at? And you? And me?
- Who is she talking to? And you?
- Is she working or travelling?
- What are you doing?

Freer speaking practice
Pairs' activity 'Describe a photo': Using action photos tell your students to ask and answer questions about what is happening. To ensure plenty of variety tell them to write some questions beforehand using question words such as 'what', 'who', 'where', 'when', 'how many', 'how much' and so on.

Group activity: Question practice

Tell your students a story using continuous and elicit what the question would be.

For example:

Teacher: 'My friend John is going to Thailand.'

Tom: 'Where is he going?'

Teacher: 'He is packing two pairs of shorts and a towel.'

Sarah: 'What is he packing?' Or 'Why is he packing a towel?'

And so on. Be inventive to make sure they ask questions using all the question words.

1.27 Language function: The weather
How to teach it

As a class brainstorm weather vocabulary but divide the words into nouns, adjectives and verbs in a table that should look something like this:

Noun	Verb	Adjective
Rain	To rain	Rainy
Sun	-	Sunny
Cloud	-	Cloudy
Wind	-	Windy
Snow	To snow	Snowy
Fog	To fog	Foggy
Ice	To freeze	Icy
Thunder	To thunder	-
Lightning	-	-
Flood	To food	-

In addition write some temperature adjectives in a cline like this:

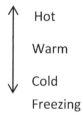

Hot

Warm

Cold

Freezing

Next, go down the noun column and elicit whether they are countable or uncountable. They are all uncountable except for 'storm' and 'flood'. Elicit or explain that with weather uncountable and singular nouns in present are expressed with 'there is' and plural (if it applies) 'there are'. For example, 'There is a storm tonight.'

If your class is ready you could also explain that in past this changes to 'there was' or 'there were' and future, 'there will be.'

Elicit or explain that weather verbs are expressed in continuous form such as 'It is raining today' rather than, 'It rains today.' Again if your class is ready you could explain that this changes to past continuous when expressing the past and to 'will' when speaking about the future.

And finally, we use 'to be' for adjectives, for example, 'It is sunny today.' This changes to 'was' for past and 'will be' for future.

Questions

Write on the board, 'Today it is cloudy and cold' and elicit the question 'What is the weather like today?' This won't make any sense to your students as they associate 'like' with personal taste. Explain that 'like' also means 'similar to' and so the question they are really asking is 'What is the weather similar to, today?' They will probably still protest but this is the question and they have to get used to it.

For a more advanced class you could also write, 'Yesterday it was raining and warm' and elicit the question, 'What was the weather like yesterday?' And for the future, 'The weather will be sunny and hot tomorrow' with the question, 'What will the weather be like tomorrow?' Note that 'will' and 'be' are separated by the noun making this harder to remember.

Freer speaking practice
Pairs' activity 'Global weather': Print out some weather forecasts from different parts of the world and tell your students to ask each other about the weather, noting also the temperature and wind direction, the previous and following day.

1.28 Comparative adjectives

In comparative sentences we modify the adjective. For example, 'hot' becomes 'hotter', 'small' becomes 'smaller' and 'difficult' 'more difficult'.

But why?

How to teach it

Hand out pictures of opposing landscapes or situations such as a city and country, nightclub and fishing scenes and ask the class brainstorm adjectives. Add to their knowledge with this list.

Tall/short, long/short, easy/difficult, hard/soft, fast/slow, cheap/expensive, young/old, new/old, thick/thin, simple/complicated, high/low, good/bad, rich/poor, clean/dirty, hot/cold, wet/dry, light/dark, ugly/pretty, fat/slim, fast/slow, safe/dangerous, weak/strong, noisy/quiet, near/far, relaxing/stressful, important, interesting, beautiful, intelligent, famous, popular, elegant, economical, comfortable.

Adjectives with one syllable

Now write on the board, 'Fishing is quieter than dancing in a nightclub'. Underline 'quieter' and elicit or explain that this is a comparative sentence; 'quiet' only has one syllable and so we add 'er' to make it comparative. This holds true for all regular comparative adjectives. For example, 'Spain is hotter than Ireland'.

One syllable spelling rules

You'll notice in the above sentence that 'hot' became 'hotter', doubling the constant. We do this when the original adjective is spelt with a consonant-vowel-consonant pattern. For example, 'wet' becomes 'wetter' and 'big', 'bigger'.

Adjectives with two or more syllables

Now write, 'London is more expensive than Madrid.' Underline 'more expensive' and elicit why this sentence contains 'more'. The answer is that 'expensive' has more than two syllables (in this case three) and so must be preceded by 'more' to make a comparative.

Adjectives ending in 'Y'

Now write, 'The country is prettier than the city'. There are two syllables in 'pretty' and so why is the comparative with 'er' instead of 'more'? The answer is if the adjective ends in 'y' you take the final letter away and add 'ier,' for example, 'happy' becomes 'happier' and 'busy', 'busier'.

Less + adjective

Now reverse the sentence with 'Madrid is less expensive than London'. Underline less and explain that it means a lesser quantity. It is used with two or more syllable adjectives, but not one. 'Ireland is less hot than Spain' is a very unnatural sentence.

The Irregulars

Not all adjectives fit into this pattern. Write this table to highlight the exceptions:

Adjective	Comparative
Good	Better
Bad	Worse
Far	Further
Fun	More fun
Little	Less

Controlled speaking practice

Using a world map give your students two places and one adjective and ask them to make a sentence. For example:

Teacher: 'Norway, Portugal and snowy.'

Tom: 'Portugal is snowier than Norway.'

Teacher: 'The city, the country and dangerous.'

Sarah: 'The city is more dangerous than the country.'

Teacher: 'And the reverse?'

Sarah: 'The country is less dangerous than the city.'

Practice 'near' and 'far' + preposition by giving your students two points and asking which one is the nearer and further from the city. For example:

Teacher: 'Madrid, Barcelona, our city and far.'

Sarah: 'Madrid is further *from* our city than Barcelona.'

Teacher: 'And the reverse?'

Tom: 'Barcelona is nearer *to* our city than Madrid.'

Freer speaking practice
Pairs' roleplay 'Making a decision': Use the comparison activity sheets at the end of the book to compare holidays and decide which one you want to buy.

1.29 Comparatives with 'as' and 'as'
In a separate lesson highlight the second way to use comparatives with 'as' and 'as'.

How to teach it

Write on the board, 'Spain is hotter than Ireland.' Elicit or explain the second way to make this sentence; 'Ireland is not as hot as Spain.' Highlight that the nouns have reversed and the adjective is in its <u>original form</u>. Preceding and following the adjective are the adverbs 'as'. In this sentence we show that Ireland is colder than Spain by using 'not'. If we omit it then we are saying that Ireland and Spain are equal in temperature.

Controlled speaking practice
Again, using a world map state two locations and an adjective and tell your students to make a sentence. For example:

Teacher: 'Oklahoma, Los Angeles and windy.'

Tom: 'Los Angeles is not as windy as Oklahoma.'

1.30 Superlative adjectives

Superlatives express the one in the group that is the most, for example, 'Mount Everest is the highest mountain in the world'. In other words ou
t of the group of things we call mountains, Mount Everest has the most height.

How to teach it

Spread out a map of your students' city or country (or speak from memory) and make some comparisons. For example, in Barcelona the cathedral Sagrada Família is taller than Casa Milá.

Now write on the board, 'Which one is the tallest?' Underline 'tallest' and elicit or explain that this means the one out of a group which has the most (height in this case). For this reason, it is also always used with the definite article 'the.'

Adjectives with one syllable

Explain that adjectives with one syllable, such as 'tall,' always end in 'est' in superlative such as 'smallest', 'biggest', 'shortest.'

Adjectives with more than one syllable

Now write, 'Barcelona is the most expensive city in Spain.' Just as with comparative, adjectives with two or more syllables are modified with a separate word, but this time instead of 'more' we use 'most.'

Adjectives that end in 'Y'

Despite having two syllables, these adjectives also change to 'est' in superlative, by substituting the 'y' for 'i'. For example, 'prettiest', 'busiest' and 'ugliest.'

Irregulars

The same words are irregular in superlative as in comparative. Highlight it with this table.

Adjective	Comparative	Superlative
Good	Better	The best
Bad	Worse	The worse
Far	Further	The furthest
Fun	More fun	The most fun
Little	Less	The least
A lot	More	The most

Controlled speaking practice

Using your city map tell your students to ask and answer questions on what they think is:

- The most exciting bar
- The most relaxing park
- The quietest neighbourhood
- The most dangerous neighbourhood
- The best place to buy food
- The worst place to play basketball
- The most fun way to pass their time
- The least fun way to pass their time
- The largest shopping mall
- The smallest restaurant

And so on...

1.31 To be in past

Just as with the present tense, 'to be' verb should be the first thing your students practice for the past.

How to teach it

First brainstorm a list of emotions or states such as: Tired, bored, angry, hungry, thirsty, relaxed, stressed, excited, sick and ill and ask your students to write the words on slips of paper.

Write on the board, 'I am relaxed today' and then, 'I was stressed yesterday.' Underline the second sentence and elicit the tense. Now, elicit the question (from your most knowledgeable student) 'Why were you stressed yesterday?' And tell them a simple story.

Elicit the negative 'I wasn't stressed yesterday' and another with 'were,' for example, 'We weren't stressed yesterday.' Write the following table:

	Present	Past
I	am	Was
You	are	Were
He	is	Was
She	is	Was
It	is	Was
We	are	Were
You	are	Were
They	are	Were

Controlled speaking practice

Vocabulary: Yesterday, last night, last week, last month, last year.

Take the slips and ask your students questions about them, their family and their colleagues to use all persons of the verb. For example:

Teacher: 'Sarah, were you bored last week?'

Sarah: 'No, I wasn't bored last week.'

Teacher: 'And your sister?'

Sarah: 'Yes, she was bored last week.'

Freer speaking practice
Pairs' activity 'Past states and emotions': Next, give each pair a copy of the emotions and state vocabulary (or write them on the board for a large class) and tell them to ask and answer questions using different persons of the verb. Extend the activity by adding 'why' and 'because.' For example:

Tom: 'Why were you tired last week?'

Sarah: 'Because I was sick.'

1.32 To be born
I have had students who have studied English for 10 years and still struggle with this grammar point, particularly the question 'When were you born?'

How to teach it

Write on the board 'I was born on (and your full date of birth)' and elicit the question. Elicit or explain the meaning and that the day of birth is not expressed with a verb, as in many languages, but rather 'to be' verb in past + the adjective born.

Controlled speaking practice

Next tell your students to ask each other where and when they, their parents, siblings and children were born. Try to use as many persons of the verb as possible.

Practice this for five minutes at the end of the lesson every week for at least the first term, if not longer.

Putting it together: 'To be' in past and 'to be born'

> **Freer speaking practice**
> **Pairs' game 'Guess the historical figure':** Hand out the name of a well-known historical figure to Student A and tell them keep it secret. Using 'to be' in past, Student B must ask questions to discover the identity. Question examples: 'Was it a man or woman?' 'When was she born?' 'Was she French?' 'Was she rich or poor?'

1.33 There was, there were

The next basic past is 'There was' and 'There were' + noun. Your students may already be familiar with this from the Weather lesson but it is good to practice.

How to teach it

Place some objects on the table and write on the board, 'There is a pen on the table.' Take the pen away and elicit the sentence, 'There was a pen on the desk.' Elicit the negative, 'There wasn't a pen on the desk' and the question, 'Was there a pen on the desk?'

Now write, 'There are two pencils on the table.' Take them away and elicit, 'There were two pencils on the table.' Elicit the negative, 'There weren't two pencils on the table' and the question, 'Were there two pencils on the table?'

Controlled speaking practice

Now take out your picture cards as you are going to play a game. Place eight cards on the table (make sure a couple show something plural) and tell your students they have 30 seconds to memorise them.

When the time is up, take the cards away and ask them to recount what was there. Elicit the use of negative by asking questions about cards you know were not on the table. Encourage your students to ask each other questions also.

For example:

Tom: 'There was a chair card and a tree card.'

Teacher: 'Was there an umbrella card?'

Sarah: 'No, there wasn't an umbrella card.'

Do this again, making it progressively harder with more cards.

Part II

2. The Past

Your students have passed the basics and are now on the next big grammar topic; the past. They will be eager to get started as they will understand that much of conversation is about telling stories — recounting your own and commenting on others — all of which needs to be done in some form of past.

2.1 Past simple

The past simple refers to something that occurred in the past and is now finished. For example, 'The dog ate my homework.' The dog is not still eating my homework, the action is finished.

Its structure runs:

Subject pronoun/noun + verb in past + infinitive or noun (if needed)

Example: 'The girl bought a bike.'

Verbs in past simple are either regular with an 'ed' ending (for example 'played') or irregular. There are so many irregular verbs in English that it is better to start here as students might find it dispiriting to learn them after the comparatively easy 'ed'.

How to teach it

Write, 'I played football last Saturday' on the board.

Elicit the tense and whether the action has finished or still continues.

Elicit the negative, 'I didn't play football last Saturday,' and the question, 'Did you play football last Saturday?'

Highlight that both negatives and questions are relatively easy in English — you simply change 'do' for 'did' and there is no change for third person.

Highlight that third person in affirmative doesn't change either. Write, 'The boy played football last Saturday' and, 'The girl played football last Saturday.'

Vocabulary

Introduce time markers such as 'yesterday', 'last week', 'last month', 'last year,' and their position at the end of the sentence. For example, 'I went skiing last year.'

Make sure that your students understand that it is 'last week', rather than '*the* last week,' which is common in many languages.

2.1.1 Irregular verbs

Now your students understand the structure, move on to irregular verbs.

How to teach it

Firstly, find out what they know. Schools spend years drilling irregular verbs into students and so you will be surprised that even the weakest student may know an irregular verb or two.

Hand out slips of paper and ask your class to write as many irregular verbs as they know <u>in present</u>. Collect them up as material for the lesson.

Controlled speaking practice

You may have 30 verbs, you may have five. In either case, it is better not to bombard your students with too many at once (remember this is the group's knowledge of English, not an individual's) and so select ten of the most common to practice. Put the others away to use the following class.

The verbs that I typically select first are: Go, eat, drink, buy, see, have, read, write, cost and take.

If you find that a student has written a verb in past, write it again in present. Place the papers where everyone can see (if it is a big class, write them on the board). Tell your students that you are going to ask them questions and <u>they have to answer in the affirmative.</u>

Look at your strongest student and ask, 'How many apples did you eat yesterday?' Elicit something like, 'I ate two apples.'

Answering in the affirmative forces the student to use the irregular verb. If they don't know the verb, help them. Use a variety of questions words such as: How many, how much, where, when, what and why.

Use all persons of the verb. For example, 'Where did your sister run yesterday?'

With stronger students continue with a further question to give them a taste of a real conversation. For example, 'Why did she run in the park?' Elicit something like, 'She ran in the park because it is close to her house.'

Freer speaking practice
Pairs' activity 'Speaking in past': Once you are confident that your students know these 10 verbs, practice a more normal conversation with questions and answers.

Divide your students into pairs and give them a topic. For example:

Your last holiday, The last special occasion you went to, Your last day off, The last time you were sick.

Ask them to brainstorm questions using the irregular verbs. For example, 'Where did you go?' 'What did you eat/drink?' 'How many coffees did you have?' 'Who did you go with?' Remember to highlight the preposition at the end of the sentence.

Ask your students to read out some of their questions to check the grammar and tell them to have that conversation. Ask them to make it the most natural conversation possible with additions such as, 'Oh really, why?' or, 'That's interesting because I went there too.'

Further speaking practice
As your students learn more verbs, practice with the below activity:

Class activity 'Making a story': Put all of the irregular verbs they've studied on the table (or write on a board for a large class). Challenge students to make stories with two verbs, then three, then four and so on. They cannot use a verb twice and they cannot use an infinitive, and it must make sense. For fun, give a point for each verb. The winner is the student who manages to string together the longest sentence.

So, for example, a story for 'go', 'see', 'say' and 'do' could be, 'There once was a girl, who <u>went</u> to school, she <u>saw</u> her teacher and <u>said</u> she <u>did</u> her homework.' The student receives four points.

2.1.2 Regular verbs

Regular verbs will naturally occur in past speaking exercises. With their 'ed' endings they are easy to memorise. The difficulty your students will have is with the pronunciation. You must correct this as soon as possible – it is not acceptable for a student to continue to say 'ask*ed*' when the actual pronunciation is *'askt'* with a 't' sound. Luckily there are some simple rules.

Pronunciation rules

'T' sound: If the root verb ends with a 'k', 'p' or 'h', the past tense of the verb is pronounced with a 't' sound. For example, 'worked', 'stopped' and 'laughed' are pronounced 'workt', 'stopt' and 'laught'.

'Id' sound: If the verb ends in either 't' or 'd', the past is pronounced with an 'id' sound. For example, 'wanted' and 'decided' are pronounced 'wantid' and 'decidid.'

'D' sound: For all other verbs the past is pronounced with a 'd' sound, omitting the 'e.' For example 'stressed', 'rained', 'closed' are actually pronounced 'stress'd', 'rain'd' and 'clos'd'.

How to teach it

Draw three columns on the board and head each one with a sound. Explain the rules and ask your students to fill the columns with the appropriate verbs. Here are examples:

Verbs which end with K, P and H: To ask, to check, to cook, to escape, to finish, to help, to hop, to jump, to laugh, to like, to look, to park, to pick up, to push, to reach, to stop, to talk, to walk, to wash, to watch, to work.

Verbs which end with T and D: To act, to add, to attend, to avoid, to cheat, to create, to contact, to count, to defend, to decide, to depend, to divide, to hate, to include, to invite, to last, to paint, to print, to rent, to start, to taste, to treat, to wait, to waste.

Other verbs (a selection): To agree, to answer, to arrive, to believe, to carry, to call, to change, to deliver, to explain, to listen, to kiss, to play, to pull, to save, to show, to try, to travel, to use.

Putting it all together: Regular and irregular verbs in past

Freer speaking Practice with Regular and Irregular verbs

Pairs' activity 'Guess my celebrity': Ask your students to write the name of a celebrity and keep it secret. Now, in pairs, get them to ask and answer questions to guess the person. To get some ideas flowing, first ask your students to change the following vocabulary to past with correct pronunciation: *To be born, grow up, go to school, leave school, get married, get divorced, have children, travel, work, spend time in, buy, retire.*

2.2 Past continuous

Grammatically, the past continuous is fairly easy.

Its structure runs:

'To be' in past + verb in gerund

For example, 'She was studying.'

Its usage, however, is not so clear and must be taught. The basic cases are:

a) Duration: To show something was happening continuously over a long period of time, but has now finished. For example, 'I was working all weekend'.

b) Context: To provide the context for the story, such as, 'He was running in the park when he saw his friend.'

c) Two events: To use with 'while' to show that two separate actions were happening at once. For example, 'She was looking after the baby while she was cooking.'

How to teach it

A) Duration

This is not so common among native speakers, but important to know. To teach it, first write, 'I was working all weekend,' on the board and elicit whether the event is finished or continues.

Next elicit the structure (above), the negative 'I wasn't working all week-end,' and the question, 'Were you working all weekend?'

Now elicit the difference between 'I was working all weekend' and 'I worked all weekend.' The answer: 'I was working all weekend' emphasises the duration of the action.

Here you must be careful. You don't want your students to walk out of the classroom thinking they can substitute past continuous for past simple. It is not correct to say 'She was watching a film yesterday.'

You must emphasise that you only use past continuous when there is a very long action, done continuously. And even then it is probably better to substitute it for another past. For example, 'She used to live in Paris,' is much better than 'She was living in Paris.'

Question practice
Pairs' activity 'Past continuous interview': Questions are important. To start, write a sentence on the board and tell your students to ask you questions about it. Correct them when the question should be in past simple.

For example: 'I was walking in the park.'

Tom: 'Where were you walking to?'

Teacher: 'I was walking to my Grandmother's house.'

Sarah: 'Why were you visiting your Grandmother?'

Teacher: 'Because I was bringing her a cake.' And so on.

Next ask your students to think of a past continuous statement and in pairs ask and answer as many related questions as they can.

B) Context
This is the most common way we use the past continuous. To start, write 'He was running in the park when he saw his friend,' and elicit the number of actions in the sentence. The answer: two.

Explain that one action provides the context of the sentence while the other is the event.

Ask the class to tell you which is which. Elicit, 'Running' is the context while 'Saw his friend' is the event.

Emphasise that the second verb (the event), is <u>always</u> in past simple.

Freer speaking practice

Lay out some pictures on the table, together with the irregular verbs you have been studying. The images must contain at least one action, maybe a sporting event, a scene from a film, or a news story. Ask your students to invent single sentence stories using the past continuous for context and the irregular verbs for events. For example, 'The politician was speaking when the protesters entered the building.'

Practice questions by telling your students to ask questions for both the context and the event. For example, 'Where were they running?' and, 'What did they do?'

C) Two events

This usage is most often expressed in literature. To teach it write, 'She was looking after the baby while she was cooking.'

Elicit the amount of actions in the sentence. The answer: two.

Elicit the negative, 'She wasn't looking after the baby while she was cooking,' and the question, 'Was she looking after the baby while she was cooking?'

Ask, 'What is the difference between this sentence and the previous context/event sentence, "He was running in the park when he saw his friend"'?

Elicit or explain that here there is no context; both actions are the event and have equal importance. They are connected by the word 'while', which means 'at the same time' and is often (though not always) used with a continuous tense.

Freer speaking practice
Pairs' activity 'Two event stories': Spread out your irregular verbs on the table. Ask your students to make sentence-long stories about two actions happening at once. Get their partners to ask questions. For example, 'He was eating a sandwich while he was driving a bus.' Question: 'Why was he eating a sandwich while driving a bus?' Answer: 'Because he didn't have lunch.'

2.3 Present perfect

The present perfect provides the bridge between the past and the present and is very common in English, if not all European languages.

Its structure runs:

Subject pronoun/noun + have + verb participle

For example, 'She has played tennis today', or 'Tom has seen Rocky V'

The verb participle is not the same as past. The past of 'see' is 'saw' while its participle is 'seen.' For a list of irregular verbs go to common irregular verbs in the appendix.

'Have' is not a normal verb here, but an auxiliary verb, which makes the tense.

The present perfect has two meanings:

1) To express something that started in the past but in a time that continues to the present. For example, in the case of 'She has played tennis today,' it happened in the past but 'today' still continues.
2) To express something that happened in the past but you don't know (or it is not important) when. In the example of 'Tom has seen Rocky V', we don't know when Tom saw it, and it is probably not important. The important thing is that it happened.

How to teach it

Write, 'She has played tennis today' on the board and elicit whether it is past, present or future. Answer: past.

Write, 'She played tennis yesterday.' Ask, 'What is the difference between these two sentences?'

Elicit or explain that the first action started in the past but in a timeframe that continues ('today' continues) while the second action is finished ('yesterday' is gone).

Now write, 'Tom has seen Rocky V.' Elicit whether it is the past, present or future. Now ask, 'When in the past?'

Elicit or explain that we don't know and it is not important.

Elicit the structure and give examples with other persons of the verb, highlighting the difference with 'have' in first and third person. For example, 'I *have* exercised this week' and 'she *has* exercised this week.'

Elicit the negative, 'She hasn't played tennis today' and the question, 'Has she played tennis today?'

Explain that 'have' <u>in this case</u> is an auxiliary verb and so we modify it to make negatives and questions. You must stress that outside of the perfect tense, 'have' is a normal verb and requires 'do.' If you don't do this, they will start saying 'Have you a pen?' or 'I haven't a pen,' which is something you should stamp out.

Controlled speaking practice

Lay your irregular verbs out on the table. Again, many of your students will have had irregular verb participles drilled into them at school, so it is important to find out what they know. Explain to them that you are going to do a question exercise and they can answer in positive or negative.

Pick up the verb 'eat', look at your strongest student and ask them, 'How many apples did you eat yesterday?' Elicit something like, 'I ate two apples.' Now ask them, 'And today?' Elicit, 'I have eaten one apple' or 'I haven't eaten any apples.'

Continue like this with 'How many' past simple and present perfect questions with time expressions such as 'today', 'this week', 'this month' and 'this year'. To save your voice and provide more practice get your students to ask questions also. <u>Remember to practice third person as well.</u>

For example:

Teacher: 'Sarah, ask Tom, how many coffees he has drunk this week.'

Sarah to Tom: 'How many coffees have you drunk this week?'

Tom: 'I have drunk eight coffees this week.'

Teacher: 'And your sister?'

Tom: 'She <u>has</u> drunk two coffees this week.'

Irregular verb question examples:
How many:

- Pairs of boots he/she wore yesterday. And today?
- Bananas he/she ate yesterday. And today?
- KMs he/she ran yesterday. And today?
- Coffees he/she drank last week. And this week?
- Cups he/she broke last week. And this week?
- Presents he/she gave last year. And this year?
- Keys he/she lost last month. And this month?
- Bills he/she paid last month. And this month?
- Hours of yoga he/she did last week. And this week?
- Friends he/she met last month. And this month?

- Cakes he/she made last year. And this year?
- Books he/she read last month. And this month?
- Hours he/she slept last week. And this week?
- Birthdays he/she forgot last year. And this year?
- Emails he/she wrote yesterday. And today?
- Sentences he/she said yesterday. And today?
- Times he/she came back home last week. And this week?
- KMs he/she drove last month. And this month?
- Sweets you bought last month. And this month?
- TV channels you chose to watch yesterday. And today?

2.3.1 Mistakes to watch out for: 'Can'

'Can' presents problems. Its strange infinitive 'to be able to' means that in present perfect it is 'I have been able to do my work today.'

To practice, ask students the following questions with 'Could you.'

For example:

Teacher: 'Sarah, could you do your work this week?'

Sarah: 'Yes, I have been able to do my work this week.'

Sometimes, you will stretch the grammatical point: 'Yes I have been able to pass my driving test,' is not very normal, but it is important that they practice.

'Could you...' sentences:
Practice with 'today', 'this week', 'this month' and 'this year.'

- o Pass your driving test
- o Learn English
- o Travel
- o Find a good beach
- o Learn to ride a bike
- o Write all your emails
- o Feed the dog
- o Have lunch
- o Win the lottery
- o Tidy your flat

2.3.2 The difference between past simple and present perfect

The difference between these two tenses is not obvious and so needs to be taught. Past simple refers to finished actions that occurred in something called 'closed time'. Present perfect, on the other hand, happened in the past but continues until the present. These actions happen in what's called 'open time'. For example, 'This week I *have spoken* to the teacher,' but 'Last week I *spoke* to the teacher.'

Have a look at the table on the next page:

Closed time	Open time
Yesterday	Today
Last night	Tonight (if it is tonight)
Last week	This week
Last month	This month
Last year	This year
This morning (if it's afternoon)	This afternoon(if it's afternoon)
One hour ago	In the last few days, months.
10 minutes ago	So far (as in, 'until now')
Two seconds ago	

How to teach the difference between past simple and present perfect

Ask your students to make a sentence in past simple using 'yesterday'. Next ask them to make the same sentence with 'today'. Elicit that the sentence is normally in present perfect because 'today' continues. Next ask your students to make a sentence using 'this week', (present perfect), ask them to make the same sentence again with 'last week' (past simple).

Finally, share some of the time markers above and ask your students if they think it is 'open time' or 'closed time.' Reinforce the point by asking students to make an example sentence for each time marker.

2.3.3 Never

'Never' is an adverb and is used to express negative in the perfect tense.

In the present perfect its structure runs:

Subject pronoun/noun + have + never + participle

Example: 'She has never eaten a pineapple.'

How to teach it

Write, 'I have been to New York' on the board and elicit the negative, 'I haven't been to New York.' Elicit or explain that there is a second negative with 'never' placed between the auxiliary and main verb.

Highlight that it can only be used with the affirmative auxiliary. 'I haven't never been to New York' is a double negative and very bad English.

Controlled speaking practice

Ask your students the following questions eliciting the negative with 'never' – for example 'I have never met the President of the United States.' Get your students to ask each other questions also, to practice.

When was the last time you:

- o   Met the President of the United States?
- o   Wrote an email to Madonna?
- o   Took the bus to China?
- o   Bought a Ferrari?
- o   Broke your best friend's motorbike?
- o   Came back to the English academy at 2am?
- o   Flew an aeroplane?
- o   Began building a car?
- o   Fell down a mountain?
- o   Went to the moon?
- o   Chose a pink and orange sweater for your father?

2.3.4 Have you ever...?

'Have you ever...?' means 'has it happened, once in your life?'

Its structure runs:

Have + subject pronoun/noun + ever + participle

Example: 'Have you ever seen a Star Wars movie?'

How to teach it

Write again, 'I have been to New York' and elicit the question, 'Have you been to New York?' Elicit or explain that there is a second question to mean, 'Has it happened?' and that is, 'Have you ever been to New York?'

Emphasise that this question is very common.

Freer speaking practice: Never and Have you ever...?
Pairs' activity 'Adventures': Tell your students to ask each other 'Have you ever...?' questions. For example, 'Have you ever lived in another country?' If that's a 'no', then they must answer 'No, I have never lived in another country.' If they have, then their partner must ask more questions. For example, 'When did you go to New York?' <u>Note:</u> They must switch to past simple, because now they are referring to finished past.

Further speaking practice
Pairs' activity 'Have you ever' game: Give your students a topic and three minutes to find five things they have in common using 'Have you ever...? They cannot be negative things in common such as 'We have both never had a dog.' Topics: Work, travel, dangerous activities, embarrassing situations.

2.3.5 Present perfect with for and since

The present perfect is often used to express ongoing time with the prepositions 'for' and 'since.'

'For' means duration; 'I have studied medicine for six years,' while 'since' answers the question 'When did it begin?' For example, 'I have studied medicine since I was a teenager.' 'Since' is often used with dates and ages – 'since 2007' or 'since she was 12.'

How to teach it

Write the above 'for' sentence on the board and elicit or explain the meaning.

Now write the 'since' sentence and elicit or explain the difference between 'since' and 'for.'

Explain that because 'for' and 'since' often express something that started in the past and continues to the present, they are most commonly used with present perfect. For example, 'I have lived in London since 2003'.

Elicit the question for the above sentences which is the same for both statements: 'How long have you studied medicine for?'

Note the 'for' at the end of the sentence. Students will often omit it, but this is bad English.

Freer speaking practice
Pairs' activity 'How long...?': Tell your students to ask each other 'How long...?' questions and answer with 'for' or 'since'. Below are some examples.

How long have you:

Known: Other students in this class, your oldest friend, me.

Lived: In your current city, at your current house.

Be: At this school, married, in your profession.

Had: Your car, the shoes you're wearing, your watch.

Liked: Your football team, a celebrity, a sport, TV programme.

2.4 Present perfect continuous

The present perfect continuous is an extension of the present perfect but with the participle 'to be' and the verb in continuous form.

Its structure runs:

Subject pronoun/noun + have + to be participle (been) + verb in gerund

For example: 'I have been working at my company for five years.'

The continuous form is very common and emphasises action; the above sentence, for example, is far more dynamic and interesting than 'I have worked at my company for five years.'

Note: The present perfect continuous is never used with the question 'Have you ever...?' or 'Never.'

How to teach it

Write the example sentence on the board and elicit the tense. Now write 'I have worked at my company for five years' and elicit or explain the difference between the two. Emphasise that the continuous form is very common – more common even than the present perfect for action verbs.

Elicit the negative: 'I haven't been working at my company for five years' and the question: 'How long have you been working at your company for?' Elicit a 'since' sentence such as, 'I have been working at my company since 2011.'

Freer speaking practice
Pairs' activity 'Speaking about hobbies': Tell your students to find out more about each other with the following questions. Make sure that they ask the complete 'How long...' question with 'for' at the end.

Questions:

How long have you been...?

Watching your favourite TV series.

Living in your house.

Reading your current book.

Doing your job.

Playing a sport.

Studying English.

2.5 Action verbs vs state verbs

There are some verbs, however, that cannot be put into the continuous form. These are known as state verbs – they are verbs where there is no action. For example, you cannot say 'I have been liking football for five years.' This is because 'like' is an opinion or state.

Common state verbs are:

Opinions: To appear, to believe, to have, to like, to love, to prefer, to seem, to suppose, to think (as in opinion).

Descriptions of things: To be + adjective, to belong, to consist, to contain, to exist.

Also: To have (as in possession), to know, to remember, to understand.

State verbs that double as action verbs
Some verbs, however, can be either an action or a state as they have two meanings. These are:

Think: Is a state when it is an opinion; 'She thinks France is a lovely country' and an action when speaking about ideas; 'He is thinking about going on holiday.'

Have: Is a state when it talks about a possession; 'He has a car' and an action when talking about 'having food' or 'having a good time.'

Remember: Is a state when talking tasks; 'Remember to turn off the light' and an action when talking about memories; 'He sat on the porch, remembering his Grandfather.' This is mainly used in literature.

The senses
Senses are also state verbs. This is because the person experiencing the sense does no action, but rather the sense arrives to them. However, be careful as many sense verbs have another meaning that is an action verb. These verbs are:

To see: It is, 'I see a ship,' not, 'I am seeing a ship.' However, 'To see' is also a synonym of, 'To meet' and in this case it is used in gerund – for example, 'I am seeing my friends this weekend.'

To hear: It is, 'I hear a train coming' and never, 'I am hearing a train.'

To taste: It is, 'She tastes orange in this cake' and not, 'I am tasting orange.' However, if you move your body while tasting something then it can be in gerund. For example, if someone phones you in a restaurant and asks you what you are doing you could reply, 'I am tasting the soup.'

To smell: It is, 'I smell home cooking' and never, 'I am smelling home cooking' because the smell comes to you. However, if you were in a garden and actively decided to bend down to smell the roses you could say, 'I am smelling the flowers.'

To feel: It is, 'This jumper feels like wool,' not, 'It is feeling like wool.' However 'feel' is used for emotions and sickness and in that case it can be used in gerund. For example, 'He is feeling sick.'

How to teach it

First explain the meaning and use of a state verb. Now, lay slips of paper on the table with state verbs and the same number of action verbs. In pairs ask your students to separate the verbs into action and state. Correct any mistakes and highlight the state verbs that double as action verbs. You may want to leave sense verbs for another lesson.

Impress upon your students they must memorise the list for homework to eliminate these mistakes.

Speaking practice

Pairs' game 'Celebrity interviews': Give each student the name of a famous person and tell them to keep it secret. Now, using action and state verbs with the present perfect and present perfect continuous (where possible), ask your students to interview each other as if their partner were that person, to discover their identity.

Question examples: 'Where do you live?' 'How long have you been <u>living</u> in XXX for?' 'Are you married?' How long have you been married for?', 'How long have you <u>known</u> XXX for?', 'Have you been <u>training</u> today?', 'How long have you <u>liked</u> your sport for?'

2.6 Past perfect

The past perfect is not as common as its present perfect counterpart; nevertheless it carries a very distinctive meaning and must be taught.

Its structure runs:

Subject pronoun/noun + had + participle

For example: '_I had eaten breakfast_ before I went to work,'

It means an action before another action. In the above sentence there are two actions 'eating breakfast' and 'going to work.' Past perfect expresses the first action, while the past simple expresses the second.

How to teach it

Write the above sentence on the board and elicit the amount of actions it contains. Next, ask your students to label the first and second action.

Underline the past perfect and elicit the tense and structure. Elicit or explain that the past perfect is made in the same way as the present perfect but with 'had' instead of 'have.' In every past perfect sentence there are two actions; the first is represented by the past perfect, while the second is in past simple. Emphasise that the second action is always in past simple, as not all languages work this way.

Elicit the negative, 'He hadn't eaten breakfast before he went to work,' and the question, 'Had he eaten breakfast before he went to work?'

Controlled speaking practice: The one hour later drill

To practice, give your student a sentence and ask them to retell the story, but one hour after it has happened.

For example, the teacher says: 'I drank coffee and now I am going to work.' The student imagines that it is one hour later replies, 'I _had_ drunk coffee before I _went_ to work.'

Two event sentences

- I drank coffee and now I am going to work.
- I walked the dog and now I will see my mother.
- She took out the rubbish and now she will clean the flat.
- We gave the cat food and now we will write emails.
- She chose a wedding gift for her friend and now she will ring her.
- They spoke with their boss and now they are promoted.
- I made dinner and now my parents will arrive.
- They passed the exam and now they will get their licences.
- He booked the hotel and now he has to buy plane tickets.
- We learnt our grammar and now we will write a letter.
- I hoovered the flat and now I will watch TV.
- She broke her leg and now she will go to hospital.
- He passed his exam and now he is a lawyer.
- They wrote the email and now they will buy the house.
- He found the receipt and now he will take back the jumper.
- We learnt English and now we will move to the USA.
- He bought the car and now he will pick up his mother.
- The dog bit the boy and now it is being sold.
- She fell down the mountain and now she will catch the train.

Freer speaking practice

Pairs' activity 'Two action stories': Lay out a mix of adjectives and nouns on the table. Mine include: Ford Fiesta, iPad, drunk taxi driver, bucket of paint, hospital, happy dentist, angry mother-in-law, hoover, bear, new job, plane, holiday, priest, coffee, new shoes.

Ask your students to add verbs to make the opening line of a story. For example, 'He had visited the happy dentist before he went on holiday...'

Mistakes to watch out for

Some students will get too ambitious and try to fit two past perfects into one sentence. This isn't possible. Equally, saying two past perfect sentences after one another isn't normal and you must guide them to use their common sense.

2.7 Past perfect continuous

I teach the past perfect continuous together with the past perfect as its meaning is exactly the same but with continuous to emphasise the action.

Controlled speaking practice
Ask your students to change these sentences as if they were speaking one hour later. For example, 'She was cycling to work and then she sees an accident,' changes to 'She had been cycling to work when she saw an accident.'

- o She was cycling to work and then she sees an accident.
- o He was doing his homework and then the phone rings.
- o They were building a house and then there is an earthquake.
- o We were having breakfast and then the police arrive.
- o I was speaking with my friend when we see a robbery.
- o You were walking to work and then an explosion happens.
- o They were watering the plants when a dog jumps over the fence.
- o We were watching TV and then the oven explodes.
- o I was finishing the exam when my mobile rings.
- o He was buying apples when the thief appears.
- o She was presenting the meeting when the boss falls over.
- o You were feeding the cats when you discover the treasure.

Freer Speaking Practice

In the same way as before, ask your students to use random nouns and adjectives to create an opening line of a story, this time in continuous form.

Example: 'He had been buying an iPad when he saw the robbery.'

2.8 Used to
'Used to' refers to repetitive action in past and its structure runs:

Subject pronoun/noun + used + infinitive with 'to'

Example: 'She used to swim when she was a teenager.'

In fact, it's a modal verb, but a strange one as it still requires the auxiliary 'do' to make questions and negatives. 'Used to' only means past – its present equivalent is the adverb 'usually.' It is for actions that are completely finished. The above sentence means the girl is either no longer a teenager *or* no longer a teenager and no longer swims.

How to teach it

Write the above sentence on the board and elicit whether it is past, present or future. Next elicit whether the action finished or continues.

Now write 'She swam when she was a teenager,' and ask: 'What is the difference between these two sentences?'

Elicit or explain that 'used to' implies a repetitive action while the past simple sentence means (most of the time) one time only.

Here, it is a good idea to find out what tense 'used to' represents in the students' own languages. In Spanish it is the imperfect tense; other European languages will have their equivalents also. A common mistake among second language speakers is to ignore it in favour of past simple, making their sentences sound static and lifeless. Emphasise that it is commonly used.

Explain that 'used to' is a modal verb and so cannot be coupled with another modal ('She used to should exercise' is impossible, for example) but it still requires 'do' for the interrogative and negative.

Elicit or explain the negative, 'She didn't used to swim when she was a teenager,' and the interrogative: 'Did she use to swim when she was a teenager?'

For further understanding, elicit or explain the present of this sentence, 'She usually swims as she is a teenager.'

Controlled speaking practice

Ask your students to reverse these 'anymore' statements with 'used to.' To practice the auxiliary, ask them to give you the negative and question as well.

For example, 'Brazil is not the best football team in the world anymore' which is also therefore 'Brazil used to be the best football team in the world.' In negative, 'Brazil didn't use to be the best team in the world,' and interrogative, 'Did Brazil use to be the best team in the world?'

- o Andre Agassi is not a tennis champion anymore.
- o Sarah isn't a lawyer anymore.
- o Simon doesn't play tennis anymore.
- o Now Maria is no longer slim.
- o She can ride a bike now.
- o They don't live in France anymore.

- o Fred and Beatrice don't go to school anymore.
- o We can speak English now.
- o They can sing now.
- o He doesn't like chicken anymore.
- o I don't like swimming anymore.

- o My husband doesn't go to school anymore.
- o I can speak Spanish now.
- o Gladiator tournaments are no longer popular in Rome.
- o She doesn't enjoy scuba diving anymore.
- o Maria doesn't drive a motorbike anymore.
- o My brother isn't slim anymore.

Mistakes to watch out for

Pronunciation: 'Used to' is notoriously difficult to pronounce. Eliminate this problem right away by writing in big letters 'Youst-tu' next to the word and get them to say it out loud.

Questions and negatives: Remember that the interrogative and negative is made with the auxiliary with 'use to' in infinitive form. For example, 'I didn't used to study,' is not correct, it is 'I didn't use to study.' This can be tricky to remember as the pronunciation does not differ significantly.

To be: We use 'used to' with both action and state verbs, 'I used to know the answer,' for example, is just as correct as 'I used to play tennis.' However, when using 'to be' verb, be careful.

'Used to' can be used with states that have since changed such as old professions or characteristics – for example, 'He used to be a doctor' or 'They used to be shy.'

However, it cannot be used for things that are normally permanent, such as gender, nationality, skin colour and height, even if the person is dead (and the action finished) as it means that at some point they ceased to have this characteristic.

For example, my grandmother was Spanish and lived to 81. She is dead now, but I cannot say that 'She used to be Spanish,' because that means that at some point she changed her nationality. You must instead say, 'She was Spanish.' Likewise, I cannot say 'My brother used to be tall as a teenager,' as that means he is no longer tall. It is, 'He was tall as a teenager.'

But, remember, how you use 'used to' with 'to be' very much depends on the context. If someone is born male and then, after an operation, becomes female then it is perfectly acceptable to say 'She used to be male.' On the other hand, the statement 'My (dead) Grandfather used to be a man,' simply makes no sense.

Freer Speaking Practice

Pairs activity 'Sports stars roleplay': Ask one student to pretend to be a retired sports person of their choice. The other student is the interviewer who must ask questions about their previous sport's routine. Encourage the interviewer to be ambitious with questions such as 'How long did it use to take you to run 100 metres?' 'How far did you used to swim?' and 'How often did you use to train?'

Variation on the task: Give Student A the name of a famous retired sports person and ask them to keep it secret. Student B must guess who they are by asking questions. Example question, 'Where did you use to train?' Answer: 'I use to train at Camp Nou in Barcelona.'

Further speaking practice: Tell your students to speak in pairs about how they have changed over the years with sports, TV series, pets, hobbies, haircuts, clothes, phobias, ambitions and foods.

3. The Future

English is a dynamic language. The present is a fleeting moment (spoken in continuous, not present simple) which means if we are not speaking in past then we are speaking in future. This can be difficult for students to grasp, as many languages are spoken primarily in present to refer to both now and the future. The four main future structures are 'going to', 'will', 'continuous as future' and present simple. In the next chapter I will go into each one in more detail. I have also included the future perfect for higher level students.

3.1 Going to
'Going to' means a fixed plan in the future.

Its structure runs:

Subject pronoun + 'to be' + going + infinitive

Example: 'He is going to play football on Saturday.'

'Going to' has its equivalents in other languages and students normally get the meaning quickly but it's still worth doing the groundwork.

How to teach it
Write the above sentence on the board and elicit whether it is past, present or future.

Elicit or explain that we use 'going to' for plans or for something that is definitely going to happen.

For example, if you see a dark cloud on the horizon you can say, 'It is going to rain.' However, you can't say, 'Do you think it is going to rain tomorrow?' because rain is too uncertain. Instead we use 'will' for prediction.

Elicit the negative, 'He isn't going to play football on Saturday' and the question, 'Is he going to play football on Saturday?'

Controlled speaking practice
Ask your students the following questions. Ask them also to ask each other and don't forget to use different subject pronouns.

For example:

Teacher: 'Tom, ask Sarah if she is going to study this weekend.'

Tom to Sarah: 'Are you going to study this weekend?

Sarah: 'No, I am not going to study this weekend.'

<u>Now practice the third person</u>

Teacher: 'Sarah, ask Tom if his <u>brother</u> is going to work this afternoon.'

Sarah to Tom: '<u>Is</u> your brother going to work this afternoon?'

Tom: 'Yes, he is going to work.

More question examples: Add a different subject pronoun as appropriate to practice I, you, he, she, it, we and they.

If he/she is going:

- o Back to work after class.
- o To do their homework.
- o To drive home.
- o To see their family tonight.
- o To snow tonight.
- o Enjoy their weekend.

- o To eat dinner tonight.
- o To celebrate their birthday this year.
- o To vote in the next election.
- o To start a new hobby next year.
- o To eat sushi this week.
- o To go to the cinema this weekend.

Freer Speaking Practice
Pairs' activity 'Discussing plans': Get your students to speak about their plans for the week, the weekend, next summer, next Christmas and so on. To practice the third person, tell them also to ask and answer questions about a sibling or other family member.

3.2 Will

'Will', also expresses future but there is a difference between, 'I am going to catch the bus this afternoon' and, 'I will catch the bus this afternoon.' The first expresses certainty while the second includes an element of doubt.

Its structure runs:

Subject pronoun + will + infinitive (no 'to')

'Will', in fact, has three distinctive meanings all based on probability. These are:

Intention: 'She will study this weekend (provided that she doesn't get distracted)', 'We will go for a picnic this afternoon (provided that the weather is good).'

Offer of help: 'I'll open the door for you,' 'They'll take you to the airport this morning.'

Prediction: 'I think Brazil will win the championship,' 'It looks like it will rain tomorrow.'

It also forms the first part of something called the First Conditional, the meaning of which we will discuss in the Conditionals chapter.

'Will' is a modal verb. This means that the question and negative are made within the verb (rather than using an auxiliary) and its tense cannot be changed.

How to teach it

Write on the board 'I will catch the bus this afternoon' and elicit whether it is past, present or future.

Now write 'I am going to catch the bus this afternoon,' and elicit the difference. Elicit or explain that 'going to' expresses certainty, while 'will' is a *probable* future and often dependent on something else happening.

For example, 'I will catch the bus this afternoon, provided that I get there on time.' We don't say the second half of the sentence but that is what we *mean*.

Elicit the negative: 'I will not catch the bus this afternoon,' and with contraction 'I won't catch the bus this afternoon,' and the question, 'Will you catch the bus this afternoon?'

Highlight the affirmative contraction. Rub out 'I will catch the bus,' and put 'I'll catch the bus.' Elicit or explain the contractions for all subject pronouns.

Explain that 'will' is a modal verb; it therefore cannot be used in the same sentence with an auxiliary verb such as 'do' or another modal.

Now explain the different meanings of 'will'; write an intention, an offer of help and a prediction sentence on the board and elicit the differences.

Distinguishing between present simple and future

Ask your students, 'When do we use the present simple?' Elicit or explain it is usually used only to express routines such as, 'Every day I go running,' or the imperative, 'Go to the door.'

Emphasise that the present moment hardly exists in English (if it does it is expressed in continuous form) and so the comment, 'I'll take the books for you,' (at this moment) is expressed in future (as an offer of help), even though it is in happening now. This is important as many languages would express this in present.

Controlled speaking practice

Ask your students the following questions. Ask them also to ask each other and don't forget to use different subject pronouns. If possible, get them to invent the second clause of the sentence using 'if' or 'provided that'. For example:

Teacher: 'Sarah, ask Tom if he will eat spaghetti tonight.'

Sarah to Tom: 'Will you eat spaghetti tonight?'

Tom: 'Yes, I will eat spaghetti tonight.'

Teacher: 'You will eat spaghetti tonight if...?'

Tom: 'I will eat spaghetti tonight *if I have the ingredients.*'

Now practice the third person

More question examples: Add a different subject pronoun as appropriate to practice I, you, he, she, we, they.

If he/she/it will:

- o Take the bus home
- o Eat spaghetti tonight
- o Take up salsa dancing
- o Send an email after this class
- o Emigrate to another country after they finish this course
- o Go to the supermarket
- o Have six kids
- o Retire when they're 50
- o Drink a coffee tonight
- o Rain tomorrow
- o Start their own business
- o Open a French restaurant

3.2.1 Introducing may and might

'May' and 'might' are also modal verbs, they refer to either the present or future but with more doubt than 'will.' For example, 'We might to go the cinema tonight,' means that it is a possibility not an intention.

Their structure runs:

Subject pronoun/noun + might/may + infinitive (no 'to')

How to teach it

Write, 'We might go to the cinema tonight' and 'We will go to the cinema tonight' on the board and elicit the difference.

Now write, 'We may go to the cinema tonight.' Elicit or explain that 'might' and 'may' mean exactly the same thing (students often worry about this).

Elicit the negative, 'We might not go to the cinema tonight' and, 'We may not go to the cinema tonight.'

Note: There is no contraction between 'might/may' and 'not'. 'Mightn't' is not possible.

Elicit the question: Logically this would be 'Might we go to the cinema tonight?' But it's not. It is *possible* but when was the last time you heard it? The real question is 'Do you want to go to the cinema tonight?'

Controlled speaking practice

Ask your students to ask each other normal future questions with 'going to' and 'will.' If the answer is a possibility get them to answer with 'might' or 'may.' Don't forget to use all subject pronouns.

If he/she/it will or is going to:

- ○ Go to the cinema this month.
- ○ Watch a film tonight.
- ○ Cut their hair.
- ○ Dance the salsa this weekend.
- ○ Cook tonight.
- ○ Learn another language.
- ○ Join a new social network.
- ○ Make a cake this weekend.
- ○ Snow in December.
- ○ Wear jeans tomorrow.

Putting it all together: Will, won't, may and might

Freer speaking practice

Pairs' activity 'Your future': Tell your students to make predictions, intentions and possibilities about their life in one, five and ten years. To help prompt a conversation write some ideas on slips of paper and place them in the middle of the table. For example: Get married, have kids, learn to drive, graduate from college, travel around the world, write a book, live abroad.

Tell them to extend the conversation by using a variety of question words. For example:

Tom: 'Will you live abroad, do you think?'

Sarah: 'Yes, I might live abroad.'

Tom: 'Great, where might you live?'

3.2.2 Adding hypothetical future: Would like to

'Would like to' can either mean a polite request; 'I would like a coffee,' or a hypothetical future; 'I would like to travel next year.' Your students already know the request 'Would like' in the Language function: Ordering in restaurants lesson. Now it is time to introduce the other meaning.

Its structure runs:

Subject pronoun/noun + would + like + infinitive (with 'to')

For example: 'She would like to buy a dog.'

How to teach it

Write on the board, 'I would like to travel next year' and elicit whether it is past, present or future. Ask, 'Is this real or hypothetical?' Elicit, 'Hypothetical.'

Elicit or explain that 'would' is a modal verb that means either hypothetical present or future if placed with a future time marker ('next year,' 'tonight', 'next week' and so on.) It is never placed with an auxiliary or another modal. Instead the negative and question are made within the verb.

Elicit the negative, 'I wouldn't like to travel next year,' and the question, 'Would you like to travel next year?'

Controlled speaking practice

Get your students to ask each other questions. Don't forget to cover all subject pronouns.

If he/she would like to:

- o Go skiing next year.
- o Swim with sharks.
- o Buy a new digital device.
- o Eat ice cream after class.
- o Earn more money.
- o Buy a new car next year.
- o Learn to play an instrument.
- o Start horse-riding lessons next summer.
- o Fly to Japan and some point in the future.
- o Live in a tent.

Freer speaking practice

Pairs' activity 'Things I would like to do before I am...': Ask your students to create a list of things they would like to do before they are 30, 40, 50 and retired. Next, get your students to ask each other questions about their lists. Don't forget to use lots of question words.

Example:

Tom: 'I would like to go travelling to the USA before I am 30.'

Sarah: 'How long would you like to go travelling for?'

3.3 Present continuous for future
We use present continuous for future in much the same way as 'going to'; that is, for plans and certainties.

Its structure runs:

Subject pronoun/noun + 'to be' + verb + gerund + future time marker

For example: 'John is taking his driving test next week.' The test is booked, and he will definitely take it.

How to teach it

Write the example sentence on the board and elicit whether it is past, present or future. Ask 'How do you know it is future?' Explain or elicit that we know it is future because of the time expression 'next week.' Take that away and it means that John is taking his driving test *now*.

Ask: 'Is this a prediction, intention or a certainty?' Elicit: 'Certainty.' Elicit or explain that present continuous is used like 'going to' for things that are definitely going to happen.

For due diligence, elicit the negative, 'John isn't taking his driving test next week,' and the question, 'Is John taking his driving test next week?

Controlled speaking practice
Get your students to ask each other questions using present continuous + future
time expression. Don't forget to practice all subject pronouns.

If he/she is:

- o Working tomorrow?
- o Driving home?
- o Spending Christmas with his family?
- o Going to the circus this weekend?
- o Making dinner tonight?
- o Making a cake this weekend?

- o Cycling to work tomorrow?
- o Buying a car this weekend?
- o Coming to class on Wednesday?
- o Skiing this winter?
- o Travelling this year?
- o Watching TV tonight?
- o Doing this weekend?

Freer speaking practice
Pairs' game 'One lie and two truths': Ask your students to write two things
that are true and one that is a lie about the future. They must not reveal which is
false. Their partner must now ask questions in present continuous (where possible) to discover which one is the lie.

For example:

Sarah: I am travelling to Indonesia next year.

Tom: OK, *Where* are you staying and *how long* are you staying for?

3.4 Present simple for future

By now your students should be trained to use some form of future to express
the distant future, the near future and even the present moment. They should
know also that we only use present simple for routines and imperative and never
for future.

96

But there is just one thing: we do. When speaking about a written schedule, such as a bus timetable or a cinema programme, it is perfectly acceptable to use present to mean future.

For example, 'The bus leaves at 8pm tonight.' Tonight is the future, but I am speaking in present because this information comes from a timetable that will not change in the immediate future. Equally you can say, 'The film starts at 7pm on Tuesday,' or, 'The flight arrives at 4am tomorrow morning.'

How to teach it

I usually explain this final future in the way that I have explained it above. There is no real need to practice as they already know the present simple.

Freer speaking practice

If you wish to practice, bring some bus or train timetables to class. If you have the Internet, ask them to look up the local cinema listings. In pairs, get them to ask each other questions about bus, train or film times.

3.5 Future perfect

The future perfect expresses a future action that will happen *before* another future action. For example: 'I <u>will have saved</u> enough money to go travelling before I quit my job.'

There are two future actions in this sentence: 'Saving money' and 'quitting my job.' We understand from the tense that 'saving money' will occur before 'quitting my job.' In this way it is the reverse of the past perfect.

Its structure runs:

Subject pronoun/noun + will + have + participle + object + a 'time clause' + subject pronoun/noun + present simple

Example: 'I will have spent all my money this month *before* I get paid

<u>It is important to note</u> the second half of the sentence is in present, not future, even though both actions occur in the future.

The reason is that after time clauses we never express future (though you can express past).

For example: 'We will have a meeting when we *will* know the answer,' is not correct. It is 'We will have a meeting when we know the answer.'

Do not confuse time clauses with time markers. Time clauses are: 'when', 'while', 'before', 'after', 'by the time', 'as soon as', 'if' and 'unless'.

Time markers are: 'everyday', 'today', 'tomorrow', 'next week', 'next month' and 'next year' and so on. With these you can use future.

How to teach it

Write, 'I will have saved enough money before I quit my job,' and elicit whether it is past, present or future.

Ask, 'How many actions are in this sentence?' and elicit: 'Two.' Elicit which is the first and second action.

Ask, 'What tense is this?' Elicit or explain that it is the future perfect. The first part of the sentence (the future perfect) expresses the first action, while the second expresses the second action. The two actions are separated by a time clause (in this case 'when'). You can never use future after a time clause and so the second action is in present simple.

Elicit the structure, the negative, 'I won't have saved enough money before I quit my job,' and the question, 'Will you have saved enough money before you quit your job?'

Controlled speaking practice

I do this with the time clause 'by the time' or 'by' + time marker. For example 'By Saturday, I will have done my homework.'

Explain that both 'by the time' and 'by + time marker' marks a time in the future when you will have completed something.

Now using all subject pronouns get your students to ask each other questions.

For example:

Teacher: 'Sarah, ask John if he will have eaten dinner by seven o'clock tonight?'

Sarah to John: 'Will you have eaten dinner by seven o'clock tonight?'

John: 'No, I won't have eaten dinner by seven o'clock tonight.'

Questions

If he/she/we will have:

- Eaten dinner by seven o'clock tonight.
- Retired by the time they're 65.
- Done homework by the weekend.
- Finished his/her studies by the time they're 25.
- Cleaned the house by next week.
- Discovered a cure for all diseases by next century.
- Booked a holiday by next month.
- Bought presents by Christmas Day.
- Learnt to drive by the time they're 21.
- Repaired the hole in the ozone layer by the time they're 80.

Freer speaking practice

Pairs' activity 'Milestones': Now introduce a further concept 'By the time I turn + age.' Explain that 'to turn' means to reach an age and is often used with future perfect. For example, 'By the time I turn 60 I will have travelled the world.'

Ask your students to talk with their partner about future milestones (you will have to explain the word) they want to achieve. For example, 'By the time I turn 35 I will have bought a house,' or if it is not for certain, 'By the time I turn 35, I may have bought a house.'

Further speaking practice

Pairs' debate 'Our planet': Write these statements on the board and ask your students to speak in pairs about whether they agree or disagree.

By 2020 the economy will have improved.

By 2050 Japan's population will have shrunk.

By the end of the century sea levels will have risen.

By the time I have grandchildren world poverty will have disappeared.

By the time I turn 70 the world will have got warmer.

Ask them to clarify their thoughts with the phrase 'In the long run' which means 'In the distant future.' For example, 'In the long run the world will have got warmer.'

4. Gerund vs Infinitive

In all sentences with at least two verbs we modify the first verb to make the tense while the second remains in its original form, known as the infinitive. For example 'She wants to go to school.' Here 'wants' makes the tense (present, third person) while 'to go' is the infinitive.

This is pretty straightforward, the only problem is that English there are two infinitives; one with the verb in its original form (as demonstrated above) and one with verb + 'ing' called 'gerund.' To distinguish between the two, from now on I will refer to the verb in original form as 'infinitive'.

4.1 The rules
Gerund

1. After certain verbs

Gerund occurs after verbs expressing 'like and dislike.' These include:

To fancy, to enjoy, to hate, to like, to love, to not mind, to not be able to stand, to prefer.

For example, 'He fancies having a coffee,' or 'She hates dancing.'

It is also used with verbs that express 'stop' and 'start.' These include:

To begin, to finish, to start and to stop.

You will have noticed that with some of these verbs you can use both the infinitive and gerund form. For example, 'He likes to ski' and 'He likes skiing' are perfectly correct as is 'She begins to study' and 'She begins studying.'

However, it is much better to teach the gerund form only, as it is a) more common and b) applies to all of the verbs above, whereas this is not the case with the infinitive. You cannot say 'He enjoys to ski,' for example, or 'She stops to study.'

You will also have noticed that there are many more verbs that are followed by gerund. This will be addressed in the Gerund vs Infinitive advanced lesson. For now, stick with the verbs above.

2. After preposition

Gerund is also used after prepositions. This happens in all cases, without exception. For example, 'She is scared <u>of</u> flying,' or, 'They are thinking <u>about</u> going on holiday'.

Common prepositions are: Above, ago, as, at, below, between, by, for, from, on, off, in, into, past, since and with.

Infinitive

1. After certain verbs

The infinitive occurs after verbs such as: To decide, to forget, to offer, to learn, to need, to plan, to try, to want, would like.

Unfortunately, there is no way to categorise these verbs. Students must simply memorise them. This is also only the basic list, but I will cover more in the advanced lesson.

2. After adjectives

The infinitive with 'to' is always used after adjectives – for example, 'It is easy <u>to learn</u> English when you are young', or 'It is impossible <u>to drive</u> to Jupiter.' This happens without exception.

Common adjectives used with verbs include: Better, difficult, easy, hard, important, impossible and possible.

How to teach it

Write on the board: 'Sarah likes skiing' and 'Sarah wants to ski.' In each sentence underline the verb 'ski' and elicit the form of the verb.

Elicit or explain that the first verb is in gerund and the second is in normal infinitive with 'to.' Technically both these endings are types of infinitives, but telling your students this will confuse them so it is better to stick with 'gerund' and 'infinitive.'

Explain that certain verbs are followed by gerund and others are followed by infinitive. In the case of gerund, these verbs often express a 'like' or 'dislike,' or 'start' or 'stop.' Infinitive verbs, however, cannot be categorised and must be learnt.

Pairs' task 'Gerund or infinitive?'

Hand out slips of paper with the above verbs or for larger classes write them on the board. In pairs, ask your students to separate them into gerund and infinitive. When everyone has finished write two columns on the board, labelled 'Gerund' and 'Infinitive,' and write the table out as a class.

Now write, 'It is easy to learn English when you are young' and 'she is scared of flying' on the board. Ask them to identify the form of the second verbs. Now ask, 'Why is the first sentence in infinitive while the second one gerund?'

Elicit or explain that infinitive with 'to' always comes after adjectives while gerund always comes after prepositions.

Now with more slips of paper ask the pairs to come up with six-to-eight questions using gerund and infinitive verbs. Ask them to use different subject pronouns (not just 'you') and question words.

This is a good time to go through some prepositions and teach some meanings. For example, 'To be good at a subject or task,' 'To be frightened/scared of something scary,' 'To think, worry, speak about a subject.'

Controlled speaking practice: Putting it all together

Collect and redistribute the slips of paper and in pairs tell your students to ask each other the questions. Don't forget to get them to ask questions about brothers, sisters, parents, friends and colleagues to practice different subject pronouns. To make the task more interesting add your own with the question endings below:

Questions

If he/she:

- Finds it difficult to remember peoples' names.
- Thinks women are better at drawing than men.
- Thinks it's difficult to learn to cycle at 30.
- Thinks it's possible to learn a foreign language without going to the country.
- Has any advice for someone who is scared of flying.
- Has ever forgotten to turn off his mobile during a meeting.
- Is good at speaking another foreign language.
- Needs to fly this week.

- o   Would like to fly this week.
- o   Minds flying.
- o   Will finish doing his homework tonight.
- o   Likes studying at night.
- o   Worried about something when they were a teenager.
- o   Knows some good subjects to talk about when meeting someone for the first time.
- o   Dreams of doing when they retire.
- o   Worried about making mistakes in their English class.

Freer speaking practice
Pairs' roleplay 'The careers councillor': Student A is a school-leaver, while Student B is a careers councillor. Using gerund and infinitive questions, the councillor must ask questions about the student's likes and dislikes to discover their ideal career.

Example questions: Would you like to travel as part of your job? Are you worried about making mistakes? Are you good at sitting at a computer for a long time? Do you like working with people? Do you need to earn a certain amount of money?

Further speaking practice
Pairs' roleplay 'Speed dating': Move the tables into a line and seat half the class while the half will rotate. Tell your class that this is a 'speed dating' exercise. Each pair has three minutes to ask and answer questions to work out whether they are the ideal person for them. To make it clear that this isn't a real dating exercise, assign each student a character. To make it even more fun, reverse the genders – give male roles to female students and vice versa.

Example questions: What do you like doing in your free time? Do you think it is important to earn lots of money? Where are you thinking of going in your next holiday?

4.3 Negative infinitives

When expressing negatives, students who speak romantic languages (such as French, Spanish and Italian) will often insert a 'that' after the verb to say, 'I try that I don't speak Spanish in my English lesson,' instead of the correct way, 'I try not to speak Spanish in my English lesson.'

To eliminate this mistake, say these sentences and ask your students to make them negative using a negative infinitive.

Example sentences:

- It's better to drive in the city – *it's better not to drive in the city.*
- She tries to eat lots of chocolate – *she tries not to eat lots of chocolate.*
- They decided to go to the party – *they decided not to go to the party.*
- It's important to get nervous in an exam – *it's important not to get nervous in an exam.*
- We try to spend lots of money – *we try not to spend lots of money.*
- It's impossible to laugh at that film – *it's impossible not to laugh at that film.*

4.3 Object + infinitive

Next tackle the object + infinitive problem. Students who speak romantic languages often say, 'I want that they call me tomorrow,' instead of the correct way, 'I want them to call me tomorrow.'

To eliminate this mistake, say the badly constructed sentence with 'that' and ask your students to correct it. This way, when a student makes a mistake in the future, they can self-correct without a reminder from the teacher.

Example sentences:

- I would like that he comes to the office early tomorrow – *I want him to come to the office early tomorrow.*
- I need that she buys me some bread – *I need her to buy me some bread.*
- I want that they don't tell the others about the problem – *I want them not to tell the others about the problem.*
- I would love that we visit New York – *I would love us to visit New York.*
- She needs that you take them out for coffee – *she needs you to take them out for coffee.*
- He would like that she picks up the package – *he would like her to pick up the package.*

4.4 Gerund vs infinitive advanced

There are many more verbs that can only be used with either gerund or infinitive, and so around upper-intermediate level, I recommend returning to it again.

In addition, there are verbs that can be used with *either* gerund or infinitive but will change their meaning depending on which one is used.

Infinitive advanced list

To afford, to agree, to appear, to arrange, to deserve, to expect, to fail, to hope, to manage, to promise, to prepare, to remember, to refuse.

Gerund advanced list

To avoid, to imagine, to involve, to miss, to practice, to regret, to resist, to risk, to spend, to tolerate, to understand.

Also: To admit, to advise, to encourage, to mention, to present, to propose, to suggest.

I have separated the above seven verbs into an 'also' list because students often find it difficult to accept that they are with gerund. However, it is not 'I recommend to go to the beach,' it is 'I recommend going to the beach.'

Likewise, it is not; 'She suggested to buy apples,' it is 'She suggested buying apples.'

The confusion arises because the infinitive after these verbs can be split with a noun or object pronoun. When this happens, you use a normal infinitive with 'to.'

For example: 'I recommend <u>to her</u> to go to the beach,' or 'she suggested <u>to him</u> to buy apples. '

<u>Note:</u> With these verbs we use '<u>to</u>' before the object pronoun. You must highlight this to your students or they will omit it. The same is true with 'propose' ('propose to them'), 'admit' ('admitted to us'), 'mention' ('mentioned to me') and 'present' ('present to you').

After 'encourage' and 'advise' there is no 'to'. 'I encourage <u>them</u> to run.' Likewise; 'I encourage running.' 'She advises <u>him</u> to study.' Likewise; 'She advises studying.'

For more information on where and where not to put 'to' before objects see Direct and Indirect Objects, chapter 31.

Verbs that change their meaning depending on gerund or infinitive

Remember: 'To remember' plus infinitive refers to tasks. For example, 'Remember to take out the rubbish.' Plus gerund, however, refers to memories – for example, 'He remembers reading with his Grandmother.'

Try: 'To try' plus infinitive refers to intention – for example, 'She tries to learn a little vocabulary every night.' Plus gerund, however, it refers to 'to trial'. Example: 'Have you tried cooking Chinese food?', or 'I want to try skiing when we go on holiday.'

Like, love, hate: To like, to love, to hate plus infinitive means that you think something is a good or bad idea – for example: 'She likes to do her homework before dinner,' 'They hate to think badly of people,' or 'We love to eat out at least once a week.'

Plus gerund, however, means you actually like or hate doing something; 'I hate cleaning,' or 'She likes going to restaurants.'

Stop: 'Stop' plus infinitive means that the person stopped what they were doing to give information – for example, 'She stopped to mention that the football match was cancelled.'

'Stop' plus gerund means to stop in general. 'He stopped smoking,' or 'She has stopped going to dance classes.'

How to teach it

Review previous gerund and infinitive verbs with a table on the board. Now place the new verbs in the centre of the table and ask your students to separate them into gerund and infinitive. Once the list is correct and any objections dealt with, teach the verbs that change meaning with infinitive or gerund.

Controlled speaking practice

Hand out slips of paper and, in pairs, ask your students to make six to eight questions with both gerund and infinitive verbs. Try to use as many question words as you can and different subject pronouns.

Now get your students to ask each other the questions. For variety add some of your own to the pile.

Freer speaking practice
Pairs' roleplay 'Digital nomads': Tired of the routine, Student A has quit their job, given away their possessions and moved to Thailand. They are poor but make enough to survive on the Internet as a digital nomad. Student B, a friend from Student A's old life, has arrived and, using gerund and infinitive verbs, will try to convince them to return.

Example questions: 'How do you imagine retiring if you are not earning any money?' 'Are you avoiding living in the real world?' Example answers: 'My friend, try waking up every day to the sound of the ocean,' 'I miss seeing my friends but...'

---

5. Modal verbs in present

5.1 Obligation

Obligation verbs are the modals 'must' and 'should,' and also 'have to,' which is <u>not</u> a modal but essential in this grammar function.

'Must' is the strongest obligation; 'She must pay her taxes.' This is followed closely by 'have to' and then 'should,' which refers to advice. For example, in the sentence, 'He should see a doctor;' there is no obligation for him to see a doctor but it is probably a good idea. Finally there is 'don't have to' which means no obligation. For example, 'They don't have to study this weekend;' they could study but they are under no obligation to do so.

How to teach it

Write sentence with each verb on the board, such as:

'She must go to school,' 'She must see her teacher,' 'She should bring a healthy snack,' 'She doesn't have to eat potatoes for lunch.'

Now place slips of paper on the table with the verbs 'must', 'have to', 'should' and 'don't have to' (or write them on the board for a big class). Ask your students to put them in a cline with the most intense obligation at the top and the least at the bottom. You should end up with something like this:

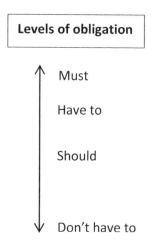

Levels of obligation

↑ Must

Have to

Should

↓ Don't have to

Place 'must' and 'have to' close together to indicate that their meaning is similar. Elicit or explain that 'I have to work today' relates to strong obligation while 'I don't have to work today' means its exact opposite, no obligation.

Elicit the question for each of the above sentences: 'Must she go to school?', 'Does she have to see her teacher?' , 'Should she bring a healthy snack?' , 'Does she have to eat potatoes for lunch?'

Note: Because 'must' and 'should' are modals the question is made in the verb. However, 'have to' is a normal verb still requiring the auxiliary 'do' for questions and negatives.

Now elicit the negative of each sentence: 'She mustn't go to school,' 'She doesn't have to see her teacher', 'She shouldn't bring a healthy snack.'

Highlight 'mustn't' and 'shouldn't' and elicit their meanings. You will see that the 'shouldn't' sentence just like 'don't have to' means the exact opposite ('shouldn't' is advice to say 'no').

The 'mustn't' sentence, however, is a trick. 'Mustn't' does not mean the opposite of 'must' (no obligation) but rather prohibition. You are saying that she is forbidden to go to school.

To make this clear, draw the below cline on the board.

Levels of prohibition

Mustn't

Shouldn't

Don't have to

Controlled speaking practice

Ask your students the following questions using 'can' so as not to give away which verb to use. Student must select the correct obligation verb to use for their answer. Do not accept illogical answers. For example:

110

Teacher: 'Sarah, can you buy me a Christmas present?'

Sarah: 'Yes, I must buy you a Christmas present?'

Teacher: 'Really Sarah, must you?'

Sarah: 'OK, I should buy you a Christmas present.'

Teacher: 'Really?'

Sarah: 'No, I don't have to buy you a Christmas present.'

Teacher: 'Exactly, well done.'

Questions 'Can you...?':

- Smoke in academy?
- Buy me a Christmas present?
- Sit down on an aeroplane?
- Park on the motorway?
- Watch TV all day?
- Drink two bottles of gin a day?

- Steal from shops?
- Do your homework?
- Eat every day or not?
- Drive at 200 mph on the highway?
- Drink beer every day or not?
- Have a Ferrari or not?

- Drink every day or not?
- Speak French to live in your city or not?
- Buy a new car every year?
- Exercise?
- Earn 100,000 dollars a year to live in your city?
- Remember your mother's birthday?

- Go to the doctor for a cold?
- Go to the doctor for a broken leg?
- Obey traffic rules?

- Drink alcohol if you are 12?
- Cut your hair every week?
- Go to the beach without sun cream?

- Buy a dog?
- Drive without a licence?
- Swim outdoors in February?
- Buy new clothes every day?
- Eat chocolate all day?
- Carry your mobile at all times?

- Wear a coat in winter?
- Speak English in class?
- Buy all your food at the supermarket?
- Visit Scotland?
- Walk on the motorway?
- Speak your language in your country?

Freer speaking practice
Pairs' activity 'Giving Advice': Give your students situations and ask them to advise each other on the things they must, mustn't, should, shouldn't, have to and don't have to do.

Situation examples: Buying a car, sightseeing in Paris, forgetting your partner's birthday, finding a new apartment, going on a first date, finding yourself shipwrecked on a desert island.

Further speaking practice
Pairs' activity 'Guess my location': Give a secret location to Student A. They must then help Student B discover where it is by saying things that you mustn't, must, should, shouldn't, have to and don't have to do in that particular place.

For example, if the location is 'Your sister's wedding,' a student may say, 'You shouldn't get too drunk,' 'You mustn't get dirt on her dress,' 'You don't have to kiss the groom.'

Locations: The academy, police station, the beach, the supermarket, a court room, a kindergarten, your parents-in-law's house, a school bus, a plane, a public toilet.

5.2 Shall

Shall is a modal verb used to make requests such as 'Shall we go to the cinema tonight?' It is more polite than 'Do you want to...?' as shall expresses more uncertainty, meaning; 'Do you want to go to the cinema tonight, if you would like to?' This is a particularly British way to speak, but it is useful as it allows the speaker to make requests without an auxiliary verb. It only refers to present and past. Its negative is shan't.

Its structure runs:

Shall + present

How to teach it

Write on the board 'Shall we go to the cinema tonight?' and 'Do you want to go to the cinema tonight?' and elicit the differences.

Elicit the positive: 'Yes, we shall go to the cinema tonight.' Highlight that, though possible, 'shall' in negative is not common. Explain also that it only means present or future.

Elicit its structure and explain its meaning and limitations.

Without any interesting way to practice I usually leave it to my students if they want to use it.

Note: In exams, examiners particularly like it if your students use the phrase 'Shall I start?' to begin the oral test – something to remember at the end of the course.

5.3 Deduction and possibility

The other way we use modals is to express deduction and possibility.

Imagine you are in a hospital, you see a professional-looking woman in a white coat, carrying a stethoscope and treating patients. You would think 'Ah, she must be a doctor,' or at least 'She must be a medical professional.' This is a deduction – making a reasonable judgement on what you believe to be true based on the information at hand. Look at the language: 'She *must* be a doctor.' This is not 'must' for obligation.

Now you see the same woman take off her coat, grab someone's handbag and run away chased by security guards. Now you think, 'Ah, she can't be a doctor.' Look again at the language; there is no 'mustn't' here, but rather 'can't' as we substitute the verb in negative. 'Mustn't' means prohibition as in, 'You mustn't smoke in the building.'

The final way we use modals is for possibility.

Now you go outside and see a film crew filming the woman's escape. Suddenly you think, 'OK, she might be an actress,' and 'This may be a movie set.' You might also think, 'She might not be a criminal after all.'

'May' and 'might' refer possibility. Don't forget they cannot be contracted in negative; 'mightn't' and 'mayn't' do not exist.

How to teach it

Explain the concept of deduction by telling your students the story above. Now lay pictures from the deductions worksheet at the back of the book and elicit positive deductions in present.

Write on the board one of those deductions. For example: 'She must be a school teacher.'

Now ask: 'Is she a builder?' Elicit or explain the negative: 'No, she *can't* be a builder.' Elicit or explain that we substitute 'must' for 'can' in negative. 'Mustn't' is not possible as it means prohibition.

Ask: 'Is she good at his job?' Elicit or explain that 'She may be good at his job' or 'She may not be good at his job.' This is a possibility, as there is not enough information to know for sure. Explain that 'may' and 'might' both mean the same thing and that there is not contraction with 'may not' and 'might not.'

Controlled speaking practice

Ask your students to make deductions and possibilities with the following sentences. Tell students to come up with imaginative answers but they must be logical. I have included some deductions in brackets, but these are not the only ones possible. All answers must be in present.

 For example:

Teacher: '"He lives on the streets." Any deductions?'

Sarah: 'He must be poor.'

Tom: 'He can't be warm at night.'

Teacher: 'Good, any possibilities?'

Sarah: 'He may be depressed.'

Teacher: 'Good, and in negative?'

Tom: 'He might not have any parents.'

Deductions

- He lives on the streets. Deduction: *He must be homeless.*
- She eats 2kgs of chocolate every day. *She must be overweight.*
- He cycles 25kms every day to work. *He must be fit.*
- They take two children to school every day and they live with them. *They must have children.*
- She is a brain surgeon. *She must be intelligent.*
- He as a plane licence. *He must fly planes.*
- He doesn't eat meat. *He must be a vegetarian.*
- She has a coffee machine and buys a lot of coffee. *She must like coffee.*
- He is wearing a crown. *He must be the king.*
- I have a British passport. *You must be British.*
- They make money by taking photos. *They must be photographers.*
- He is coughing and sneezing. *He must be ill.*

Freer speaking practice
Pairs activity 'Making deductions': Go back to deductions worksheet and ask your students to make more deductions and possibilities from the pictures. For a more dynamic class you could even play them the first 30 seconds of a funny YouTube video and ask them to deduce what is happening. Then play the rest of the video to see if they were right.

6. Modal verbs in past

When I did my teacher training, my instructor told me that one of the hardest things to grasp for students are modal verbs. At the time I found this difficult to believe; modals require no auxiliary, they carry no preposition and they can be used interchangeably to mean present and future.

However, as soon as I started teaching I realised what she meant. Modals may be fairly simple in present but in past they are mind-bogglingly complicated and take a lot of practice to get right. For this reason I recommend only tackling this topic at a B2 level onwards.

6.1 Obligation

Obligation in present is made of 'must', 'should' and the non-modal 'have to.'

If one day at the office you suddenly fall down a flight of stairs and hit your head badly against the floor, your colleagues would say 'You must go to the hospital.' Simple so far, but a week later, how do you recount this story to your friends?

Usually, to make a modal past you add 'have' plus participle. So, can you say? 'Well, I fell down some stairs and I <u>must have gone</u> to the hospital.' No, that doesn't work as 'must' here does not mean obligation. To make this sentence work you have to substitute 'must' with 'had' to make, 'I fell down some stairs and I <u>had</u> to go to hospital.'

Now imagine you have a terrible cold and a concerned colleague says, 'You should go to the doctor.' This is not obligation now, but advice. How do you recount that to your friends a week later? Well, in this case you add 'have' + participle to make 'I should have gone to the doctor.'

<u>Note:</u> This does not mean that you went to the doctor but rather it was a good idea to do so.

Now imagine that you did something that was prohibited or a bad idea, like smoking in the office toilets. You are caught by a security guard who says 'You must not smoke in the toilets.' A week later you recount the story, but how? You cannot substitute 'must' again for 'have' as 'I didn't have to smoke in the toilets' means you had no obligation to, not that it was prohibited.

You must, in fact, substitute the verb again to 'shouldn't' to make 'I shouldn't have smoked in the toilet.'

Confused yet? Let's recap:

Present:

'I must go to the hospital.'
'I should go to the doctor.'
'I mustn't smoke in the toilet.'

Past:

'I had to go to hospital.'
'I should have gone to the doctor' (you didn't).
'I shouldn't have smoked in the toilet.'

How to teach it

Write the above sentences on the board one at a time. Use the story above to explain to your students the verb changes. Don't forget to tell your students that 'should have + participle' talks about something that didn't occur, but was supposed to.

Controlled speaking practice
Ask your students to change these sentences to past.

- I must call him.
- He mustn't look in the cupboard.
- She mustn't argue with my neighbour.
- We must buy a new sofa.
- He should apply for the job.
- They mustn't throw stones from the balcony.
- I must study next weekend.
- You must not sit there.
- They shouldn't get married too early.
- They must water the plants next week.
- We must not tell him.
- She should wear a jacket.

Freer speaking practice

Class activity 'Should have, shouldn't have, could have': Below are six simple stories, read each aloud and ask for advice on things you should have done, shouldn't have done and could have done (third conditional with 'could') to salvage the situation. For example:

Teacher: 'I became obsessed with the gym and spent all my free time there and my boyfriend/girlfriend broke up with me.'

Sarah: 'You should have talked to your boyfriend more.'

Tom: 'Your boyfriend could have come with you to the gym.'

Reading these two-line passages is excellent comprehension practice for your students. But if they don't understand you or you have a very big class, you could write them on slips of paper and work in pairs.

Stories

1. I became obsessed with the gym and spent all my free time there and my boyfriend/girlfriend broke up with me.

2. I woke up late and missed my train, and so I spent $50 on a taxi to get to work on time.

3. I was alone and my car broke down on the top of a mountain at night and my phone battery was dead.

4. I hated my maths teacher. I only went to half my classes and failed my exams.

5. My boyfriend hates flying. I booked a holiday to New York but when we arrived at the airport he wouldn't fly. I went on holiday alone.

6. I wanted to impress my boss. I invited him to my house for dinner but when he arrived I discovered he was a vegetarian and I had cooked steak.

6.2 Deduction and possibility

As we have already seen in present, 'must' makes a positive deduction, for example, 'He must be a policeman, he is wearing the uniform,' and 'can't' the negative. 'He can't be a policeman, he is robbing a bank.'

This idea continues in past by adding 'have' + participle.

For example, 'He <u>must have been</u> a policeman, he wore the uniform' and, 'He <u>can't have been</u> a policeman, he robbed a bank.'

Because 'can' is such a strange and irregular verb you can also say, 'He couldn't have been a policeman.'

Possibility is expressed with 'may' and 'might,' for example, 'She might/may be a famous athlete (she looks fit and I just saw her signing autographs)' and in negative 'She might/may not be a famous athlete (I just saw her scoffing a McDonald's).'

Again this continues in past with 'may'/ 'might' + 'have' + participle.'

For example, 'She <u>might/may have been</u> a famous athlete, I saw her signing autographs,' or, 'She <u>may/might not have been</u> a famous athlete, she used to eat a lot of McDonald's.'

How to teach it

Write on the board, 'He must be a policeman, he is wearing the uniform,' and elicit the negative, 'He can't be a policeman, he is robbing a bank.'

To review the verb substitution, go back to deduction and possibility in present chapter and redo the controlled speaking exercise. Now elicit or explain the past of these two sentences:

'He must be a policeman, he wears the uniform,' and 'He can't be a policeman, he robs a bank.'

Now go on to possibility. Write, 'She might/may be a famous athlete, I saw her signing autographs', and elicit the past affirmative and negative.

Elicit or explain that modal verbs have no past tense and so the only way to make them so is with have + participle.

Controlled speaking practice

Ask your students to make past positive and negative deductions and possibilities with these statements. There is no right answer here, but they must be logical. For example:

Teacher: 'He cycled to work and he didn't have a driver's licence (not drive a car).'

Tom: 'He couldn't have driven a car.'

Sarah: 'He must have been fit.'

Tom: 'He might have failed his driving test.'

Sarah: 'He might not have liked cars.'

Statements

- She wore a crown and was married to the king.
- He cycled to work and he didn't have a driver's licence (deduction: he didn't drive a car).
- She was allergic to dogs and didn't like them (deduction: she didn't have a dog).
- He bought a new car every year.
- They spoke Chinese and lived in China.
- The boat did not arrive at the port. It has disappeared (deduction: it sank or got lost).
- He spent a lot of time in hospital.
- The sky is grey, there is water on the ground (deduction: it rained).
- There is no longer a cake on the table, my cat is looking fat and guilty (deduction: the cat ate it).
- She was a secretary and now she is a manager.
- The baby is crying, my son has the baby's favourite toy.
- There is a traffic jam. Two cars have stopped in the road, there is glass everywhere.
- My cup is broken. My daughter was doing the washing up.
- Fernando Alonso is very happy, spraying champagne on the Grand Prix podium.

Freer speaking practice
Pairs' activity 'Looking into the past': There are many famous photos and paintings that tell us a lot about a person or situation. Print some out and get your students to make deductions and speculations in past.

Suggested photos:

'Migrant Mother' and 'Bud Fields' 1935 by Walker Evans, 'The shell-shocked Soldier' by Don McCullin and 'The Construction of the GE Building at Rockefeller Center' by Charles C. Ebbets by 1932.

Suggested paintings:

'Las Meninas' by Velazquez and 'American Gothic' by Grant Wood 1930

Freer speaking practice
Pairs' activity 'The Case of John Roberts:' Deduction and possibility in past lends itself naturally to the topic of crime. Tell your students to imagine they are member of a jury. Using this fictional crime in the appendix ask your students to deduce what crime (if any) John Roberts is guilty of.

7. Still and Anymore, Already and Yet

'Still,' 'anymore,' 'already' and 'yet' are adverbs used to express *when* something happens and if it continues. They can be confusing so it is better to split them into two lessons: 'still' and 'anymore' first and then 'already' and 'yet.'

How to teach it: Still and anymore

'Still' means to continue while 'anymore' means to discontinue.

Write on the board, 'John is still working.' Underline 'still' and elicit its meaning: That John continues to work either today or generally in his life.

Elicit or explain that you place 'still' before the main verb. In the above example, 'working' is the main verb while 'to be' is the auxiliary. The exception arises when 'to be' is the only verb in the sentence, for example 'He is still a boy.' In this case 'still' goes after the verb.

Elicit or explain that because 'still' means to continue it is almost always placed with a continuous tense (present or past) or present simple, to express routine.

Elicit the question: 'Is John still working?'

Elicit the negative: This is actually a trick because 'still' is not generally used in negative. 'John is still not working' in this context doesn't make sense.

The real negative is in fact, 'John is not working anymore.'

Underline 'anymore' in the above sentence and elicit what it means. Elicit or explain that it means that John used to work but this has since finished. Elicit or explain that 'anymore' must be placed at the end of the sentence.

Elicit the question: Though it is possible to say, 'Is John not working anymore?' it is generally not a common. The normal form would be, 'Is John still working?'

How to teach it: Already and yet

'Already' expresses an affirmative answer that 'yes, it has happened,' while 'yet' forms the negative and the question.

Write on the board, 'Yes, I have already done my homework.' Highlight 'already' and elicit or explain the meaning.

Elicit or explain that 'already' goes before the main verb, just like 'still.' In the sentence above, 'do' is the main verb, while 'have' is the auxiliary used to form the tense.

Elicit the negative. This is a trick. The negative is 'I haven't done my homework yet.' Highlight 'yet' and note the placement – always at the end of the sentence. Elicit or explain that 'yet' forms the negative and also the interrogative, meaning that the question to this sentence is 'Have you done your homework yet?

Elicit the tense of the above examples – the present perfect. Impress upon your students that 'already' and 'yet' are not *always* used with the perfect tense but it is the most common.

Controlled speaking practice

Using the already and yet picture at the back of the book make sentences about what the teenager has already done, hasn't done yet and possibly is still doing. Give your students each a sentence below and tell them to turn it into a question for another student. For example:

124

Teacher to Tom: 'Turn on computer'

Tom to Sarah: 'Sarah, has she turned on her computer yet?'

Sarah: 'Yes he has already turned on the computer.

Teacher to Sarah: 'Pack school bag.'

Sarah to Tom: 'Tom, has she packed her school bag yet?'

Tom: 'No, she hasn't packed her school bag yet.'

Sentences

- Make the bed.
- Turn on her computer.
- Pack school bag.
- Set up speaker.
- Go outside.
- Put on shoes.
- Tie shoelaces.
- Wake up.
- Take the dog for a walk.
- Put her clothes in the cupboard.

- Tidy his desk.
- Do the washing.
- Practice the guitar.
- Brush hair.
- Take off pyjamas.
- Get dressed.
- Decorate room.

Freer speaking practice

Pairs' activity 'What have you done this week?': As a group think of all the tasks you usually do in a week. Using 'already' and 'yet' tell your students to ask each other about which they have completed this week and which are still pending. For example:

Tom to Sarah: 'Have you walked the dog today yet?

Sarah: 'Yes, I have already walked the dog.'

Putting it all together: Still, anymore, yet and already

Tables are an excellent way to clarify information. Using everything they have learnt get your students to write this table together as a group.

Positive	Negative	Question
Already	Yet	Yet
Still	Anymore	Still

If your class shares a language ask them to write example sentences of each in their own language and read them to other students to see if they can agree on a translation.

Freer Speaking Practice

Pairs' roleplay 'The Flatmates': First, as a class, brainstorm household chores, then explain the scenario. The student and their partner share a flat. Student A's parents are coming to visit and the flat is a mess. Speak together about which chores you have already done, which chores you haven't done yet, what you are still doing and what you won't do anymore. For example:

Sarah: 'My parents are coming, have you cleaned the toilet yet?'

Tom: 'I always clean the toilet, I am not cleaning the toilet anymore.'

Chores: Hovering, cleaning the windows, washing up, dusting, mopping, making the bed, washing the clothes, cleaning the bathrooms, taking out the bin, loading the dishwasher.

8. Uses of Just

8.1 Just as adverb

'Just' refers to the very recent past. Like 'already' and 'yet' its most natural tense is the present perfect, though this is not the only possibility; present simple, past simple and continuous are also possible.

Its structure runs:

Subject pronoun/noun + have + just + participle

Example: 'He has just finished his dinner.'

How to teach it

Write on the board, 'I have just arrived at the academy' and elicit the meaning. Elicit the tense and the structure. <u>Note</u>: 'Just' goes before the main verb.

Elicit or explain that 'just' has no real negative. Elicit the interrogative, 'Have you just arrived at the academy?'

Controlled speaking practice

Ask your students to change these sentences with 'just' using present perfect. For example, 'It starts raining' changes to 'It has just started raining.'

- o   It starts raining.
- o   I finish making the dinner.
- o   He starts cleaning the kitchen.
- o   She gets to work.
- o   We arrive at the library.
- o   They start preparing the lesson.

- o   He finishes playing the flute.
- o   They get to Barcelona.
- o   I am taking out the rubbish.
- o   She leaves for work.
- o   He stops eating chocolate.
- o   She starts exercising more.

- o   He gives up smoking.

- o She takes up cycling.
- o They set up a business.
- o We get to San Sebastian.
- o She feeds the cat.
- o They arrive at the airport.

Freer speaking practice
Pairs' activity 'What has just happened?': Using the deduction and possibility worksheet at the back of the book ask your students to speak together about what they think has just happened. Alternatively you could use a current news story or action photos to prompt a discussion.

8.2 Just about to

'Just about to' means the subject is at the point of doing something. For example, 'I was just about to call you' or 'It is just about to rain.' It is only used with 'to be' verb in present and past.

Its structure runs:

Subject pronoun/noun + to be + just + about + infinitive

How to teach it

Place your bag on the table and write on the board, 'I am just about to pick up my bag,' then pick up your bag. Explain its meaning giving plenty of examples. Elicit its structure and explain that it is only used in present and past.

Elicit the negative: 'I am not just about to pick up my bag' and the interrogative 'Are you just about to pick up your bag?'

Controlled speaking practice

Place five picture cards in front of Student A and ask them to write on a slip of paper which card they will pick up and what they will do with it. Now using 'just about to' ask the class to predict what Student A will do. For example, 'He is just about to pick up the hat card and put it under the desk.'

8.3 Other uses of just

Just also means:

'Only' – 'There is just one biscuit left.'

In close proximity – 'The post office is just opposite my house'

A synonym of 'really' – 'The house is just beautiful.'

'Exactly' or 'precisely' – 'The ball landed just on the line.'

9. Relative Clauses

Relative clauses are the connectors 'that', 'who', 'which', 'when', 'whose' and 'where' that we use to define the preceding noun.

For example, 'My teacher who helps me with my English' – the second clause, after 'who', answers the questions, 'Who is my teacher? And what does she do?' Answer: 'She is the one who helps me with my English.'

'The academy where I take my tennis classes' – the second clause, after 'where', answers the question, 'What is this academy and why is it important? The answer: 'It is the one where I take my tennis lessons.'

9.1 The Rules of Relative Clauses

Relative clauses are divided into two categories; defining and non-defining.

Defining relative clauses

In a defining relative clause you cannot omit information from the sentence and have it still make sense.

For example, 'People who play the piano are often good at typing' – all of the information in this sentence is needed; you cannot bracket off a section with commas or omit anything.

With defining relative clauses it is acceptable (and very common) to substitute 'who' and 'which' for 'that'.

For example, 'The man <u>who</u> walks my dog' and 'The man <u>that</u> walks my dog' are both possible, as are 'The car <u>which</u> I drive' and 'The car <u>that</u> I drive.'

Non-defining Relative Clauses

In non-defining relative clauses the connector is placed between commas as extra information which can be omitted. For example:

'The academy, where we play tennis, is next to my house.' It is equally possible to omit 'where we play tennis' and have the sentence still make sense.

With non-defining relative clauses you must use 'who' for a person and 'which' for a thing. 'That' is not acceptable. For example:

'Cycling to school, which is healthy, is becoming more and more common,' or 'Mother Teresa, who was a nun, made a real difference to the word.'

Finally, if the relative clause refers to the object of the sentence, you don't need it. For example,

'The film which we are going to see is called Jaws' or 'The café where I go to serves great coffee.'

How to teach it

Write the connectors on the board and elicit what each is used for:

- o Who/that are for people.
- o Which/that are for things.
- o Where is for location.
- o When is for time.

Whose is for possessive. Example: 'My neighbour whose daughter is a doctor.'

Now write, 'My neighbour who teaches me English' and, 'My neighbour, who teaches me English, is a very nice person,' and elicit the difference – the first is a defining clause and the second a non-defining clause.

Elicit or explain that with defining clauses, 'that' is an acceptable substitute for 'who' and 'which' while in non-defining clauses you must use 'who' and 'which.'

Controlled speaking practice

Ask your students to fill in the blanks with the appropriate connector. The exercise contains defining and non-defining clauses. For example:

'Someone, _____ speaks English very well, is a member of your family.'

Possible answer: 'My uncle, who speaks English very well, is a member of my family.'

'Something, _____ you have had for a long time.'

Possible answer: 'My sunglasses are something which I have in my bag right now.'

Sentences

Someone _____you trust to keep a secret.
Somewhere_____you can buy English books.
Something_____helps you to save time in the day.
Someone, _____speaks English very well, is a member of your family.
Somewhere_____you can get a good coffee.

Someone_____you can talk to.
Someone_____child works in medicine (whose).
Something, _____is in your bag right now, you have had for at least a year.
Something_____you don't leave the house without.
A company _____logo is yellow (whose).

Someone_____you have known since childhood.
Something, _____keeps you warm, is in your closet.
Somewhere_____you can have a good time without spending money.
Something special_____you have given to someone else.
Someone, _____has inspired you, is still part of your life.

Freer Speaking Practice
Pairs' activity 'Think of definitions for these words': Ask your students to come up with definitions for the following ideas: A secret, a good person, a great career, a garden, a wedding, a misunderstanding, a successful marriage, war, their boss, a good parent, a start-up company, a school.

Encourage them to try both defining and non-defining descriptions. For example, 'A secret is information that other people don't know about' or 'A secret, which is sometimes a good thing, is information that other people don't know about.' ('That' can be omitted here).

---

10. Indirect Questions

English is a very indirect language. Direct questions such as 'What is the time?' can often seem rude, particularly when asking strangers. To resolve this, native speakers will often soften questions with a beginning clause such as '*Do you know* what time it is?' or '*Could you tell me* what time it is?' But what happens to the structure when you do this?

Well as we know, an affirmative statement runs: Subject pronoun/noun + verb and an interrogative: auxiliary verb + subject pronoun/noun.

For example, 'She can dance' in affirmative becomes, 'Can she dance?' in interrogative and 'It is red' becomes 'is it red?'

In indirect questions, however, the original question remains in its affirmative order connected by 'if.' For example:

'<u>Is it</u> red?' becomes 'Do you know if <u>it is</u> red?'

'<u>Can she</u> dance?' becomes 'Can you tell me if <u>she can</u> dance?'

'<u>Are you</u> cooking tonight?' becomes 'Could I ask if <u>you are</u> cooking tonight?'

'<u>Has she</u> taken the class?' becomes 'I was wondering if <u>she has</u> taken the class?

Finally, if the direct question uses the auxiliary 'do,' you omit it or replace it with 'if' for the indirect question. For example, 'Does this work?' becomes 'Do you know <u>if</u> this works?' or 'How long does it take to drive to Barcelona?' becomes 'Could you tell me how long ~~does~~ it takes to drive to Barcelona?'

How to teach it

Write on the board 'What is the time?' and 'Do you know what the time is?' and elicit the difference in meaning and structure.

Now write, 'Does she like ice cream?' and 'Do you know if she likes ice cream' and do the same, highlighting the absence of 'do.'

Emphasise that English is a very indirect language and we often use indirect questions because they are more polite.

Examples of the beginnings of indirect questions are:

- 'Do you know...?'
- 'Do you happen to know...?'
- 'I was wondering...?'
- 'Could you tell me...?'

Controlled speaking practice

Give your students the following direct questions and ask them to make polite indirect questions:

- What is your name?
- How old is your mother?
- Can you speak English?
- Do you like hip hop music?
- Do you drive?
- Are you going out this weekend?

- Are jeans suitable for work?
- Have you ever lost your wallet in the street?
- What is your boyfriend's/girlfriend's worst personality trait?
- Will you buy a new car next year?
- What is the most powerful country in Europe?
- Can I have your lunch?

Freer speaking practice
Pairs' roleplay 'Awkward situations': Tell your students they have to pretend to be British for the day (this is sure to get some laughs). On slips of paper give them some difficult situations which they have to politely resolve. Student A is the polite one trying to solve the situation while Student B is obstructive and difficult.

Awkward Situations

You and your flatmate have a cleaning rota. You always do your share. He/she has done the cleaning but they haven't done it very well.

Your neighbour lets their dog poo outside the communal doorway of your building. They don't think it's a problem, you do.

The colleague next to you keeps distracting you by talking. When they are not talking they are speaking loudly on the phone or playing loud music on their headphones.

Your child and your neighbour's child play together. One day he/she steals your child's favourite toy. They are very upset. You confront the child but they deny it and the parent believes them.

11. Adverbs

While verbs express *what* you do, adverbs express *how* you do it. For example, with the phrase 'I am driving a car', it is clear that you are driving – but how are you driving? 'I am driving *slowly,'* on the other hand gives us the full picture.

Adverbs can modify verbs, adjectives or other adverbs. For example:

Verb modification: 'She speaks *quickly*', 'He walks *carefully*,' 'They cry *loudly.'*

Adjective modification: 'Your cat is *quite* naughty', 'The house is *pretty* small,' 'Your answers are *always* correct.'

Adverb modification: 'He says *most* things *correctly*' – here 'most' modifies 'correctly'. 'She is *almost always* late.' Here 'almost' modifies 'always'.

11.1 Different kinds of adverbs

There are seven types of adverbs, these are:

Interrogative: When, where, why, who, how, which, what.

Degree: Fairly, hardly, rather, pretty.

Place: By, down, here, there.

Time: Now, soon, still, then, today.

Frequency: Always, never, occasionally.

Manner: Bravely, happily, well, badly.

Sentence: Certainly, suddenly, luckily, surely.

What the adverb modifies and where to place it, depends on its type. For example, adverbs of frequency are placed before the main verb such as 'She <u>always</u> goes swimming on Saturday' while adverbs of manner are usually placed after the verb, 'She dances <u>happily</u>.'

You should never try to teach all adverbs at once. The knowledge of which adverb to use and where to place it usually comes with practicing different grammar points.

I recommend, however, teaching adverbs of manner and sentence as a separate grammar point.

11.2 Adverbs of manner and sentence

Adverbs of manner are placed after the verb they modify. For example, 'The chef laughed loudly' or 'The girl sings well.'

Adverbs of sentence usually go at the front of the sentence (though they can go at the end) and describe the 'mood' of a phrase. For example, 'Suddenly, the police arrived' or 'Luckily, they didn't find out.'

Spelling rules

Most manner and sentence adverbs are derived from adjectives. If the adjective ends in 'y' then add 'ily.' For example, 'happy' changes to 'happily'. If the adjective doesn't end in 'y' add 'ly'. For example 'quiet' becomes 'quiet*ly*.' This is not an absolute rule and there are exceptions.

How to teach it

Write an example sentence of an adverb of manner and an adverb of sentence on the board. Highlight the adverb and elicit their functions.

Elicit or explain the placement of manner and sentence adverbs and what information they bring to the sentence.

Highlight that adverbs usually come from adjectives and explain the spelling rules.

Freer speaking practice

Pairs' activity 'Making adverbs from adjectives': Hand out a selection of adjectives and ask your students to make the adverb. Ask them, where possible, to make both the positive and negative version. For example, with the adjective 'patient' students can make the both adverbs 'patiently' and 'impatiently.' Ask them to make sentences, and check the placement is correct.

Adjectives: Lucky, fortunate, patient, comfortable, careful, sudden, immediate, dangerous, small, good, bad, fast.

Mistakes to watch out for

Students will often use the adjective when they mean the adverb. For example, 'He speaks bad,' is wrong as the adverb here is 'badly.'

Common adjectives and their irregular adverbs

Good – well

Bad – badly

Fast – quickly (In this case, 'He drives fast' is also acceptable as 'fast' is now also an adverb).

Freer speaking practice

Further pairs' activity 'Change the sentence': Give each pair a print out of these sentences (or write them on the board). Ask them to modify the meaning with adverbs. In some cases, they can use more than one adverb in a sentence.

He didn't come to the party.

She speaks too fast, I can't understand her.

He saw the problem.

The police arrived.

She understands me.

He drives not well.

He tidied up because his mother was arriving.

She didn't see her birthday present.

She skis.

I understood what I had to do.

Adverbs: Quietly, quickly, well, badly, immediately, unfortunately, suddenly, luckily, quickly, sadly, happily, surely, currently, actually, lightly, separately, suitably, currently, actually.

Examples: 'Luckily, he didn't come to the party,' or 'Sadly, he didn't come to the party.'

12. Modifiers

Modifiers are adverbs that modify adjectives or nouns to express a degree. For example, 'It is <u>quite</u> hot.' 'Quite' is the adverb that modifies the degree of hot.

12.1 Modifiers + adjectives
I usually teach modifiers + adjectives at A1 level, when students learn basic adjectives.

Basic modifiers are:

Really, very, quite, not very, a little, a bit.

   <u>Note:</u> Though 'really' can be used as a substitute for 'very' – 'not really' cannot be used in place of 'not very.'

12.2 Modifiers + nouns
Basic modifiers for countable nouns are:

Loads of, a lot of, quite a lot of, not many, a few, several, a few, very few, a couple of.

Basic modifiers for uncountable nouns are:

Loads of, a lot of, quite a lot of, not much, a little, very little, a bit of.

   <u>Note</u>: Most of the time you must include 'of' before the noun.

12.3 Modifiers advanced
Modifiers add personality and playfulness to speech and we natives use them all of the time. Without them English lacks its nuances, its richness and its famous sense of humour, and so once your students are speaking with confidence teach them some more.

Advanced modifiers can only be used with adjectives. They include:

Absolutely, totally, incredibly, rather, pretty, fairly and for the most part.

Which modifier you use, however, depends on the adjective. 'Absolutely' and 'totally' can only be used with extreme adjectives, while the rest can be used with normal adjectives.

For example, you wouldn't say, 'It is totally cold outside,' you would say, 'It is totally freezing.' Equally you wouldn't say 'It is absolutely hot,' but rather, 'It is absolutely boiling.'

Likewise, 'Rather freezing' sounds ridiculous, as does, 'Incredibly boiling' so there are clear 'dos and don'ts' that govern which modifier and adjective you select.

How to teach it

Put the modifiers on the table and ask your students to put them in order of intensity. They should end up with something like this:

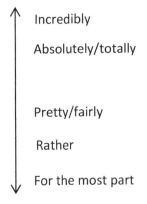

Incredibly

Absolutely/totally

Pretty/fairly

Rather

For the most part

Elicit or explain that 'absolutely' and 'totally' can only be paired with extreme adjectives. To demonstrate what these are, tell your students a 'normal' adjective and get them to come up with the extreme version.

Normal and extreme adjectives

Cold – freezing, hot – boiling, scary – terrifying, beautiful – stunning, good – amazing/wonderful/incredible, bad – terrible / horrific, tired – exhausted, upset – devastated, angry – furious, sad – miserable, excited – thrilled, happy – delighted, surprised – astonished.

Mistakes to watch out for: Incredibly

Note that although 'incredibly' is an extreme modifier it is not used with extreme adjectives. I think the reason for this is that 'incredibly' is just too extreme and so you have to tone it down with a normal adjective. For example, 'She was incredibly exhausted' sounds crazy, while, 'She was incredibly tired' sounds fine.

Note: English speakers often use less intense modifiers to mean 'very' rather than 'not very.' For example, 'It was pretty cold last night' actually means it was *very* cold last night. 'The tickets were rather expensive,' mean that they were *very* expensive.

Freer speaking practice
Pairs' activity extreme situations: Get your students to ask each other about the last time:

> They experienced extreme weather.

> Bought something unusually cheap or expensive.

> Worked really hard.

> Had an incredible experience.

> Had a terrible shock.

Further speaking practice
Pairs' roleplay 'Launching a product': You have an idea for a product but must convince investors to invest $100,000 to launch it. In pairs, first come up with your product. It must be either:

> A children's game.

> A piece of exercise equipment.

> A new web service.

> A household appliance.

Now each pair must present their product using plenty of modifiers to support their case. For example, 'We have created an incredibly exciting children's toy.'

The other pairs are the investors and must ask the presenters lot of questions to determine whether they will invest. Each investor has $10,000 to invest. They can invest in one project or divide the money between several. The winner is the pair who receives the most investment.

---

13. Quantifiers

13.1 Too, too much, too many, enough

'Too,' 'too much' and 'too many' mean more than is needed while 'enough' means sufficient. 'Too' is only paired with adjectives such as, 'Too hot,' or 'Too expensive,' while 'Too much' is paired with uncountable nouns; 'There is too much traffic' or 'He has too much money,' and 'too many' countable nouns; 'There are too many people in the street,' or 'You can't eat too many vegetables.'

'Enough,' however, is a little more complicated. When paired with an adjective, 'enough' comes after the word – for example 'It is cheap enough.' When paired with a noun, however, 'enough' goes before the word. For example, 'She has enough time,' or 'Is there enough food?'

How to teach it

Write a sentence for each quantifier on the board and elicit the meaning. For speakers of European languages saying that 'enough' means 'sufficient' is usually enough information, as 'sufficient' is a Latin cognate meaning that there is a similar word in all Latin based languages. Elicit the structure for each quantifier paying particular attention to 'enough.'

Controlled speaking practice

OK, so they know the theory, now teach them in practice.

Try to pick up the table. You can't – elicit why from your students; 'It's too heavy' or 'You're not strong enough.'

Try to fit the chair into your bag. You can't – elicit why; 'Your bag is too small,' 'The chair is too big' or 'Your bag is not big enough.'

You want to go to The Maldives on holiday but you can't. Elicit why; 'It costs too much money,' 'You are not rich enough,' 'You don't have enough money' or 'It is too far.'

You want to have a party with 500 people in the classroom in an hour but you can't. Elicit why; 'There would be too many people,' 'The classroom is too small', 'There is not enough time to organise it,' 'There is too much to organise' or 'The room is not big enough.'

Continue like this until everyone can think of at least three examples of why not, for your proposals.

13.2 So, so much, so many, so few, so little, such

The 'so' and 'such' quantifiers are basically modifiers amplifying or dampening the following word. But when we already have so many modifiers ('very', 'really', 'quite'), why do we need 'so' and 'such'? The reason; they make it personal.

Imagine that it is a hot day; you come to class sweating and say 'It is very hot outside.' 'Very hot' is a general observation of the weather, you are making no reference about how it affects you. Now imagine you say 'It's *so* hot outside.' You are now saying something subtly different – that the heat has affected you with the second part either stated or implied. For example 'It's so hot outside that I can't concentrate,' or 'It's so hot outside (look at me I am sweating).'

The same is true for 'such' (and all of the above quantifiers). 'It is very tasty food' is different from 'It is such tasty food (with either stated or implied) that I am going to eat it all up!'

The structure of 'so' and 'such' quantifiers run:

'So' + adjective: Example, 'Your brother is so handsome (that I am going to ask him on a date)' or 'That concert ticket is so expensive (that there is no way I am going with you).'

So many + countable noun: Example, 'There are so many people who want to learn English (that I might be in work forever)' or 'She gets so many Christmas presents (that she is getting spoilt).'

So few + countable noun: Example, 'There are so few blue whales left (that they might become extinct) or 'There are so few restaurants that serve Mongolian food (that I will never get to try this cuisine).'

So much + uncountable noun: Example, 'There is so much pollution in this city (that I am leaving)' or 'They drink so much sugary drink (that their teeth are going to rot).'

So little + uncountable noun: Example, 'My son does so little housework (that I am going to kick him out when he turns 18)' or 'They eat so little meat (that they should become vegetarian).'

Such a + adjective + <u>singular, countable noun</u>: Example, 'He is such a good dog (that I will look after him for you over the holidays),' or 'This is such a beautiful beach (I never want to leave).'

Such + adjective + <u>plural or uncountable</u> noun: Example, 'This is such delicious fruit (that I will buy more)' or 'You have such well-behaved children (I wish mine were like that).'

How to teach it

First write a 'so' sentence on the board and its equivalent with 'very.' Explain or elicit the difference – that 'very' expresses a general statement, while 'so' how something personally affects you. Emphasise the difference by writing a 'that' clause after the 'so' sentence. Now elicit the structure.

Continue with 'so much,' 'so many,' 'so little' and 'so few.' Elicit examples of sentences from your students.

Now, when they are comfortable with this concept, move on to 'such'.

Write 'They have such a beautiful house', and 'Their house is so beautiful' on the board. Elicit the difference in meaning – essentially there is none and the difference is in the structure; 'such a' is followed by adjective and single noun, while 'so' is followed by adjective.

Now write, 'It is such tasty food,' and 'He has such fast horses,' on the board. Circle the 'a' in the previous sentence and ask why there is none here. The answer is that there is no 'a' when 'such' is paired with an uncountable noun (food) or a plural noun (horses).

<u>Note</u>: 'Such' can be paired with 'a lot of' for both countable and uncountable nouns.

Controlled speaking practice
Read these sentences aloud to your students. Ask them to change them with 'so' and 'such' and add their own 'that' clause at the end to make it personal. For example:

Teacher: 'She knows a lot of people.'

Tom: 'She knows so many people *that she can't remember everyone's birthdays.*'

<u>Note</u>: There are often two ways to express these sentences so ask your students to explore all the possibilities. For example, 'It is such a hot day' and 'The day is so hot.'

- ○ She knows a lot of people.
- ○ I give a lot of advice.
- ○ He makes a lot of suggestions.
- ○ They read a lot of news.
- ○ We don't go to many parties.
- ○ She listens to a lot of reports.
- ○ It's a very hot day.
- ○ He is a bad mechanic.

- ○ The house is very dirty.
- ○ The food is very spicy.
- ○ The trip is very exciting.
- ○ The film is very boring.

- You have a lot of energy.
- He doesn't have a lot of money.
- I spend a lot of time doing my homework.

- There are a lot of cars in the city.
- I eat a lot of food.
- They make a lot of mistakes.
- He doesn't use a lot of paper.
- She knows a lot about software.
- There is a lot of pollution in London.

- He drinks a lot of cups of coffee.
- She takes a lot of risks.
- We don't make a lot of decisions.
- She has made a lot of appointments.
- He took a lot of buses to get to Madrid.

Freer speaking practice
Pairs' activity 'Comparatives': Give pairs pictures of two objects or places and ask them to come up with comparatives. This is excellent practice for oral exams, where essentially your students will have to do this very task. For example: 'The Fiat 500 is so much smaller than the Mercedes that I don't know how we will fit everyone in,' or 'There are so many more people in China than in Russia that I think China will do better in the Olympic Games.'

Further speaking practice
Pairs' roleplay 'The Travel Agent': Ask your students to name somewhere where they would like to go on holiday and somewhere where they really wouldn't. One person is the travel agent and the other the client. The travel agent has to convince the client to buy a holiday to the unattractive destination, while the client must argue for their preferred destination. For example:

Travel Agent: 'There are so few spoilt beaches in North Korea, I know this is the place for you.'

Client: 'Yes, but there are so many military police, I would really prefer to go to Tenerife.'

Travel Agent: 'There are so many discos in Tenerife, you wouldn't get any sleep.'

'That'

Finally, this little golden nugget is for students who want to learn English to the highest level:

Native speakers substitute 'so' in negative sentences for 'that.' For example, 'My French exam wasn't *that* bad,' or 'The flight to Paris wasn't *that* expensive.'

13.3 Fewer, less, not as much, not as many

'Fewer,' 'less,' 'not as much,' 'not as many' all make negative comparisons with nouns. For example, 'Los Angeles has fewer bears than Alaska,' or 'Fruit salad doesn't have as much fat as ice cream.'

The structures run:

'Less' and 'not as much' + uncountable noun

'Fewer' and 'not as many' + countable noun

How to teach it

I always teach this with advanced weather vocabulary as it helps students see how to practically apply this grammar to a sentence.

First write a three-column table on the board and label the columns, 'Nouns', 'Verbs' and 'Adjectives'.

Now elicit weather vocabulary, getting your students to tell you the corresponding noun, verb and adjective for each word. When they run out of vocabulary, give them some more. You should end up with a table that looks like this:

Noun	Verb	Adjective
Rain	To rain	Rainy
Snow	To snow	Snowy
Wind	To blow	Windy
A storm	-	Stormy
Ice	To freeze	Freezing
Hail	To hail	-
Fog	To fog	Foggy
Frost	To frost	Frosty
Lightning	-	-
Thunder	To thunder	-
A Flood	To flood	-
A drought	-	-
A hurricane	-	-
Tornado	-	-
A gale	-	-
A blizzard	-	-
A heatwave	-	-

This is, in fact, a good opportunity to practice comparatives with adjectives also and so first write the names of two countries with radically different climates (let's say Norway and Portugal) and ask your students to make some normal comparisons. For example, 'Norway is snowier than Portugal,' and 'Portugal is not as snowy as Norway.'

Note: Always practice the 'as/as' comparative also, or your students will forget.

Now go through the nouns and elicit from your students whether they are countable or uncountable (Note: Any noun preceded by 'a' or can be made plural it is countable). Mark a 'C' next the countable and a 'UC' next to the uncountable.

Now ask: 'How do we make comparisons with nouns?' One of your brighter students will say something like 'Norway has more snow than Portugal.' Write this on the board.

Next ask: 'What is the reverse of this statement?' Elicit or explain that it is 'Portugal has less snow than Norway.'

Now write 'Portugal has more heatwaves than Norway.' Elicit or explain the reverse 'Norway has fewer heatwaves than Portugal.' It is 'fewer' in this case because 'heatwave' is countable.' 'Less' appears in the example before, because 'snow' is uncountable. Elicit or explain the other way to say these sentences: 'Portugal does not have as much snow as Norway,' and, 'Norway does not have as many heatwaves as Portugal.'

Controlled speaking practice
Give your students two other places, let's say Oklahoma and Morocco, and a noun and ask them to compare the climates. For example:

Teacher: 'Drought.'

Sarah: 'Oklahoma has fewer droughts than Morocco', or, 'Oklahoma does not have as many droughts as Morocco.'

Teacher: 'Lightning.'

Tom: 'Morocco has less lightning than Oklahoma,' or 'Morocco does not have as much lightning as Oklahoma.'

Freer speaking practice

Pairs' roleplay 'Let's relocate': Tell your students that they are a pair of work colleagues who have been given the chance to work somewhere else for six months. One student wants to go to Alaska, while the other prefers the Philippines. Ask them to debate the weather of each one and try to convince their partner that their country is better. For example:

Tom: 'There are fewer blizzards in the Philippines than in Alaska.'

Sarah: 'Yes, but there are not has many hurricanes in Alaska as there are in the Philippines.'

14. Take for Time and Last

14.1 To take

'Take' for time is a difficult grammar point and students will often struggle. It expresses duration, but only for actions (verbs), never for nouns.

Its structure runs:

It + takes (in third person) + object pronoun/noun + time + infinitive (with 'to')

Example: 'It takes him 30 minutes to get dressed in the morning.'

How to teach it

Write the above sentence on the board and elicit whether it is past, present or future.

Now underline 'take' and elicit what it means. Emphasise that this is not 'take' as in, 'Take this pen' but rather the duration of an action. 'Take' represents time and for this reason it is always expressed with the subject pronoun 'it.' The subject of the sentence is the object pronoun (me, her, him and so on) or noun while the action itself is expressed in the infinitive. For example: 'It takes her 45 minutes to get to work.'

Elicit the negative: 'It doesn't take him 30 minutes to get dressed in the morning,' and the question: 'How long does it take him to get dressed in the morning?'

Controlled speaking practice

It is important to practice all the object pronouns, so the teacher must control the questions. If left to the students, all questions would be 'How long does it take you...?' and all answers 'It takes me...'

Ask your students the following questions. To practice the interrogative, also get your students to ask each other questions you provide them.

How long does it take...?:

- o You to have breakfast in the morning.
- o Your brother/sister to get to work/school.
- o Your friend to do his/her homework.
- o Your favourite sports team to complete a match.
- o Your teacher to prepare a lesson.
- o Your parents to make dinner.

- o People to drive to the next city.
- o Your colleagues/classmates to finish their work for today.
- o You to return to your house.
- o Your friends to choose a holiday destination.
- o The government to organise an election.
- o The class to prepare themselves for the next lesson.

Adding other tenses

Once your students have got used to 'take,' add other tenses. I recommend doing this in a different class. Introduce the tenses your students know, for this reason the class needs to be an intermediate level or above before you teach this language point.

How to teach it

Write on the board 'It takes her 30 minutes to get to work.' Elicit the structure, once again. Now elicit the different tenses.

Past simple: 'It took her 30 minutes to get to work.'

Present continuous: 'It is taking her 30 minutes to get to work.'

Present perfect: 'It has taken her 30 minutes to get to work.'

Past perfect: 'It had taken her 30 minutes to get to work.'

Used to: 'It used to take her 30 minutes to get to work.'

Future (will): 'It will take her 30 minutes to get to work.'

Future (going to): 'It is going to take her 30 minutes to get to work.'

Second conditional: 'It would take her 30 minutes to get to work if... (your student thinks of the next clause).'

Third conditional: 'It would have taken her 30 minutes to get to work if... (your student thinks of the next clause).'

Controlled speaking practice
Ask your students the following and tell them to ask each other questions you provide them.

How long...?

- o It took you to get to work this morning.
- o It will take your classmates to get home.
- o It used to take your sister/brother to walk to school.
- o It usually takes to drive to Paris.
- o It took us to learn the last grammar point.
- o It used to take your parents to prepare dinner for you.
- o It has taken me to do this lesson.
- o It is going to take your classmates to do their homework.
- o It would take your brother/sister to make a cake.
- o It has taken your parents to raise you.
- o It would have taken another student to arrive at the academy if he/she had gone by bus.

Freer speaking practice
Pairs' activity 'Tell me about your life': Ask your students to ask and answer 'take' questions in different tenses on the subjects of:

Work: Example, 'How long did it take you to complete your last

project?'

Travel: Example, 'How long will it take you to fly to Sydney next year?'

Hobbies and studies: Example, 'How long has it taken you to learn the violin?'

14.2 To last

A common question from students is, "What is the difference between 'take' and 'last'?" Well, put simply, both express duration but 'take' is + verb while 'last' is + noun.

Some nouns name objects; 'table', chair' and so on – others, however, are events and feature time; these are the ones you use with 'last'. For example, 'How long does a football match last?' or 'The swimming lesson lasts 45 minutes.'

'Last' exists in most tenses, but not *usually* continuous. 'How long is this film lasting?' is not correct. It is 'How long does this film last?'

Its structure runs:

Pronoun/noun + last + time

How to teach it

Write on the board 'The film lasts two hours.' Underline 'last' and elicit the meaning. Elicit the negative: 'The film doesn't last two hours,' and the question: 'How long does the film last?'

Controlled speaking practice

Ask your students the following questions:

How long does...?

- o   A football match last?
- o   A flight to New Zealand last?
- o   A train journey to the capital last?
- o   A meal last?
- o   A typical exam last?
- o   A doctor's shift last?

Adding other tenses

Go back to 'The film lasts two hours' and elicit:

The past: 'The film lasted two hours.'

The future: 'The film will last two hours.'

The present perfect: 'The film has lasted two hours.'

Used to: 'The film used to last two hours.'

Usually: 'The film usually lasts two hours.'

Second conditional: 'The film would last two hours, if we went to see it.'

Third conditional: 'The film would have lasted two hours, if we had seen it last week.'

Controlled speaking practice
This time ask your students: 'How long did the last class last?'

This question is likely to silence the room for a moment. Give them time to work it out; the first 'last' is an adjective to mean the 'class before,' the second is the verb.

The answer is: 'The last class lasted an hour and a half' (or whatever is correct for you.)

Ask them: 'How long did the last film you watched last?' And elicit an answer.

Now ask: How long....?

- ○ Will the next film you watch last?
- ○ Has the last class you have taken lasted?
- ○ Will the next exam your sister or brother takes last?
- ○ Did your lessons at school used to last?
- ○ Does adolescence usually last?
- ○ Did your last journey last?
- ○ Do your lessons at the academy last?
- ○ Has this course lasted?
- ○ Would your lessons last if I wasn't here?
- ○ Would your lessons have lasted last week if there had been an earth-quake?

Freer speaking practice
Pairs' activity 'durations': Tell your students to ask and answer duration questions for:

    Sports events.
    Flights/train journeys/travel.
    Work shifts/ work days/ projects.
    Films/plays/ concerts.

When using past, encourage your students to use the phrase 'How long did the last...last?' to practice this strange sounding but perfectly normal construction.

15. Reflexives and Get + Adjective

15.1 Reflexives

We use reflexives when you (or someone else) is both the object and the subject of an action. For example take the sentence, 'I cut myself yesterday.' 'You' (the subject) did the action to 'you' (the object).

The reflexive pronouns are: Myself, yourself, himself, herself, ourselves, yourselves and themselves. They are always placed after the verb they modify.

While reflexives express interaction with 'the self', I teach alongside it 'each other' which means interaction with one other. For example, 'They looked at each other,' or, 'My children play with each other often.'

How to teach it

Write on the board 'I am cutting my friend's hair.' Now stand in front of the class and make a sawing action with your hand, on top of your other hand. Elicit or explain what you are doing: 'I am cutting myself,' and write it on the board.

Elicit the difference between the two sentences; the first is you interacting with someone else, while the second is you interacting with you.

Now lightly start tapping your shoulder and elicit what you are doing: 'I am hitting myself.'

Now write out the table below. Elicit as much as content as you can.

Subject pronoun	Reflexive
I	Myself
You	Yourself
He	Himself
She	Herself
It	Itself
We	Ourselves
You	Yourselves
They	Themselves

Finally elicit the word for an interaction between two people: 'Each other.'

Common reflexive verbs
Accident verbs: To burn, to cut, to hit, to hurt, to kill.

Others: To amuse, to behave, to blame, to dry, to enjoy, to express, to introduce, to help, to prepare, to paint (a self-portrait), to teach, to time.

Controlled speaking practice
As a class, or in pairs ask your students to describe, using reflexives, what is happening in the pictures in the Reflexives Worksheet at the back of the book.

Freer speaking practice
Pairs' activity 'Reflexive questions': Write on the board the following questions:

How do you enjoy yourself in your free time?

How do your parents introduce themselves to a group of strangers?

How does Fernando Alonso (or the sports person of the day) prepare himself for a race?

Do your neighbours spend time with each other?

Now ask your students to ask each other these questions and come up with three more of their own. Encourage them to use more reflexives rather than just 'yourself.'

Further questions

A time when you accidentally hurt yourself.
A time when a loved one hurt him/herself.
Ways to express yourself when you go to a foreign country.
Something your friends have taught themselves in the past.
If her colleagues like each other.
If she behaved herself when she was a child or was she bad.
How she expresses herself when she doesn't know a word in English.
If she has ever cut herself while cooking.
If he has ever painted himself (portrait).
Something you want to teach yourself in the future.

15.2 Get + adjective
Mastering 'get' + adjective is one of the keys to unlocking the English language. But what does it do?

'Get' basically has four meanings. These are:

To obtain – 'Get me a pen, would you?'

To receive – 'I get an email from them every morning.'

To arrive – 'When are we going to get to the airport?'

Process – 'I get tired at the end of the day.'

It is this final meaning expressed with 'get' + adjective that I will deal with in this section.

Imagine that you get up in the morning feeling as fresh as a daisy and go to work. At the beginning of the day you don't feel tired, but at the end of your particularly hard 12 hour shift, you *do* feel tired. How did this happen? Well, at some point in the afternoon, let's say at about 4pm, you *got* tired.

This is what 'get' + adjective is – it is the process of *becoming* (in this case tired). A diagram of your day would be like this:

7am wake up	**4pm coffee break**	**8pm end of shift**
I am not tired	I am getting tired	I am tired

'Get' + adjective, however, only expresses 'becoming' in impermanent things such as moods and physical states. You cannot say, for example, 'He is getting to be a doctor,' as becoming a doctor is a permanent thing.

How to teach it

Tell the story above and write the diagram on the board. Circle, 'I am getting tired,' and elicit what it means – process or 'becoming'. Now write, 'She is getting to be an engineer,' and ask if that sentence is possible. Elicit why it is not possible; 'get' only expresses the process of impermanent moods or states, while to be an engineer is permanent.

At this point your students may understand the idea of 'get' but they may not realise it applies to all tenses. To highlight this, take the above sentence and ask them to make it:

Past: 'I got tired/ I was getting tired.'

Future: 'I will get tired/ I am going to get tired.'

Present perfect: 'I have got tired.'

Used to: 'I used to get tired.'

Second and third conditional: 'I would get tired if.../ I would have got tired if...'

Now elicit other mood and state adjectives until you have a list similar to the one below:

Angry, hungry, bored, tired, sleepy, lost, confused, irritated, jealous, stressed, excited, light, dark, dirty, wet, worried, drunk, sick, ill, better, worse, depressed, ready.

Note: You cannot say 'Get happy.' This is because, in English, 'happiness' is a reaction to something else, not a process. For this reason instead we use the verb 'make.' For example, 'My family makes me happy,' or 'Our jobs make us happy.' You can, however, say 'Get sad' though it is arguably not good English. It is better to say 'Something makes me sad.'

Common questions
"But 'lost' is the participle of the verb 'to lose' not an adjective, isn't it?"

Yes they are right – it is the participle, however, it is also an adjective. We know this because it can be paired with 'to be' verb to make 'I am lost.'

Controlled speaking practice
The following questions have been written using a variety of tenses. Use them with your students and encourage them to use a variety with each other. Don't forget to use different subject pronouns.

- o   If she/he would get lost without a map in Barcelona.
- o   If she/he gets stressed when she has lots of work to do.
- o   If she/he used to get confused when people spoke quickly in English.
- o   What time it gets dark/light in New Zealand in the summer.
- o   When the last time she got sick was.

- o   How long it takes her/him to get ready in the morning.
- o   How often she/he gets lost in their city.
- o   If she/he ever gets angry with the traffic when driving.
- o   Which is worse to get wet when walking to work or to get dirty.
- o   If she/he would get drunk tonight if you didn't have an English class.
- o   If the global economy is getting worse or getting better in his/her opinion.

Freer Speaking Practice

Pairs' roleplay 'I can't sleep!': One student is a doctor and the other the patient. The patient is an insomniac and the doctor must ask them questions to determine how it is affecting their life and how they can solve the problem. Don't forget to encourage a variety of question words.

Example questions: How often do you get tired? When was the last time you got dizzy? Do you ever get hungry at night? How long does it take you to get to sleep at night?

A further doctor/patient roleplay can be done with the problem 'I can't stop eating!'

15.2.1 Get + comparative adjectives

'Get' is also commonly used with adjectives in comparative to indicate a change in size, speed, temperature or form.

The structure runs:

Get + adjective (comparative)

Example: 'The world is getting hotter,' or 'It is getting more expensive to live in London nowadays.'

How to teach it

Write the above sentences, highlight the comparative form, and elicit the meaning. Your students will not find this difficult to grasp as they will probably have something similar in their own language using a different verb.

Controlled speaking practice

Now ask the following questions:

- If the climate is getting hotter or colder.
- If the internet in your area is getting faster or slower.
- If English is getting easier or more difficult.
- If the cost of living in their country is getting cheaper or more expensive.
- If winters in their city are getting wetter or drier.

- If they are getting younger or getting older.
- If their native accent when speaking English is getting weaker.
- If their knowledge of English is getting stronger.
- If the kids in their family are getting taller or shorter.

16. Reported Speech

We use reported speech to recount previous conversations. For example, a direct question 'Do you <u>have</u> a pen?' would later be recount as 'The teacher asked me if I <u>had</u> a pen.'

When we retell the story we use one tense back from the tense that was originally used. In the above example, the question was in present simple. When recounted, however, it changes to past simple.

16.1 The reported speech table
Present simple changes to **past simple:** 'I like films' – 'She told me that she liked films.'

Present continuous changes to **past continuous:** 'I am eating an apple' – 'She told me she was eating an apple.'

Present perfect changes to **past perfect**: 'I have done my homework' – 'He told us he had done his homework.'

Present perfect continuous changes to **past perfect continuous**: 'We have been skiing for 12 years' – 'They said they had been skiing for 12 years.'

Past simple changes to **past perfect:** 'We bought a dog' – 'They said they had bought a dog.'

Past continuous changes to **past perfect continuous**: 'I wasn't feeling well' – 'He said he hadn't been feeling well.'

Past perfect remains **past perfect**: 'We had had breakfast before the mail arrived' – 'They said they had had breakfast before the mail had arrived.'

Will changes to **would**: 'I will go running tomorrow' – 'She said that she would go running the next day.'

Present perfect future changes to **would + present perfect**: 'By tomorrow I will have completed the project' – 'He told us that by tomorrow he would have completed the project.'

May changes to **might**: 'I may go to France next year' – 'She said that she might go to France the following year.'

Imperative changes to **infinitive**: 'Pick up the pen' – 'She told me to pick up the pen.'

Time markers
'Today' changes to 'that day.'

'This morning/this afternoon' changes to 'that morning/that afternoon.'

'Tomorrow' changes to 'the following day.'

'Yesterday' changes to 'the previous day.'

'Here' changes to 'there.'

'Now' changes to 'then.'

How to teach it

Elicit or explain that we use reported speech to recount what is said. With the help of your class write the reported speech table. Now say sentences with different tenses and ask your students to recount them. For example:

Teacher: 'I like chocolate.'

Tom: 'The teacher said that she liked chocolate.'

Teacher: 'Yesterday, I was cooking when the phone rang.'

Sarah: 'The teacher said the previous day she had been cooking when the phone had rung.'

Continue like this to cover all tenses.

16.2 Reported speech questions
Do/Does: For questions with 'do', take away the auxiliary and change it to the reported speech tense. For example:

'Where does Peter live?' changes to 'She asked ~~did~~ where Peter lived. 'What did you do yesterday?' becomes 'He asked what we had done the previous day.'

To be/Can: With 'to be' and 'can', change the subject and verb back to affirmative order and change it to reported speech tense. For example:

'Who <u>are you</u> talking to?' becomes 'She asked who <u>I was</u> talking to.'

'What <u>is your</u> name?' becomes 'He asked me what my name <u>was</u>.'

'How old <u>is your</u> mother?' becomes 'He asked me how old my mother <u>was</u>.'

'When <u>can we</u> have dinner?' becomes 'He asked when <u>they could</u> have dinner.'

'How tall <u>were you</u> when you were eight?' becomes 'She asked me how tall <u>I had</u> been when I was eight.'

<u>Note:</u> In the above sentence, the second past 'were eight' stays in past simple as 'had been eight', though correct sounds strange.

Yes or no questions: Here, take away the auxiliary and add 'if'. For example:

'Do you speak English?' becomes 'She asked me if I spoke English.'

'Did you like ice cream as a child?' becomes 'They asked me if I had liked ice cream as a child.'

How to teach it

Just like the sentences, ask your students questions and get them to recount them in reported speech. For example:

Teacher: 'Tom, how old are you?'

Tom: 'The teacher asked me how old I was.'

Controlled speaking practice: Crime

Reported speech naturally pairs itself with the vocabulary topic 'Crime'. To add more flavour to your lesson, teach the names of some crimes and criminals at the beginning.

Now practice reported speech by reading this dialogue line by line between a thief and a policeman and go around the class asking your students to recount it back to you. For example:

Teacher: 'I was waiting in the rain when I saw the man.'

Tom: 'The thief said that he had been waiting in the rain when he had seen the man.'

Teacher: 'I wanted to go to Disneyland.'

Sarah: 'The thief said that he had wanted to go to Disneyland.'

Dialogue: A policeman's interrogation of a thief

The thief said to the policeman: 'I was waiting in the rain when I saw the man.'

'I wanted to go to Disneyland.'

'The man looked rich so I hit him on the head and stole the money.'

The policeman said: 'I have called your lawyer.'

'He may not be here for an hour.'

The thief: 'Then I will call my mother.'

The policeman: 'Sit down and tell me the truth.'

'Your mother will be waiting for you after the interview.'

'By then she will have been informed by my colleague about what you have done.'

The thief said: 'Call her now.'

Policeman: 'Not until you have confessed.'

The thief said: 'This may take a while, do you have a cigarette?'

Freer speaking practice
Pairs' activity 'Create your own crime dialogue': In pairs, ask your students to create their own crime related dialogue, at least 10 lines long. When everyone is finished, one pair will read the dialogue line by line while another pair recounts it in reported speech.

Further speaking practice
Class game 'Alibi': This game does not require reported speech but it is fun and fits with the crime theme. You can always inject grammar into the task by asking the interviewers to recount what the suspects have just said.

Write 'Alibi' on the board and explain the meaning. Explain that a crime has been committed and tell your students what it is and where it happened. For example: A bank robbery across the street.

Pick two suspects and the rest of the class will be the police interviewers (divide large classes into smaller groups). Send the suspects out the room to decide on an alibi – tell them to make it as detailed as possible and to anticipate all the questions they may be asked. Meanwhile the police decide what they are going to ask the suspects.

Each suspect is interviewed separately, while the other remains out of the room. Through questioning, the police must look for inconsistencies in the suspects' story. For example:

Both suspects say that they couldn't have committed the crime as they were at the cinema. However, if one says they were watching a horror movie while the other says it was a comedy, they are clearly lying. If the suspects' stories match then they cannot be charged and have won the game. If the police uncover inconsistencies then they win.

17. Used to, be used to, to get used to

Have you ever noticed how many times native speakers use 'used to'? By now, your students will know the verb 'used to' for repetitive past as in 'I used to play tennis.'

There is, however, another 'used to'; an adjective which means to be accustomed to, or familiar with something so that it no longer seems difficult or strange. For example, 'I am used to playing tennis,' or 'He is used to driving to work.'

English speakers understand the difference from their structures, which are:

'Used to' for time: Subject pronoun/noun + used + infinitive (with 'to')

Example: 'He used to drive to work.'

'Used to' for accustomed: Subject pronoun/noun + to be + used + verb in gerund

Example: 'He is used to driving to work.'

Finally, there is 'To get used to,' which means the process of becoming accustomed to something.

'To get used to' for process: Subject pronoun/noun + get + used to + verb in gerund

Example: 'He is getting used to driving to work.'

How to teach it

Some teachers say never teach the time 'used to' and adjective 'to be used to' together as it is confusing. I disagree. Of course, your students should know the time 'used to' before you start, but, if you don't incorporate it into the adjective 'to be used to' lesson your students will never see the difference in the structure.

First write a time 'used to' on the board with, 'She used to swim every day,' and elicit the meaning (repetitive action in past).

Now underneath write 'She is used to swimming every day.' Elicit or explain that this sentence is nothing to do with time. To emphasise this, section off the time sentence by drawing a box around it.

'To be used to' is an adjective meaning 'to be accustomed to' – speakers of European languages should understand this as 'accustomed' is a Latin cognate. For other students you may have to use a translation in their own language.

Elicit the structure of both the verb and the adjective 'used to.' Underline the infinitive and the gerund to mark the difference. Elicit the negative: 'She isn't used to swimming every day' and the question: 'Is she used to swimming every day?'

Controlled speaking practice: Used to and to be used to

Now use these ideas to ask your students questions. Alternate between time 'used to' and adjective 'to be used to' with the same verb so that they can practice the different structures. For example:

Teacher: Tom, are you used <u>to shopping</u> on the Internet?

Tom: Yes, I am used to shopping on the Internet.

Teacher: Did you use <u>to shop</u> on the internet when you were a child?

Tom: No, I didn't use to shop on the internet when I was a child.

Now ask the following questions:

- o Shopping on the Internet.
- o Eating supermarket food.
- o Taking the elevator to your office.
- o The price of petrol.
- o Not smoking in public places.
- o Watching reality TV shows.
- o The current leader of the country.
- o Not going to school.
- o Not living with his parents.
- o Drinking Starbucks coffee.
- o Having responsibility.
- o Voting in elections.
- o Earning money.

- Driving on the motorway.
- The sunny or cold weather.
- Recycling.

How to teach it: To get used to

Now write 'She is getting used to swimming every day' and elicit the difference in meaning between this and 'She is used to swimming every day.' 'She is getting used to swimming every day' means she is in the process of becoming accustomed.

Elicit the structure, the negative: 'She isn't getting used to swimming every day' and the question: 'Is she getting used to swimming every day?'

Explain that just like the 'get' + adjective grammar point ('I get lost'), 'get' can be used for all tenses. To emphasise this elicit some more tenses for the above with:

Past: 'She got used to swimming every day' or 'She was getting used to swimming every day.'

Present perfect: 'She has got used to swimming every day.'

Past perfect: 'She had got used to swimming every day before she took the class.'

Future: 'She will get used to swimming every day,' 'She is going to get used to swimming every day.'

Second conditional (if students know the grammar): 'She could get used to swimming every day if... (your student thinks of the next clause).'

Controlled speaking practice part II: To get used to

Now add 'to get used to' and work through all the different tenses.

If she/he:

- Could get used to growing their own food.
- Has got used to speaking English.
- Is getting used to climate change.
- Could get used to living without the Internet
- Will get used to being retired.

o   Is going to get used to living in a warmer climate (due to climate change).

o   Has got used to having children.
o   Got used to looking things up on the internet (when?)
o   Is going to get used to self-driving cars.
o   Has got used to being their age.
o   Got used to going to work (when?)
o   Is getting used to studying English.

Freer speaking practice
Pairs' roleplay 'The recruitment agent': A recruitment agent visits one of their former clients for whom they have recently found work to find out how they are getting on.

Hand each pair one of the following jobs: An English teacher living in Japan, a long distance truck driver and a vet in Alaska.

Before you begin, ask your students to write three questions a recruitment agent would ask a client about their new job, using 'used to', 'to be used to' and 'to get used to.' After that, ask them to make more questions during the roleplay.

For example: Are you used to eating Japanese food? Did you use to eat Japanese food in your own country? How long did it take you to get used to living in a tiny apartment?

When they have finished, change roles.

18. Passive Voice

We make the passive voice with an object, some version of 'to be' verb and the participle.

For example, 'The apple was eaten,' or 'The painting is finished.'

We use passive voice when we want to emphasise the result of an action rather than the person or subject doing the action.

For example, in the active sentence 'I did the report,' it is me who is important in the sentence and the fact that *I did* it. Change this to passive and it becomes, 'The report was done, by me.' The report is now the important part of the sentence.

Its structure runs:

Object + to be + participle

Things to remember

Adding the agent

If you want to add the 'doer' of the action (also known as the agent) it is done with 'by.' For example, 'The chair was made <u>by my father</u>' but often this information is superfluous.

The passive exists in all tenses

Too often we only ask our students to practice present, past and future passive ('The apple is eaten, the apple was eaten, the apple will be eaten'). In fact, it exists in all tenses. See activity below.

Preposition placement

If there is a preposition between the verb and object you keep the preposition *after* the verb. For example, 'They talked <u>about</u> the issue' (active), 'The issue was talked <u>about</u>' (passive).

Plurals

Remember to drill: 'The apple <u>is</u> eaten' in singular but 'The apples <u>are</u> eaten' in plural. Equally in past 'The apple <u>was</u> eaten' and 'The apples <u>were</u> eaten.'

It is very common in English

You must emphasise this to your students, but why? Whilst other languages have this structure they don't necessarily use it, preferring to speak the whole time in active sentences.

Why do we use it in English then?

The reason is partly cultural and partly because we have no subjunctive tense. Because we have no way to soften or cast doubt on our active sentences we speak in passive. 'The reservation wasn't made,' is a far softer and socially acceptable than saying 'You didn't make the reservation.' English is a very polite language (yes, it really is) and you must emphasise the importance of speaking indirectly, using 'please' and 'thank you', 'can I have' rather than 'bring me' and so on, because not all cultures operate in this way.

How to teach it

Write the following sentence on the board, 'The boy breaks the window.'

Explain that this is an active sentence. Ask a student to put it into a passive (it is a common thing to study, one person in the group is sure to know how to do it. If it is totally new, you do it).

Elicit: 'The window is broken by the boy.'

Ask: 'What is more important in this sentence, the window or the boy?'
Elicit: 'The window.'

Elicit the structure and negative: 'The window isn't broken by the boy,' and the question: 'Is the window broken by the boy.'

Ask your students to make the sentence plural. Elicit: 'The windows are broken by the boy.'

Ask them to make the sentence past simple. Elicit: 'The window was broken by the boy.'

And plural past. Elicit: 'The windows were broken by the boy.' Next elicit past simple questions and negatives.

Ask them to make it into future: 'The windows will be broken by the boy,' and do the same with questions and negatives.

Tense practice

The passive, however, exists in far more tenses. To practice, ask your students to change these sentences to passive. Stop depending on their level.

- Someone is processing it now.
- Someone processes it every day.
- Someone was processing it when she got here.
- Someone processed it yesterday.
- Someone can process it.
- Someone will process it tomorrow.
- When is someone going to process it?
- Someone has processed it.
- Someone would process it, if there were time.
- Someone would have processed it if there had been time.
- Someone may process it tonight, but I am not certain.
- Someone may have process it yesterday, but I am not certain.
- Someone must process it.
- Someone has to process it.
- Someone should process it as soon as possible.
- Someone must have processed it.
- Someone could have processed it.
- Someone should have processed it.

Controlled speaking practice

Now they have an idea of the breadth of the passive, ask them to convert these sentences into passive voice.

Remember: If there is a preposition between the verb and object you keep the preposition after the verb.

- The girl ruined her dress.
- They gave my sister a ticket too.
- She is painting the wall.
- I am doing the work now.
- I didn't write the email.
- They thought of a solution.

- She answers the call.
- They thought about the problem.
- I spoke to the teacher.
- They lost the orders.
- We arrived at an agreement.
- They have received the emails.

- The child hit his sister.
- She was looking for his phone number.
- The mechanic repaired the car badly.
- She has sent the letters.
- We spoke about the film.

Further speaking practice
Pairs' roleplay 'A bad day at work': Student A is an employee at a bank and Student B is their boss. Student A has made some mistakes in the last few days. These include:

Transferring 10,000 euros to the wrong client's account.

Accidentally deleting 2000 client files.

Forgetting to order a new watercooler.

Spilling coffee in their computer.

Losing their boss's presentation for the following day.

   The employee wants to separate themselves from these actions and so they use passive voice. The boss is angry and will use direct voice. For example, employee: 'The watercooler hasn't been ordered.' Boss: 'You didn't order the watercooler.'

19. There

By this point your students will know 'there' in present, past and future form, but it can be applied to many other tenses and to progress they need to understand all of them, even if they don't use them right away. I usually teach this at B2 level after the Modals in Past lessons.

The variations of 'there' are:

Present: 'There is/are.'

Past: 'There was/were.'

Future with 'will': 'There will be.'

Future with going to: 'There is going to be.'

Present perfect: 'There has been.'

Past perfect: 'There had been.'

Used to: 'There used to be.'

Second conditional: 'There would be / There could be.'

Third conditional: 'There would have been / There could have been.'

Possibility: 'There may / might be.'

Possibility past: 'There may / might have been.'

Deduction positive: 'There must be.'

Deduction positive past: 'There must have been.'

Deduction negative: 'There can't be.'

Deduction negative past: 'There can't have been.'

Obligation: 'There has to be.'

Obligation past: 'There had to be.'

Mild obligation (advice): 'There should be / There shouldn't be.'

Mild obligation (advice) past: 'There should have been / There shouldn't have been.'

How to teach it

You must make sure that your students understand all of the above grammatical structures (such as modal verbs in past) before you start, as the concept of 'there' is hard enough.

Write on the board, 'There is a pen on the table' and elicit the past and future. Now slowly elicit the other 'theres' until you get down to mild obligation in past: 'There should have been a pen on the table yesterday' (but there wasn't). Question your students to make sure they understand what each version means. For example:

Tom: 'There must be a pen on the table.'

Teacher: 'Is that obligation or deduction?'

Tom: 'Deduction.'

Teacher: 'Can you complete this sentence so that it makes sense?'

Tom: 'There must be a pen on the table because this is an office and there are always lots of pens around.'

Teacher: 'What is the negative of that statement?'

Tom: 'There can't be a pen on the table because I put all the pens in my bag.'

Controlled speaking practice

Ask your students the following questions. You will probably have to modify them slightly to fit your surroundings. Try to elicit as many possible answers. For example:

Teacher: 'Are there car accidents in China today?'

Sarah: 'There must be car accidents in China today.'

Teacher: 'And last week?'

Sarah: 'There must have been car accidents in China last week.'

Teacher: 'And in your town last week?'

Sarah: 'There may have been a car accident last week, I don't know.'

Questions

1. Are there car accidents in China today? (must be) And in your small town? (may be).

2. Is there a meeting at your work this week? (has/hasn't been) And next week? (will/won't) And in Microsoft last week? (may be).

3. Is there a party in the next classroom? (can't be) And this morning? (can't have been).

4. Was there an election last year? (was/wasn't) And in the 80s? (would have been).
Is there a football match in your country today? (must be) And last week? (must have been).

5. Will there be public money for schools next year? (should be) And last year? (should have been).

6. Has there been a local festival this year in your country? (has been).

7. Are there cars in the street? (must be) And elephants in the street? (can't be).

8. Did there used to be horses in the street? (used to be).

9. Will there be hospitals next year? (should be/has to be).

Freer speaking practice
Pairs' or group roleplay 'Lost on a desert island': You have landed on a desert island with 20 other people. Using 'there' discuss together:

What you need to survive.

Security issues.

How you're going to get rescued.

Items you have: A knife, paperclips and string, a lighter and a bottle.

Vocabulary: Shelter, raft, fresh water, earth quake, tsunami, sharks.

For example:

Sarah: 'We are on a desert island. There must be coconuts, we can eat those.'

Tom: 'There must be fish in the sea, we can go fishing.'

Sarah: 'There might be sharks.'

Scenarios

Now start to feed your students the following situations. Let them use their deduction and imagination to answer you. Elicit a few alternatives where possible.

Scenario 1: You hear running water. Answer: 'There must/might be a river.'

Scenario 2: The ground shakes. Answer: 'There must have been an earthquake.'

Scenario 3: You see dark clouds on the horizon. Answer: 'There will be a storm.'

Scenario 4: Two people go missing while hunting at night (they didn't take the knife), you see a happy tiger. Answer: 'They must have been eaten by the tiger' or, 'They should have taken the knife' or, 'They shouldn't have hunted at night'.

Scenario 5: You see the remains of walls formed into squares. Answer: 'There used to be village here' or 'There must have been people here.'

Scenario 6: You find an underground bunker. Answer: 'There may be people here' or, 'There must have been people here' or, 'There should be some resources we can use'.

20. Negative Answers

In English there are two types of negatives, those beginning with 'any' ('I don't know anybody who can fix my fridge') and those beginning with 'no' ('I know nobody who can fix my fridge.') But what's the difference? Well, the first sentence contains an auxiliary in negative (in this case 'don't') so the negative is an 'any' word. The second has no auxiliary and so the negative is a 'no' word ('nobody'). The full table runs:

	With auxiliary	Without auxiliary
People	Anybody/anyone	Nobody/no one
Things	Anything	Nothing
Location	Anywhere	Nowhere
Quantity	Any	None
Choice of two	Either	Neither

The quantity negative has a noun after 'any' but after 'none' the sentence stops. For example, 'She doesn't have any apples,' and 'She has none.' You can however say 'She has no apples.'

The choice of two negatives would run: 'I don't like either coffee or tea' or 'I like neither coffee nor tea.' For more information go to the Either or Neither chapter here.

How to teach it

Write the above example. Underline 'anybody' and 'nobody' and elicit the rule. Next write the above table eliciting examples of each negative as you go.

Controlled speaking practice

Practice with the negatives drill. With each of these questions students must answer in the negative. Get them to use both the auxiliary and non-auxiliary versions where possible.

- Who told you to wear those clothes this morning?
- Where do they want to go?
- Which newspaper does he read?
- What have you done today?
- How many beers have you drunk this morning?
- What were you looking at just now?
- Who did you see last night?
- How much homework did you do last week?
- Which document did you lose yesterday?

- Where were you going yesterday?
- Who have you offended this week?
- What was that email about?
- How many cars have you crashed into this month?
- Which birthday did you forget last year: mine or yours?
- What are you studying tonight?
- Who lives on the moon?
- Which of these mobile phones have you broken?
- Where are you going with that pen?

21. To Be Like and to Look Like, Senses and Adjective Order

'To be like' and 'to look like' are a great source of confusion for students. In essence, 'To be like' is for personality with the question, 'What is she like?' and 'To look like' is for appearance with the question, 'What does she look like?

We ask these two questions all the time without realising how similar they are. Your students, however, will stumble over this grammar point for years and have to put in a lot of practice before they start to get it right every time.

21.1 To look like
How to teach it

This is the perfect opportunity to either review or teach some personality and appearance vocabulary.

First let's start with appearance. In pairs or as a group ask your students to think of words for physical form. Elicit the below. For advanced groups, push it further.

Vocabulary for appearance: Bald, beard, clean-shaven, curly hair, cute, good-looking, handsome, moustache, over-weight, blond, brown, black, red and grey hair, slim, straight hair, short, tall.

Vocabulary for appearance advanced: To be in your early, mid or late 20s, 30s, 40s, beauty spot, a belly, a brunette, a red-head, freckles, fringe, muscular, skinny, wrinkles.

Now write on the board: 'She is tall with blond hair' and elicit the question, 'What does she look like?'

Explain that 'like' in this case means 'similar to' and we use the verb 'look' as we are using the sense of sight.

Now write: 'She looks like her mother' and elicit the question, '<u>Who</u> does she look like?'

Now finally write: 'She and her brother look alike.' Underline 'alike' and elicit the meaning; an adjective that means 'to be similar to each other'.

Emphasise that the verb 'look' is <u>only</u> in the question. In the answer you use 'to be' or 'to have'. For example, 'What does your mother look like?' Answer: 'She <u>has</u> short, brown hair and she is tall.' If you don't do this, your students will start saying, 'She has like short brown hair.'

Controlled speaking practice
Tell your students to ask each other the following questions. Ask them to make more questions also.

- ○ What their brothers / sisters look like.
- ○ Whether they and their siblings look alike.
- ○ Whether they look like their father or mother.
- ○ What they used to look like at school.
- ○ What their school used to look like.
- ○ What their house looks like.
- ○ What they think they will look like in the future.

Freer speaking practice
Pairs' game 'Guess my celebrity': Give your students slips of paper with the names of the following celebrities (or celebrities relevant to your students) and tell them to keep it secret. Student A must describe the person while their partner guesses their identity.

Suggested celebrities: Bruce Willis, Danny DeVito, Santa Claus, Penelope Cruz, Charlie Chaplin, Marilyn Monroe, Barak Obama, Henry IIV

21.2 Adjective order
We rarely use more than two adjectives together, but when we do they run in a particular order which is:

Opinion > Size > Age > Colour > Style or Material > Noun

Example: 'I have a beautiful, big, old, brown, Tudor style House' or, 'She has lovely, long, brown, straight hair.'

How to teach it

The 'Appearance' lesson above is a good time to highlight the order. Write on the board the above and examples. Emphasise that you would not normally put so many adjectives together but when you do use more than one, bear in mind that there are rules.

Controlled speaking practice

Using four or more adjectives, ask your students to describe:

- o Their car.
- o Their house.
- o Their hair.
- o Their office/school.

21.3 To be like

How to teach it

Now let's move on to personality adjectives. Elicit a good selection of personality adjectives from the class. For advanced students, push it further with the advanced list.

Personality vocabulary: Ambitious, bossy, brave, charming, easy-going, jealous, kind, laid-back, moody, reliable, sensitive, sensible, selfish, sociable, spoilt.

Personality vocabulary advanced: Absent-minded, arrogant, cheerful, calm, conscientious, easy-going, eccentric, forgetful, giving, grumpy, insecure, insincere, loyal, open-minded, outgoing, optimistic, smart, stubborn, talkative, thoughtful, vain, wise, witty.

Now write on the board: 'He is easy-going and charming' and elicit the question, 'What is he like?'

Explain that this expresses his permanent characteristics and 'like' again means 'similar to', rather than 'I like ice cream.'

Now write: 'He is like his brother' and elicit the question, 'Who is he like?'

Next write: 'He and his brother are alike.' Underline 'alike' and elicit what it means – again, that he and his sister are similar, but this time in personality.

188

Emphasise that the permanent characteristic question can be applied to anything; people, animals, buildings, your job, a country and inanimate objects.

To highlight this, say the following statements and elicit the questions:

'Her job is fun but stressful.'
'What is her job like?'

'Brazil used to be dangerous.'
'What did Brazil used to be like?'

'My office is light and airy.'
'What is your office like?'

'My next car will be much bigger.'
'What will your next car be like?'

Controlled speaking practice
Tell your students to ask each other the following questions and to make up their own.

- o   What their brothers / sisters are like.
- o   Whether they and their siblings are alike.
- o   Whether they are like their father or mother.
- o   What they used to be like at school.
- o   What their job / school is like.
- o   What their favourite / least favourite person is like.

Freer speaking practice
Pairs' activity 'Celebrity personalities': Print out a selection of well-known celebrities and historical figures and ask your students:

What they think they are like from their current behaviour.

What they think they were like at school.

Which one would make the best flatmate or boss.

Which would make the worst flatmate or boss.

What they currently look like.

What they looked like 10 years ago.

Further speaking practice

Pairs activity 'Personality traits': Your students must decide which personality traits are the best to have in a boss, best friend and life partner. Full roleplay found in The Ultimate ESL Book of Speaking Activities available at www.bilinganation.com.

21.4 The other senses
'Like' can also be used for other senses with the questions:

What does it: taste, smell, sound and feel like?

Controlled speaking practice
Elicit 'like' questions from the following statements:

It tastes terrible.
What does it taste like?

It feels like silk   .
What does it feel like?

It sounds like a train.
What does it sound like?

It sounded like a bus.
What did it sound like?

It smells like roses.
What does it smell like?

It tastes like chocolate.
What does it taste like?

Note: Be careful with the last two statements. To say that something smells *like* roses, means that it isn't roses, it is something similar to roses (such as perfume). If it really is roses you say, it smells *of* roses. It is the same with taste; if something 'tastes *like* chocolate' it isn't chocolate, it only tastes similar to it. If it really is chocolate then it tastes *of* chocolate.

21.5 The senses: action vs state verbs

As discussed before, verbs fall into two categories; action, which can be expressed in gerund, and state, which cannot. The senses ('to see', 'to hear', 'to taste', 'to smell' and 'to feel') are state verbs; this is because you, the sensor, do no action but rather the sense arrives to you. However, many sense verbs have another meaning that *is* an action verb and can be put into gerund.

22. As and Like

As we saw in the previous chapter 'like' is a preposition meaning 'similar to,' and commonly used in similes. For example, in the sentence 'Your father works like an ox', the father is not really an ox, but works so hard he is comparable to an ox.

We use 'as', on the other hand, for things that *are* real. It expresses five main things. These are:

Jobs – 'She works as a dentist.'

Function – 'You can use a sofa as a bed.'

At the beginning of sentences to show how things are or appear – 'As a parent, I understand what she is going through.'

Comparison – 'France is not as hot as Portugal.'

Because – 'As you know the way, you can lead us,' or, 'We can't go swimming as I have forgotten my costume.'

Note: There are a few other definitions for 'as' but these are very nuanced and would be confusing for your students to learn all at once.

How to teach it

Write on the board 'She treats me like a daughter,' and, 'She treats me as a daughter,' and elicit the difference – the first being that I am not her daughter but she treats me in the same way, the second being that I really am her daughter.

Now write an example sentence for 'like' and the definitions for 'as' along with examples.

Controlled speaking practice

Now tell your students that you will read them the following sentences and they have to fill in the blanks with either 'as' or 'like'. There are a lot of sentences so that you can do this exercise in several different classes.

_____you know I find it difficult to swim long distances.

He drives _____a racing car driver.

He works _____a racing car driver.

I am not going to the party _____I have a cold.

It's_____expensive in Madrid _____it is in Barcelona.

_____I said we should go to the cinema instead of a restaurant.

It smells_____roses.

Do_____I do.

He speaks_____his father.

_____a method of creating employment, it could be better.

_____my sister you should support me.

She looks_____her sister.

He sounds_____he is in trouble.

She dances_____a ballerina.

_____the world gets hotter, we wear more t-shirts.

_____I understand it, there is an economic crisis.

She looks_____a model.

It's_____being in the army.

He climbs_____a monkey.

She works_____a zookeeper.

_____your children grow they look more_____their father.

It's _____cold in Russia_____it is in Spain right now.

The weather is _____Russia right now.

Don't hurt yourself_____I did.

It hurts_____mad.

I did _____you told me.

You speak_____a teacher.

_____you have the food, can you prepare the picnic?

Comparative sentences are _____difficult_____conditional sentences.

He works_____a handyman.

It's_____he's a handyman, he is very useful around the house.
It wasn't_____you said, the children were very difficult.

She acts_____a child.
She works _____a waitress.
_____the best team in the world, they have a lot of responsibility.
They look_____film stars.
_____your friend I advise you not to marry him.

It tastes_____chocolate.
It sounds_____you had a good time.
We want to be treated_____adults.
I want to be treated _____a human being.
_____a dessert, it's not very sweat.

23. The Conditionals

The conditional tense refers to a future, hypothetical or impossible situation. All conditionals consist of two clauses divided by a comma: The situation, starting with 'if,' and the outcome, expressed by the conditional.

For example: 'If she goes to the meeting (situation), I will come too (outcome)' or 'If they spoke German (situation), they would live in Germany (outcome)'.

The clauses can be reversed with no change to the meaning such as, 'They would live in Germany, if they spoke German.'

Conditionals have a reputation for being hard to teach. In my experience, while it is often difficult for a student to remember word order, the actual concept they grasp immediately as (with European languages at least) the conditionals in the students' own languages connect exactly with English.

If you are teaching students with a shared language it is a good idea to get them to make translations of the sentences you give so that they can see the similarities. I start teaching the conditionals at early B1 level and finish at early B2.

23.1 The zero conditional
The zero conditional refers to a real present.

Its structure runs:

If + present + noun/pronoun (optional) + imperative

Examples: 'If you go to school, take your bag with you', 'If you like chocolate, then eat some' or 'If you bake a cake, give it to me.'

<u>Remember</u> with imperative there is no subject pronoun.

While it is good to know this structure do not spend too much time on it as in many languages, this structure means future and they may start using it as such.

23.2 The first conditional

The first conditional is with 'will' and means a possible future.

The structure runs:

If + present + noun/pronoun (optional) + will + infinitive (no 'to')

Example: 'If it rains, she will take an umbrella' or 'If we go to France, we will hire a car.'

How to teach it

Write the above first conditional sentences on the board and elicit whether it is past, present or future.

Ask: 'Do they refer to something that is definitely going to happen, or probably going to happen? Elicit: 'Probably going to happen.'

Elicit the negative: 'If we don't go to France, we won't hire a car' and the question: 'If we go to France, will we hire a car?' or 'Will we hire a car, if we go to France?' You can reverse the statement and it means the same thing.

Highlight the contraction: Rub out 'We will hire a car' from the original sentence and put 'We'll hire a car,' preferably in a different colour pen.

Controlled speaking practice

Practice by giving your students a statement that has a high probability of being true, and ask them to turn it into an 'if' clause. Your students must invent the second 'will' part of the sentence. For example:

Teacher: 'It is sunny this weekend.'

Student: 'If it is sunny this weekend, I will go to the beach.'

Teacher: 'And with contraction?'

Student: 'If it's sunny this weekend, I'll go to the beach.'

Highlight that the first conditional can also be used with the present continuous and write: 'It is snowing, so I make a snowman' and elicit: 'It is not snowing, so I won't make a snowman.'

Now go around the class and verbally give each student two or three of these sentences. If you have a large class, print out the list and ask them ask and answer each other in pairs.

- It is sunny this weekend.
- You see [insert movie or person] this afternoon.
- Your favourite team wins [insert tournament].
- Your boss gets sick next week.
- Your parents go to [insert country] this summer.
- Your brother/sister buys a new [insert object] this year.

- Justin Bieber gives up singing.
- You learn to [insert skill].
- Your brother/sister forgets their house keys tomorrow.
- You burn your dinner tonight.
- Hippie clothes come back into fashion.
- There is a huge storm tonight.

- Madonna gets married again.
- Your brother/sister adopts a stray dog.
- Your mother buys you a bright orange jumper for your birthday.
- You don't sleep tonight.
- You see an old friend in the street after class.
- I don't give you any homework today.

Highlight Can

'Can' is a very irregular verb, and therefore must be dealt with separately. The infinitive is 'to be able to.'

To practice, write on the board, 'It is raining so I can't play football this afternoon.'

Ask your students to make an 'if' clause with this statement using 'will.' 'If it is raining this afternoon, I won't be able to play football.'

'Can' statements

- ○ I am not sick so I can go to the party.
- ○ She doesn't like exercise so she can't teach gymnastics.
- ○ I am not working so I can meet you.
- ○ She can paint so she can paint a picture for her mother.
- ○ He can dance so he can teach me.
- ○ I practice every day so I can play the guitar.

Helper phrases

The first conditional is often used in conjunction with the following phrases:

As soon as: meaning 'once this event has happened the subject will do the following...' For example, 'As soon as winter comes I will buy a new jacket' or 'As soon as they call she will book the tickets.'

Just in case: meaning 'in the event that something happens.' For example, 'I will pack a sandwich just in case you get hungry' or 'We'll take an umbrella just in case it rains.'

Freer speaking practice
Pairs' roleplay 'Planning an office party': One of your most loved colleagues is retiring and you have to plan the party. Brainstorm all the tasks you need to do and, using 'as soon as' and 'just in case' plus 'will,' organise the jobs between you.

23.3 The second conditional

The second conditional, also known as the present conditional, refers to something hypothetical but possible.

Its structure runs:

If + past + would + infinitive (no to)

Example: 'If she had a bicycle she would cycle to work' or 'If they weren't allergic to animals, they would have a cat.'
How to teach it

Write the above sentences on the board and ask: 'Is this possible or not possible.' Answer: 'Possible.'

Next ask: 'Do they refer to something that is real or hypothetical?' Answer: 'Hypothetical.'

Elicit the negative: 'If she didn't have a bicycle, she wouldn't cycle to work' and the question: 'If she had a bicycle, would she cycle to work?' or 'Would she cycle to work, if she had a bicycle?' Highlight that you can reverse the statement.

Highlight the contraction: Rub out 'She would cycle to work' and put 'she'd cycle to work,' preferably in a different colour pen.

Controlled speaking practice

This time practice by giving your students a statement that is not true. They have to turn it into a second conditional 'if' clause, and invent the second part.

For example, the teacher knows that John can't speak German.

Teacher: 'You speak German.'

John: 'If I spoke German, I would look for a job in Germany.'

Teacher: 'And with contraction?'

John: 'If I spoke German, I'd look for a job in Germany.'

Highlight the continuous form by writing: 'It is not raining so we go for a picnic,' and elicit the reverse statement, 'If it weren't raining, we would go for a picnic.'

Highlight can with: 'I can paint so I can teach art' and elicit: 'If I could paint, I would be able to teach art.'

Important additions: 'To be' verb

'To be' the English language's last subjunctive verb which means its form changes in second conditional. While it is perfectly normal for native speakers to say 'If she <u>was</u> cold, she would put on a jumper,' it is grammatically incorrect.

In the second conditional, 'was' changes to 'were' in all cases. Therefore the correct way to say this sentence is: 'If she <u>were</u> cold, she would put on a jumper.'

Whether to use 'was' or 'were' when speaking is a grey area nowadays. However, you must highlight the correct, 'official' way with 'were' as in exams your students may be marked down for not using it.

Sentences

Now go around the class and verbally give each student two or three of these sentences. If you have a large class, print out the list and tell your students to work in pairs.

- You play [insert instrument].
- You speak [insert language].
- You buy a Ferrari.
- You are a politician.
- You see a famous footballer in your local supermarket.
- Your brother/sister writes a best-selling novel.

- Your friends make you go bungee jumping.
- You know how to fly a helicopter.
- There is a party in the room next door.
- You see a robbery.
- There is an earthquake in your town.
- You forget your mother's birthday.

- You break your boss's computer.
- It is snowing outside.
- You go to Brazil.
- You are wearing a red hat.
- You shrink your favourite sweater.
- Your brother/sister becomes a famous artist.

Freer speaking practice
Pairs' activity 'What would you do if?': Hand out slips of paper and ask your students to write three hypothetical situations. Collect them up and make a pile in the middle of the table. In pairs, tell your students to ask each other questions from the pile. Tell them to discard any questions that are unsuitable and encourage them to correct any mistakes.

To avoid 10 'What would you do if you won the lottery?' questions add your own.

Suggested questions

What would you do if:

Your car broke down in the middle of the night on a deserted mountain and your mobile had run out of battery?

You accidentally lost your grandmother's engagement ring?

Your partner or flatmates were in another country and you accidentally locked yourself out of the flat?

You suddenly became allergic to all dairy and meat products?

You found $50 in a cash machine?

23.3.1 The second conditional in real life

The 'What would you do if you were swimming and saw a shark?' type of conversation is all very well, but how often does it happen? When you think about it – not often. However, the second conditional is very common in real life to organise, problem-solve and debate.

While most students of a B1 level will have already had the 'What would you do if...?' class (often multiple times) they will have never been taught this and will come alive when they finally realise the true possibilities of the tense. Enjoy a great class.

Helper phrases

In the real world, conditionals are supplemented with 'helper phrases' that substitute 'if' to give the sentence a distinctive meaning. The main ones are:

Imagine that: A verb, used to convey an imaginary situation. For example, 'Imagine that you were walking in a deserted manor house and saw a ghost, what would you do?'

Supposing that: An adverb, used when negotiating but in more of a hypothetical way. For example, 'Supposing that you took the job, would we have to relocate?' Or to convey imagination; for example, 'Supposing that there were a flash flood, where would you run to?'

What if: A phrase that literally means 'if', but in more of a conversational way; for example, 'What if I failed chemistry? Would I still get on the course?' It is commonly used among native speakers and most learners will be happy to add it to their repertoire.

Freer speaking practice

Pairs' activity 'hypothetical situations': To practice I use the game Rory's Story Cubes. The cubes are nine die with a different picture on each face. The idea is that you roll the cubes and the pictures help people to tell a story. Put your students into pairs and hand them each a cube. Ask them to roll and the picture that appears should spark an idea for a question.

For example: A student sees a picture of a key and says, 'Supposing that you lost your keys and everyone you lived with was out of the country, how would you enter your house?' Or 'What if, you had no money and had to rob a bank, how would you do it?'

This method provokes a more spontaneous conversation. 'Imagine that' and 'supposing that' will have equivalents in the students' native languages and they will enjoy using it in English. Rory's Story Cubes can be bought on Amazon or in an app that you shake to 'roll the dice.' If you don't have them, then write 30 random nouns and allocate a few to each pair for the same effect.

Problem solving

Another common way we use conditionals – particularly second – is to problem solve and negotiate. For this we use the following helper phrases plus a conditional (zero, first, second, third). They can either start the sentence or connect the two clauses in the middle. These are:

Provided that: An adverb often used in negotiation or problem solving meaning; 'If you do this, I will do that'. For example, 'Provided that we went to France, I would pay for the hotel'; or 'I will do the report, provided that you organise the meeting'.

Unless: A conjunction meaning that something can only be true in a particular situation.

As long as: A synonym for 'provided that'. For example, 'I would go to the party, as long as you didn't invite my ex-boyfriend.'

Controlled speaking practice

I have designed a negotiation lesson which has proven particularly popular among business students. First explain each helper phrase – this could be tricky and so have translations on hand if needed or ask your strongest student what they think it is in their language (you need to know also, to check).

Provided that and as long as

Now practice by giving the one clause of a first or second conditional sentence and ask them to make up the other half by joining it with either 'provided that' or 'as long as'.

For example: The teacher says to a student 'I would drive...' and elicit from them something like 'I would drive as long as you <u>paid</u> for the petrol.' Make sure they use the correct conditional form. 'I would drive as long as you <u>pay</u> for the petrol,' mixes two conditionals and is not correct.

Sentences

- o I would drive...
- o She would look after your dog...
- o They will make the cake...
- o You will get promoted...
- o There won't be too many issues...
- o She would learn to play the piano...

- o They would pay for the wedding...
- o I'll be happy to do your homework...
- o We would have a picnic...
- o He would move flat...
- o He will speak to the boss...
- o It wouldn't be a problem...

Unless

Now do the same thing with 'unless'. For example the teacher says 'They won't study Chinese...' and elicits something like 'They won't study Chinese unless they move to China.'

Sentences

- o   They won't study Chinese...
- o   He wouldn't join the army...
- o   She won't live in a flat...
- o   We won't arrive on time...
- o   They wouldn't bring up the subject...
- o   She wouldn't take the job...
- o   There wouldn't be a problem...
- o   They won't change school...
- o   We wouldn't get a pay rise...
- o   There won't be another recession soon...
- o   They wouldn't get married...

Freer speaking practice
Pairs' roleplay 'Negotiations': In each of the below situations your students must negotiate an agreement using second conditional and the above phrases.

1. Student A wants to have a week long holiday in Italy but Student B is afraid to fly. If you drive it will take two days out of your already short holiday. Negotiate an agreement.

2. You have to organise an anniversary party for your parents. Your brother (who is not here) doesn't get on well with your uncle Antonio who is a drunk. Your mother wants Antonio to come. What do you do?

3. Student A and B want to set up a restaurant business together. You have the money but you both work full time in other jobs. Neither of you wants to give up your jobs in case the restaurant fails. Negotiate an agreement.

23.4 The third conditional

The third conditional, also known as the past conditional, refers to something that happened in alternative past, meaning it is therefore impossible.

The structure runs:

If + past perfect + would + present perfect

Example: 'If she had studied architecture, she would have become an architect' or 'If they had been sick, they wouldn't have come to the party.'

How to teach it

Write the above sentences on the board. And elicit whether they refer to the present, future or past. Answer: Past.

Elicit whether they are possible or not possible. Answer: Not possible. Why? Because the past has already happened.

Elicit the negative: 'If she hadn't studied architecture, she wouldn't have become an architect' and the question: 'If she had studied architecture, would she have become an architect?' or 'Would she have become an architect, if she had studied architecture?'

Highlight the contraction: Rub out 'She would have become,' and put 'She'd have become,' preferably in a different colour pen.

Controlled speaking practice

This time practice by giving your students a statement about the past that is not true. They have to turn it into a third conditional 'if' clause and invent the second part.

For example, the teacher knows that Sarah didn't grow up in the USA.

Teacher: 'You grew up in the USA.'

Sarah: 'If I had grown up in the USA, I would have gone to school there.'

Teacher: 'And with contraction?'

John: 'If I'd grown up in the USA, I'd have gone to school there.'

Highlight the continuous version with 'he was speaking so I didn't interrupt' and elicit 'if he had been speaking, I wouldn't have interrupted.'

Highlight 'can,' write: 'I could play the piano from an early age, so I could go to music school' and elicit: 'If I had been able to play the piano from an early age, I could have gone to music school.'

Sentences

- You grew up in the USA.
- You went to Tokyo last week.
- You forgot your keys this morning.
- There was a marathon in your city yesterday.
- You accidentally threw out your wallet in the trash yesterday.
- Your parents had 10 children.

- Your brother/sister ran to work this morning.
- Someone stole your car yesterday.
- You slept for two hours last night.
- Your brother/ sister took a helicopter to work.
- There was a strike at your work yesterday.
- You swam in the sea last week.

- You weren't able to start your car yesterday.
- It was snowing last week.
- Your brother/sister wrote a best-selling novel.
- You were able to go skiing last weekend.
- The other party won the election.
- The Berlin wall never fell.

Freer speaking practice
Pairs' activity 'What would you have done if...?': Hand out slips of paper and ask your students to write three third conditional questions. Remember they must place these questions in the past with a past time expression. Collect the paper and make a pile in the middle of the table. In pairs, tell your students to ask and answer questions from the pile. Tell them to discard any that are unsuitable and encourage them to correct any mistakes.

Questions to add include:

If you hadn't gone to work today, would your boss have noticed?

If you had found 100 euros in the street today, what would you have done with it?

What do you think you would have been like if you had been born a member of the opposite sex?

What would your life have been like, if you had lived in the 60s?

23.5 Mixed conditionals
If you analyse the way natives use third conditional you will often hear this. 'If I had taken chemistry instead of physics at university, I would have a better paid job now.'

This is known as a mixed conditional: The first clause is third conditional, referring to an alternative past and the second clause, second conditional referring to a hypothetical present.

Your students will understand this idea because they are sure to have it in their own languages.

Controlled speaking practice
Hand out slips of paper and ask your students to think of a third conditional clause. Now redistribute the paper and in pairs ask them to create the ends of the sentences in second conditional. Examples include:

- o   If you hadn't studied...
- o   If you hadn't had kids...
- o   If the financial crisis hadn't happened...
- o   If you had/hadn't followed your parents' advice...
- o   The internet was never invented...
- o   Hitler won World War Two...

Further speaking practice
Pairs' activity 'Turning points': Ask your students to think of three turning points in their lives. For example, graduating from college, getting their current job, not getting something, getting married and having kids. Ask them to explore what their lives would be like now if these things hadn't or had happened in the past.

For example: 'If I hadn't studied engineering, I would be a journalist now.'

Putting it all together: The conditionals
Group game 'Guess my identity with conditionals': Using only questions in conditional, the class must guess the identity of a student pretending to be a famous person.

24. As if and As though

'As if' and 'as though' are conjunctions used in place of 'like' to make a simile or metaphor. They are used with either second or third conditional (most commonly second).

They are often used to convey something negative. For example: 'She acts as if she were the queen.'

How to teach it

Write the above sentence and ask 'Is she the queen?' Elicit: 'No.' Underline 'as if' and elicit the meaning and the following tense (second conditional).

Note: In sentences with 'to be' it sounds much better to use the official 'were' rather than 'was.'

Controlled speaking practice

Ask your students to change the following statements with 'as if' or 'as though' + second conditional. For example, 'You act like my father' changes to 'You act as if you were my father.'

- You act like you are my father.
- You speak like you know the right answer.
- You behave like the king.
- You drive like Fernando Alonso.
- You look like you have seen a ghost.

- You act like you are poisoned.
- You speak to me like I am a child.
- You deal with your employees like they are idiots.
- You treat her like a maid.
- You spend money like there is no tomorrow.
- She speaks to him like his mother.

- You treat me like a slave.
- You act like Elizabeth Taylor.
- You behave like you have no money.
- You work like there is no tomorrow.
- You run like you are on fire.

Freer speaking practice

Pairs' roleplay 'Work colleague from hell': Your new colleague (who is not present) never arrives on time, doesn't do his/her work, thinks they are superior to everyone else, spends company money in expensive restaurants and drives badly. Complain to each other about the problems using 'as if' and 'as though.'

For example: 'She treats us as if we were slaves' or 'He behaves as though he were the owner of the company.'

25. Wish and Hope

'Wish' refers to a desire. It is used either for a hypothetical present or an impossible past. In present it is used with the first clause of the second conditional – for example, 'I wish you didn't eat so much chocolate'

If it is with an action verb it can also be used with 'would' or 'could' particularly to indicate routine. For example, 'I wish you wouldn't work so much' or 'She wishes we could go to the cinema.'

When referring to past it is used with the first clause of the third conditional – for example, 'I wish we had spent more time with each other last year.'

'Wish' is a normal verb and you can therefore make questions such as, 'Do you wish you had a dog?' You can also put it into past, although this is not common and mostly used in story books. For example, 'She wished there had been more to eat.'

25.1 Wish
How to teach it

Write: 'She wishes she had a dog,' and elicit whether she has a dog, the structure: 'wish' + second conditional and the meaning. Elicit or explain that it is a desire.

Elicit the negative: 'She wishes she didn't have a dog,' and the question: 'Does she wish she had a dog?'

Now write: 'I wish you would exercise more.' Explain that we sometimes use 'would' in present in place of second conditional to emphasis routine. 'I wish you exercised more' is equally acceptable.

Now write: 'I wish I could go on holiday.' Explain that we use 'could' in the same way as above but to mean 'to be able to'.

25.2 Wish in past

Write: 'They wish they had gone to France last year' and elicit the tense and structure: 'wish' + third conditional (first part only).

Ask: 'Did they go to France last year?' Elicit: 'No'. Elicit or explain that the above is an impossible desire because it refers to last year.

Elicit the negative 'They wish they hadn't gone to France last year,' and the question: 'Do they wish they had gone to France last year?'

25.3 If only...

'If only' is a synonym of 'wish' and works with the same structures. Highlight this by writing the following and eliciting the meanings.

'If only I spoke French', 'If only they would call' and 'If only I could ski' or 'If only I had passed the exam.'

25.4 Hope

'Wish' is never used for future. For future desires we use 'hope' + infinitive (no to) or 'hope' + present or 'hope' plus future. For example:

'I hope to travel to Spain next year.'

'I hope (that) we travel to Spain next year.'

'I hope we will travel to Spain next year.'

Note: Although 'will' is possible, it is not often used as 'hope' already means the future.

Write the above sentences on the board and elicit or explain that this is the future version of 'wish.' Elicit the questions: 'Do you hope to travel to Spain next year?' Note: There is no negative.

Controlled speaking practice

Ask your students to insert 'wish' + conditional into these sentences in place of 'it's a pity' or 'it's a shame.'

The second conditional

- o It's a pity they can't play tennis.
- o It's a shame he doesn't go to university.
- o It's a shame I don't know how to repair my car.

- It's a pity it's raining.
- It's a shame we don't know the answer.
- It's a shame she doesn't have a bike.
- It's a pity we don't like vegetables.

The third conditional

- It's a shame he didn't complete his course.
- It's a shame the shark ate him.
- It's a shame he fell down the mountain.
- It's a shame my jumper shrank in the wash.
- It's a shame the ship sank.
- It's a pity they didn't pass their exams.
- It's a shame the photocopier broke.
- It's a shame they got drunk.

Freer speaking practice
Pairs' activity 'Wishes and hopes': In pairs ask your students to put their wishes and hopes on paper under the themes of:

I wish I was good at...

I wish I could meet...

I wish I didn't have to...

I wish I had learnt......as a child

I wish I had......earlier in my life

And hopes for:

Travel.

Study.

Work.

Personal goals.

Further Speaking Practice
Pairs' roleplay 'The break up': You are a pair of flatmates. After many years together neither of you wants to live together anymore. You both think that the other is anti-social and has bad habits. Your flatmate did something very annoying the previous year; explain it to them using 'wish.'

For example, 'I wish you cleaned the shower' and 'I wish you hadn't invited your crazy cousin to stay.'

26. Connectors and Giving and Opinion

26.1 Connectors

If you're going to construct an argument, in writing or speech, you have to use connectors. Broadly speaking they come in four categories; 'and' (or 'one more point'), 'consequence,' 'but' and 'to conclude.'

How to teach it

Write a table headed 'And', 'Consequence', 'But' and 'To conclude' and elicit some words. Each of these words is sure to have its equivalent in the students' own languages and so have plenty of translation dictionaries and smartphones available.

If you go down the route of explaining them only in English, you're going to run into difficulty as many words are very similar and very nuanced. Therefore even if your students grasp the general meaning of a word, they might mistake it for another in their language such as by mistaking 'despite' for 'although.'

After a few minutes you should have something like the table below. Fill in any gaps yourself.

And	Consequence	But	To conclude
Additionally	Therefore	However	In conclusion
Furthermore	So	Even though	Therefore
Also	That's why	Although	To sum up
Moreover	Which means that	Despite	
In addition	Because	On the one hand	
	Consequently	On the other hand	

Now write the words on slips of paper and mix them up. Divide your students into pairs and hand each one five or six words, depending on their level. Be sure to include at least two 'and' words, two 'but' words, a consequence and/or concluding word.

Controlled speaking activity
Give each pair a simple question. For example, 'Do you recycle?' and ask them to come up with a one minute argument for why or why not, using their connectors. For example, Sarah has the words 'furthermore', 'in addition,' 'although', 'despite' and 'that's why.' Here is her answer:

Sarah: 'Yes I recycle, <u>furthermore</u>, I recycle every day, <u>although</u> I don't like doing it. I recycle because <u>despite</u> all the progress we have made we are still damaging the environment, <u>that's why</u> the climate is getting hotter and <u>in addition</u> the icebergs are melting.'

It isn't a perfect answer but it's the best she is going to do in under a minute and her use of connectors was correct.

Other example questions include: 'Do you have a dog?' 'Do you prefer the internet or TV?' 'What is your favourite country?' 'Who do you think will win the next World Cup?'

Do this activity as a class if you have a small group or in pairs if it is larger. By the end your students will have a far greater understanding of connectors.

Freer speaking practice
Pairs' activity 'The mad debate': Give your students two ideas, for example peanut butter Vs jam/jelly and using your connectors ask Student A to defend peanut butter and Student B jam in a one minute debate. For example:

Tom: 'Peanut butter is better because it gives you energy despite being a snack.'

Sarah: 'Yes, but jam is more flexible, in addition to toast you can use it in desserts.'

Other mad debate topics include: 'Cycling or going by bus', 'cats or dogs', 'burgers or salad', 'smart phone or tablet.'

26.2 Expressing your opinion

The second part of building an argument is expressing your opinion. This lesson requires some student preparation.

Tell your students to go to www.ted.com and watch the video 'Amanda Palma, The Art of Asking' before the class.

Ted is a well-respected website showing talks from various experts about science, technology and current affairs. Amanda Palma is a musician and her 20 minute long video tackles the issue of Internet music piracy from the artist's perspective. Her argument is an interesting one: namely that because you can't force people to buy music anymore you should kindly ask them to donate money instead as patrons, much in the same way as you would give money to a busker. Your students need to be at least a B2 to understand this video.

From these ideas and their own, your students will construct a debate. To facilitate the lesson, you need to have watched the video as well.

How to teach it

In the following class write a four column table on the board and elicit some words. Go through each word and ask them to think of phrases to make sure they understand the meaning.

Opinion	Agree/disagree	Structuring	Conclusion
In my opinion	I agree/don't agree	In addition	To sum up
If I were them	That's rubbish	However	To recap
As far as I know	Let's compromise	Although	In conclusion
I believe/think		Firstly, secondly	
I am in favour of		Finally	

Additional vocabulary for higher level students
Speaking generally: Generally speaking, on the whole, overall.

Your real opinion: As far as I am concerned, frankly, to be honest, personally speaking, to tell the truth.

Evaluating: After all, above all, doesn't make sense, to be pointless, in other words, to outline, whereas.

Consequence: Consequently, due to, so, so that.

Freer speaking practice
Pairs'/group activity 'The debate': Ask your students to explain Amanda Palma's argument and ask them what they thought. Now write on the board the statement, 'The Internet is killing the music industry' and explain that you are going to have a debate.

   Note: Writing a statement rather than a question is a much more effective way to provoke an opinion.

   Divide your class into those that agree with this statement and those that disagree and pair opposing views together. Ask them to write three, two line, arguments to support their point. Meanwhile facilitate ideas with these questions:

Who are the winners and losers of this situation?

Has music got better or worse since the Internet, or is it the same?

How do musicians make money nowadays?

Now using opinion vocabulary, give each side five minutes to state their case and answer questions from their opponent. When everyone is finished the class (or you) decide who has won.

---

27. Neither and Both, All and None, Most, Either or Neither

These five little words are a source of great confusion for students and so must be taught over several lessons. They essentially all express quantity though they are pronouns, not quantifiers.

27.1 Both and neither

'Both' means 'the two,' affirmative, while 'neither' means 'the two,' negative. For example, 'Both of us like coffee' (or 'The two of us like coffee'), 'Neither of us likes tea' (or 'The two of us don't like tea').

Their structures runs:

Both + of + object pronoun/noun + verb (example above) or subject pronoun + both + verb

Neither + of + object pronoun/noun + verb (example above)

How to teach it

Write the above sentences and elicit the meanings and emphasise that they only mean two.

Controlled speaking practice

Ask the following questions. Remember, you are only talking about you and the individual student.

- Which of us is female?
- Which of us owns an aeroplane?
- Who has eyebrows?
- Who lives in (your current city)?
- Who is an alien?
- Who can walk?

- Who has walked on the moon?
- Which of us is a professional basketball player?
- Which of us can read?

- Which of us has a dog called Jeff?
- Which of us breathes air?
- Which of us is going to the cinema tonight?

27.2 All, none, most

'All' means 'more than two' affirmative, while 'none' means 'more than two' negative. For example, 'All of us like music' and 'None of us like bad action films.'

'Most' means 'the majority,' for example 'Most of us own a TV.'

The structure for all of these pronouns is:

All/none/most + of + object pronoun/noun + verb

Controlled speaking practice

Ask your students the following questions. This time you are talking about you and the class.

- Which of us like football?
- Which of us are human?
- Which of us are cats?
- Which of us like ice cream?
- Which of is live...(in the country you live in)?
- Which of is live...(in a country you don't live in)?

- Which of us have relatives?
- Which of us know words in English?
- Which of us have been to Antarctica?
- Which of us have a sofa?
- Which of us have brown hair?
- Which of us like animals?

27.3 Either or neither

This is where it starts to get complicated. As before 'neither', along with 'either' are used to express 'two' negative.

When there is an auxiliary, you use 'either' and 'or' to connect your choices. For example, 'I <u>don't</u> like either coffee <u>or</u> tea.'

When there is no auxiliary, you use 'neither' and 'nor.' For example, 'I like neither coffee <u>nor</u> tea.'

For more on this see the chapter on Negative Statements.

'Either', however, has two more functions. It can be used in a question such as, 'Do you want either coffee or tea?' asking 'Which of the two?'

It can also be used in an answer such as 'Either, don't mind,' to say 'Both are good, I don't mind which one.'

How to teach it

To avoid confusion, I recommend teaching this language point in a separate lesson.

On the board write the question: 'Do you prefer either coffee or tea.' Underline either and explain that it means 'A choice of two.'

Now ask them to imagine that they don't want any. Elicit or write the sentences:

'I don't want either coffee or tea' and 'I want neither coffee nor tea.' Underline 'either' and 'neither' and elicit the difference between the two; 'either' is used with negative auxiliary and 'neither' is used without an auxiliary.

Underline 'or' and 'nor'. Elicit or explain that 'or' is used with 'either' while 'nor' is used with 'neither.'

Now ask them to imagine that they don't care which drink they receive. What would be the reply? Elicit or explain that it is, 'Either,' or 'Either please, I don't mind.'

Controlled speaking practice

Ask your students the following with 'either' in the question. In negative, get them to practice both the 'either' and 'neither' and in positive 'either.' For fun ask them why they made that choice. For example:

Teacher: 'Do you like either Justin Bieber or One Direction?'

Tom: 'I like neither Justin Bieber nor One Direction.'

Teacher: 'Or?'

Tom: 'I don't like either Justin Bieber or One Direction.'

Questions

Do you like either...?

- TV or the Internet.
- Justin Bieber or One Direction.
- American cars or French cars.
- Spiders or rats.
- Survivor or Big Brother.
- Falling down the stairs or losing your wallet.
- Game of Thrones or Lord of the Rings.
- Getting a parking fine or failing an exam.

- Breaking your leg or your arm.
- Getting stuck in a traffic jam or waiting two hours at the hospital.
- Baths or showers.
- Dogs or cats.
- This government or the previous government.
- Your electricity bill or your water bill.

Freer speaking practice: all, none, most, both, neither and either
It is difficult to find a satisfying speaking practice as these pronouns are used only as and when you need them. You could try a pairs' shop roleplay where one student is the shop assistant, asking 'Do you want either shoes or boots,' and the other is the difficult customer, who replies 'I want neither shoes nor boots,' but this may quickly become tedious.

Teaching it back

The best speaking practice, I find, is to wait a few weeks after teaching the grammar point and then get them to teach it back to you.

Split the class into pairs and give each one two corresponding pronouns such as 'both and neither' or 'none and all.' Tell the pair that they are going to teach it to the class. Let them work together for a moment to think of how they are going to do it and then ask them up to the board to give a presentation.

For large classes, ask the pairs to teach each other. For example, one pair will teach 'both and neither' while in exchange the other pair will teach 'either and neither.'

28. Phrasal Verbs Advanced

A phrasal verb consists of a verb paired with an adverb, preposition or both and by now, as your students will have no doubt have told you on numerous occasions, they are very hard to learn. The problem is that really, when you think about it, they don't make any sense. Take, 'She has taken up tennis.' 'Taken up?' – what does that mean? We understand that she has started playing tennis because at some point in history our culture equated 'take up' with 'start,' but getting your students to make that connection is not so easy.

How to teach it

Firstly, even though it is tempting, try to avoid teaching a group of phrasals because they begin with the same verb, such as 'run out', 'run into' and 'run for.' Your students will never be able to remember the difference as they look so similar. Nor will they be able to fit them into vocabulary group as they all mean different things.

The exception to this rule are phrasals with the verbs 'to fall', 'to cut' and 'to get' (see below), as within their verb group they express variations on something very similar.

The best way to teach phrasal verbs is as part of lexical sets (vocabulary groups), together with non-phrasal verbs. For example, with the topic of sport you might teach 'to kick', 'to shoot', 'to throw', 'to give up' and 'to take up' (a sport). This way your students can mentally assign 'to give up' and 'to take up' to a more concrete meaning.

Visualisation techniques

Next ask your students to create a picture in their mind to represent the verb, for example, with 'take up' they could picture themselves picking up (taking up) a tennis racquet and with 'give up', putting the racquet on the top shelf of their wardrobe, therefore 'giving it up' to their closet. This is, in fact, what many native speakers do. When I imagine the verb 'take on' as in 'to take on work' I think of loading my person or my car with a bundle of files, thereby 'taking on (loading my body with) the work.'

Everyone's pictures will be different but give them a moment to think of something plausible and share their ideas. It really works.

Pronoun problems

Where do you put the pronoun? Well, in about 80% of cases it works like this:

With a noun you have two options: 'I gave up <u>tennis</u>' or 'I gave <u>tennis</u> up.'

The pronoun, however, is placed after the verb and so it is 'I gave <u>it</u> up' or 'I will pick <u>them</u> up from the airport.' These are called 'Separable Phrasal Verbs'.

If the phrasal verb has three words, the noun and pronoun go at the end, such as 'I get on with <u>my parents</u>' or 'I get on with <u>them</u>,' 'We have run out of <u>milk</u>' and 'We have run out of <u>it</u>.'

The awkward verbs

Then finally there are a set of two-word phrasal verbs where the pronoun always goes at the end. These are called 'Inseparable Phrasal Verbs' and include: 'look after', 'run into', 'care for', 'count on', 'get on/off' and 'go over.'

Every time you teach a new phrasal verb, teach whether it is separable or inseparable.

Teaching the other meaning

Most phrasal verbs have at least two meanings. For example, 'to give away' means 'to give for free' and 'to reveal a secret'. I advise you never to teach more than one meaning at a time because getting one to stick is hard enough.

Once your students know and use one meaning here is a fun game to teach the other.

Freer speaking practice
Pairs' game 'Call My Bluff phrasal verbs': Call My Bluff is an old British TV show where the contestants must guess the meaning of obscure words.

Give Pair A a phrasal verb they know, and give them one minute to guess the other meaning (Note: They never get it). Next, give the definition to Pair B. When the minute is up Pair B must explain the verb to Pair A without using any of the words in the definition. To be sure that they have the right meaning Pair A may have to answer in their own language and so have the translation on hand to check if they are correct.

If Pair A guess correctly they receive two points, if they guess with Pair B's help both teams receive one point.

The game creates a memorable, fun experience and amazingly students almost always retain the vocabulary.

Examples of double or triple meaning phrasal verbs:

Bring up – To raise a child / To raise a subject with someone, example, 'I will bring up the problem at the next meeting.'

Give away – To give for free / To reveal a secret.

Give up –To stop doing something / To surrender.

Hang up – To hang up clothing or a picture / To put down the telephone.

Make up – To invent / To reconcile / To compensate, for example, 'I will make it up to you.'

Pick up – To collect or take something / To pick someone up in a bar for romantic purposes.

Work out – To calculate / To exercise in a gym / To result 'well,' for example, 'Taking the train worked out cheaper than the bus.'

29. To Fall, To Cut, To Get

There are hundreds of verbs in English that mean something very specific but have a very close synonym. The speaker must be very careful with the verb they select to convey the right meaning or the sentence can go completely off course. For example, there is an enormous difference between 'He cut up his leg' and 'He cut off his leg' though it is just a change in preposition. There are many verbs like this (not just phrasal verbs) but some of the most difficult come from the verbs 'to fall', 'to cut' and 'to get'. There is simply no way to teach all the meanings of 'to fall', and the rest, separately. This is one of those times when you must take a deep breath and teach them all together.

29.1 To fall
There are five main 'fall' verbs and in addition, 'to drop.' These are:

To fall in: To fall inside something – for example, 'The boy fell in the swimming pool.'

To fall out: To fall out of something you were inside, for example, 'The girl fell out of the tree.' Also, it means 'to be angry/annoyed with someone.'

To fall over: To fall when on a level or flat surface, for example, 'I fell over in the street.'

To fall off: To fall from something you were previously on, for example, 'She fell off her bike.'

To fall down: To fall from a high place *but* the sides of the thing you are falling down are vertical or at a severe angle. For example, 'He fell down the mountain,' or 'She fell down a well.' It also means 'to collapse,' for example, 'This building is so old, it is almost falling down.'

To drop: That something a person, animal or vehicle is carrying falls by accident. For example 'He dropped his wallet at the party,' or 'The lorry dropped fruit all over the street.'

How to teach it: To fall in, to fall out, to fall off

Write the above verbs and elicit or explain the definitions through drawings and examples.

Controlled speaking practice

Now tell your students that you will say the noun and they must decide which 'fall' it is. For example:

Teacher: 'A euro from my pocket.'

Tom: 'A euro falls <u>out</u> your pocket.'

Make sure you select the 'falls' at random.

To fall in: A fly into soup, with bad people, a swimming pool, a well.

To fall out: From a train, from a bus, a euro from my pocket, from a tree, hair, tooth from a mouth, a person from a window.

To fall off: From a boat, from a branch, a person from the top of a building, a hat from a head, a child from a swing, a lamp from a table, a person from a cliff, a person from a ladder, a person from a balcony.

How to teach it: To fall over, to fall down, to drop

In exactly the same way, write the above words and elicit the meanings. <u>Remember</u> 'to drop' is only used for things you carry.

Now give your students a phrase and ask them to tell you the correct verb to use.

To fall over: A lamp on the floor, a person in the street, a shopping trolley/cart.

To fall down: A person from a mountain, a person from a well (also fall in), a person from stairs, a person from a hill.

To drop: An umbrella from my hand, a person in the street, keys from my person, a bone from a dog.

29.2 To cut
The definitions of the 'to cut' verbs are as follows:

To cut down: To completely remove something that is taller, higher or wider than you: 'He cut down the banner' or 'She cut down the tree.'

To cut off: To remove a small amount from a larger entity: 'He cut off his finger,' or 'The electricity company cut off our house' (our house being a small part of a bigger network).

To cut out: To cut a shape out of something larger: 'She cut out the pattern.'

To cut up: To destroy something through cutting: 'He cut up his love letters.'

How to teach it
Elicit the definitions for the above verbs through drawings and examples.

Controlled speaking practice
In the same way as 'to fall' give your students the following phrases and ask them to respond with the appropriate 'cut' verb. For example:

Teacher: 'A hedge.'

Sarah: 'To cut down a hedge as a hedge is wider than you.'

Remember to ask the phrases at random.

To cut down: A hedge, a rope from a tree, a branch from a tree.

To cut off: Fingers, a thread from a dress, a head, a pony tail, electricity supply, water supply, gas supply.

To cut out: A pattern, template, a picture from a magazine.

To cut up: Paper, newspaper, material, jeans.

29.3 To get
Finally, 'To get' is fairly simple:

To get on: To enter something you will be on, for example, 'To get on a bus.'

To get off: To exit something you were previously on ('To get off a bus.')

To get in: To enter something that you will be in ('To get in a car.')

To get out of: To exit something that you were previously in ('To get out of a car.')

To get into: To start an interest or find yourself in trouble. For example, 'She is getting into tennis.'

Note: You are 'in' something when it is a closed space. You are 'on' something you can move about on.

Controlled speaking practice
Give your students the following nouns and ask them to respond with the appropriate 'get' verbs.

Note: Make sure they say both the enter and exit verb such as: 'To get on and off a bus.'

To get on and off: A bus, a bike, a skateboard, a horse, a plane, a ship or large boat, stage.

To get in and out: A car, a bed, a box, a shower, a cupboard, a bath, a lift/elevator, rowing boat, a submarine.

To get into: Spinning, dancing, trouble, university, work, music, tennis.

Part III: The Details

The majority of the below language points you won't find in a traditional text book. Knowing and teaching well the finer aspects of the language will distinguish you as a teacher; winning the respect of your students and boosting your earning power. It has taken years of curation and research to uncover these details, how they work and why. Now I share them with you. Enjoy.

30. High Energy Activities

Below are four high energy activities for when students are feeling tired towards the end of the class. Each take around five to ten minutes to complete but teach an important language point which will improve your students' English enormously.

30.1 On and in

What is the difference between 'on' and 'in'? Well, generally speaking 'on' is when an object is placed on top of something else, while 'in' is when it is placed inside a closed space. However, not all words follow this rule and this activity should hopefully answer any doubts.

Below you will find a list of 'on' and 'in' nouns. Dictate the words at random and elicit whether your students think it is 'on' or 'in'. To give the words context you have to say 'A person and a bike' (rather than simply 'bike') from which your student can imagine a person riding a bike and hopefully remember that the word is 'on'. Place the words into a table on the board.

On: Person and: A bike, TV, bed (above the sheets), a bus, the toilet, the telephone, the Internet, fire, boat, holiday, the floor.

The 15th of January, Tuesday, the left, the right, time (at a point of time).

In: A person and: Water, trouble, bed (under sheets), a film, tree, bath, shape (exercise), marriage, a car, a submarine, shower, the attic.

A child playing and snow, a plane and the sky.

The future, June, the eighties (80s), the centre, free time, time (within a period of time).

Common questions: 'Why is a person <u>on</u> a bus, a boat and a plane but <u>in</u> a car?'

Answer: Well even though they are all closed spaces you can walk on a bus, a boat and a plane meaning that they are less closed than a car – which is really just a box on wheels.

30.2 Make and do
Generally speaking we use 'make' when we are creating something ('make a cake') and 'do' when it is an action ('do exercise'), but the rule does not work all of the time. In exactly the same way as 'on/in', dictate to your students the following nouns at random and elicit whether it is 'make' or 'do'. Place the words in a table on the board.

Make: The bed, a change, a choice, a decision, a discovery, a fortune, an arrangement, a list, a noise, a living, a mistake, a phone call, a promise, a request, a speech, an announcement, an effort, an appointment, trouble, an offer, an excuse, an impression, a pact, a reservation.

Do: A job, a favour, business, nothing, something, exercises, homework, housework, better, your best, research, an investigation, the shopping, the dishes, the washing.

30.3 In, on and at for arrangements
This is one of the most popular activities. Making arrangements in English can be a nightmare because we use so many prepositions. Tell your students to imagine that they are going to meet their friend and must select the correct preposition for the arrangement. Write a table on the board headed 'At', 'On' and 'In', dictate the below nouns at random and elicit the preposition.

At: Christmas, New Year, Easter (festival), time, airport, cinema (outside a building), lunch (meals), weekend, the party (event), night, the concert, house/home.

On: Tuesday, 11th, my birthday, ninth floor, Christmas Day, New Year's Eve, the moon, on time (the point of time), the beach.

In: Country, city, park or plaza (open space), inside a building, morning, afternoon, evening, the future, 2015, 80s, in time (in the period of time), summer.

The rules

Only after they have completed this task, and got many wrong, tell them the rules. I recommend this way round as students learn a lot from their mistakes.

At is for festivals (Christmas, Easter and so on), events (a party, concert or conference), time (2pm, lunchtime) and the outside of a location you can see in its entirety (the airport, the cinema, the entrance to the park), the weekend and night.

On is for days, (11th, Tuesday, my birthday, Christmas day), floors in a building, planets and 'on time' – meaning the exact point in time.

In is for places you can't see in their entirety (cities, countries, parks) as well as months, years and decades, seasons, morning, afternoon, evening, the future and a period of time (for example, let's meet in time for Christmas).

Freer Speaking Practice

Group activity 'Making appointments': During the following class give your students four locations and times and ask them to select the correct preposition, starting with the phrase 'Let's meet.' For example:

Teacher: Breakfast, Saturday, New York, my Grandmother's house'

Tom: 'Let's meet <u>at</u> breakfast, <u>on</u> Saturday, <u>in</u> New York, <u>at</u> your Grandmother's house

Other locations: Fiesta, plaza, evening, 10th / Berlin, town hall, March, Tuesday /

New Year's Eve, beach, morning, water fountain / The 7th, night, park, Bruce Springsteen concert.

30.4 Plurals

Plurals are a small but tricky grammar point, which is good to practice as a standalone activity. Divide your class into teams of two or three students and tell them you will dictate the following words and they must write the plural with the correct spelling. At the end the team with the most correct plurals wins.

Words: Person, tooth, cactus, daddy, mouse, wish, foot, man, fish, woman, child, monkey, daddy, goose, country, sheep, deer, wolf, box.

The rules

Once they have completed the task reveal the spelling rules. Don't say before as, again, students learn a lot from their mistakes.

If the singular word ends in 'f', take it away and add 'ves'. For example, 'knife' becomes 'knives.' Other words include: Shelf, leaf, wolf, thief, wife.

If a word ends in 'h' or 'to,' add 'es' – for example, 'wish' becomes 'wishes,' and 'potato' becomes 'potatoes.' Other words include: Witch, wish, potato, tomato, fox, box, glass.

If a word ends in 'us,' take those letters away and add 'i'. For example 'fungus' becomes 'fungi' and cactus becomes 'cacti.'

Finally if the word ends in 'y' remove it and add 'ies'. For example, 'baby' becomes 'babies'. Other words include: fairy, fly, sky, country, story. Exceptions to this rule is monkey where you simply add 's' to the end.

Irregular plurals

There are also a few irregular plurals such as people, teeth, feet, children, men, women, geese, sheep, deer and fish (also 'fishes')

30.5 US and UK words

English teachers teach the language in their own style of speaking. US teachers teach American English, British teachers British English and Australian teachers Australian English and so on. This is perfectly reasonable but whatever type you teach don't neglect the other ways of speaking. From their exposure to TV and film your students may already know quite a few words in the other style of language.

Write the word in the language you teach on the board and elicit its equivalent in the other type of English. In the list below UK English is on the left and US English on the right.

Wardrobe/ closet flat/apartment/ lift/elevator chips/French fries taxi/cab plaster/ band aid sweets/candy to swap/ to switch nappy/ diaper biscuit/cookie autumn/fall aubergine/ eggplant petrol/gas jello/jelly jelly/jam film/movie trousers/pants football/soccer postcode/zip-code

Spelling

There are also some notable differences in spelling. UK English is on the left and US on the right.

Theatre/ theater centre/center Colour/color honour/honor organise/organize realise/realize defence/defense

Dates

Dates are also different.

UK English: Day > Month > Year. For example: 5th June 2015

US English: Month > Day > Year. For example: June 5th 2015

Freer speaking practice
Team quiz 'UK/US English': Once your students understand the difference between US/UK English divide them into teams and do a quiz. In the case of spellings, ask them to dictate both the UK and US versions of a word.

---

31. Direct and Indirect Objects

The direct object is a noun or pronoun, which is the creation, the object or the result of an action instigated by the subject of the sentence. For example, 'Laura is writing a letter'; Laura is the subject and the letter is the thing that she is creating, the object.

In this way, the direct object answers the question 'what' or 'who'. For example, 'What is Laura writing?' 'She is writing the <u>letter</u> (direct object) or 'Who are you picking up from the airport?' 'I am picking up my <u>Grandmother,</u>' (also direct object).

The indirect object is the secondary object in the sentence. This answers the question, 'For what?' or 'For who/whom?' For example, 'Laura is writing a letter for Jack.' The letter is still the direct object while Jack is the indirect object, answering the question, 'For whom are your writing this letter?'; 'For Jack.' There cannot be an indirect object without a direct object.

Direct and indirect objects are expressed in English with several different pronouns. There is no rule and so students must memorise them – a chore, I know, but worth it as it will eliminate so many small mistakes. Never teach more than one direct object rule at a time.

When teaching this grammar point I always give students all the verbs in this category and ask them to study them at home.

The direct object in the example sentences is <u>underlined.</u>

31.1 Direct object with 'for'
Structure: Subject + verb + indirect object + for + direct object

Verbs include: To look for, to search for, to pay for, to ask for, to wait for, to prepare for, to be responsible for, to work for, to vote for, to apply for, to care for.

The direct object here is expressed with 'for' – for example, 'He pays for <u>the meal</u>'. If the sentence contains an indirect object, it goes directly after the verb with no preposition.

Examples: 'He pays *the waiter* for <u>the meal</u>' or 'She asks *the teacher* for <u>the pen</u>.'

Controlled speaking practice

Ask your students about the last time they paid for something and who they paid. Tell them also to ask each other for pens, paper and so on. Ask them who they asked, and what they asked for. For example, 'I asked Tom *for* a <u>rubber</u>.'

31.2 Indirect object with 'for'
Structure: Subject + verb + direct object + for + Indirect object

Verbs include: To buy, to book, to get, to keep, to make, to pour, to save, to find, to consider, to open, to close, to check, to confirm, to build, to blame, to include.

On the other hand there is another list of verbs where the indirect object is with 'for' and the direct object has no preposition.

Examples: 'I buy a <u>car</u> for my brother'. Here, 'the car' is the direct object and 'my brother' is the indirect object.

31.3 To let
Structure: Let + pronoun/noun + infinitive (no 'to')

'To let' means 'to allow.' It is almost always expressed in imperative form. The important thing your students have to remember is that after the pronoun/noun there must be another verb in infinitive (no 'to').

For example, 'Let me have <u>the pencil</u>'. 'Let me the pencil' doesn't exist.

31.4 Object + infinitive
Structure: Subject + verb + object (pronoun) + infinitive

Verbs include: To need, to advise, to invite, to convince, to remind, to ask, to dare, to beg, to persuade, to allow, to encourage, to cause, to challenge, to force, to make (i.e. force), to help, to teach, to tell, to want.

With these verbs the direct object is placed after the verb and before the infinitive.

Examples: 'Tell <u>them</u> to go to work' or 'I want <u>him</u> to contact the office.'

31.5 Object + that + past, present or future
Structure: Verb + object + that + past, present, future

Verbs include: To promise, to inform, to warn.

This small set of verbs also place the object after the first verb but must be separated with 'that' and use a different tense.

Examples: 'Promise me that we will go skiing this weekend' or 'Warn them that the shop is closing.'

31.6 Indirect object with 'to'
Structure: subject + verb + direct object + to + indirect object

Verbs include: To explain, to admit, to apply, to propose, to suggest, to deny, to describe, to take, to conclude, to swear, to recommend, to present, to prove.

Also: To complain, to say, to speak, to talk (with 'about' for the direct object). For example, 'He complained to them about the exam.'

There is a small but important list of words where the indirect object is expressed with 'to'. For example, students often make the mistake, 'Explain me <u>the problem</u>'. This happens when the student doesn't understand that they have to use the preposition 'to' before the indirect object (the recipient of the news) 'me.'

Examples: 'He denied <u>the crime</u> to the police' or 'Describe <u>the painting</u> to them.'

31.7 Verbs that use either 'to' + indirect object or no preposition at all

Structure: verb + direct object + to + indirect object or verb + object pronoun (indirect object) + direct object

Verbs include: To give, to lend, to pass, to post, to read, to sell, to show, to send, to bring, to offer.

English is always changing and now it is acceptable to say 'Give the pen to me' or 'Give me the pen.' That said, option two is not strictly grammatically correct but commonly used when speaking (rather than writing).

Examples: 'Pass him the book' and 'Pass the book to him.' Or 'Send me the letter' and 'Send the letter to me.'

Putting it all together: Direct and indirect objects practice
Teams' activity 'The direct, indirect object challenge': Over several weeks ask your students to memorise object + infinitive verbs, ('I need him to study more'), indirect objects with 'to' (He denied the crime to the police) and indirect objects where you can use 'to' or reorder the sentence to omit it entirely, ('Send him the letter' or 'Send it to him').

Now set a light-hearted challenge by writing these verbs on slips of paper and asking your students in teams to put them into one of the three categories.

Give your students between five and ten minutes to complete the activity and hand the winning team a prize at the end.

32. Confusing Verbs

Here is a list of very similar verbs and their definitions.

Raise and rise: 'To raise' means to move something to a higher position; 'The boy raised the flag' while 'rise' means that something moves <u>itself</u> to a higher position; 'The sun rises in the morning.'

Know and meet: 'To know' means 'to have knowledge of something' or 'be familiar with' – for example, 'She knows how to speak English,' while 'to meet' means to physically meet someone or encounter someone for the first time – for example, 'Let's meet for a coffee' or 'I met my husband at a party.'

Argue, debate and discuss: 'To argue' most of the time means to shout and be angry with someone/something. 'To debate' means to have a formal and combative conversation on a topic and 'to discuss' means to have a light conversation on a topic.

Expect and hope: 'To expect' means that you think it is very probable that something will happen, often because the subject has done something to make it happen. For example, 'He expects to pass his exam.' 'To hope' is a desire which may or may not be probable. For example, 'She hopes to study in the USA.' There is nothing to guarantee that she will study in the USA, it is a wish. Both 'expect' and 'hope' in present form mean future.

Steal and rob: You steal an object and rob a person or a location. For example, 'The thief robbed the bank and stole the money.'

Manage and achieve: 'To manage' and 'to achieve' mean the same thing but 'achieve' can only be paired with a noun or adjective + noun, while 'manage' is paired with an infinitive verb. For example, 'He managed to get good grades' and 'He achieved good grades.'

Refuse and reject: 'To refuse' and 'to reject' also mean the same thing but 're-fuse' is paired with an infinitive verb while 'reject' with a noun. For example, 'She refused to work with them' and 'She rejected the offer.'

Test, prove and taste: 'To test' means to see if a hypothesis is correct, 'to prove' means to show indisputable evidence that it is true and 'to taste' is for food.

Treat and deal with: 'To treat' is for medicine and the way someone behaves towards someone/something else. For example, 'They treat me like a slave.' 'To deal with' means to manage a difficult person or situation. For example, 'I will deal with the problem.'

Cure and heal: 'To cure' means that the patient has been given something that fixes the illness – 'The doctor cured the girl's headache' while 'to heal' means that the body fixes itself; 'I didn't go to the doctor, the cut healed itself.'

33. Movement Phrasal Verbs: Back, In and Out

'Back' means to return, while 'in' means to enter a close space and 'out' to exit. Selecting which phrasal to use for which movement is complicated, however, most students will have been taught the phrasal verb 'come back' at A2 level but it does not apply to every type of return. For example, if you were at your work and you said to your boss that you were 'coming back home' it wouldn't make any sense; the verb you need is 'go back.'

How to teach it

Below are six sets of movement verbs. Teach one set at a time and only move on to the next one once your students fully understand.

33.1 Been and gone

Write, 'She has been to the shops' and 'She has gone to the shops.' Elicit the difference:

With 'been' the person went to a location and came back, while with gone, the person went and is still there.

Controlled speaking practice

Ask your students to make two example sentences of each.

33.2 Go back and come back

'After spending the day at the office, the man said to his boss, "I am going back home",' and 'After spending the day at the office, the man called his children and said "I am coming back home"'. So what's the difference? Well, this is where it gets tricky.

Roughly speaking 'go back' means to leave, while 'come back' means 'to return.' However, the verb you select depends upon the perspective of the person you are talking to.

For example, at the end of a day at the office, you say to your boss, 'I am going back home' because from *his* perspective you are leaving. If your kids call a few minutes later, you tell them, 'I am coming back home,' because from *their* perspective you are returning. If once you have arrived home, your boss calls about a problem, you would then tell him, 'I am coming back in the morning,' because from *his* perspective you are returning.

Illustrate this point with a diagram of an office, a house and a couple of stick men.

Controlled speaking practice

Ask your students to give you two examples of each sentence.

Freer speaking practice
Pairs'/group activity 'Explain your movements': Ask your students to explain their movements for the day from the perspective of themselves and the people they live with. Remember, from the class's perspective they are coming back to class and will later go back home.

33.3 Go in and come in
'To go in' means to enter a closed space like a room, a building or an elevator.

'To come in' means that someone is already in the closed space and observes you enter. Illustrate this point by asking two students to leave the room; one enters while the other waits outside. Ask from the perspective of the class, and that of the person outside, whether the student has come in or gone in and why. Teach this grammar point along with 'to go out' and 'to come out' below.

33.4 Go out and come out
Teach 'to go out' and 'to come out' along with 'to go in' and 'to come in.'

'To go out' means to leave a closed space from the perspective of those in the closed space with you.

'To come out' means that someone on the outside observes you exiting a closed space. It is also when a news story, company figures, programme, product, a film or a rash is published, launches or appears.

Teach this grammar point with the example above ('to go in'/ 'to come in') when two students leave the room. From the perspective of the class, does the student 'go out' or 'come out'? From the perspective of the student already outside, what happens?

33.5 Give back, put back, take back

'To give back' means to return something to the owner. It is separated by the object pronoun of the one you must give the item to. For example, 'Give <u>him</u> back the pen.'

'To put back' means to return something to its original place. For example, 'Put it back on the shelf.'

'To take back' means to return something which was originally taken from another location, or to withdraw an insult. It is mainly used when returning items in shops. For example, 'She wants to take back the trainers.'

Ask your students to give each other something, to take something from the classroom (for 'put back') and, if possible, to take something from another classroom (for 'take back'). Now tell them to ask each other to 'give,' 'put' and 'take' the objects back. Remember to use all persons of the verb, not just 'me.' While the student is in the middle of the action, ask them what they are doing. For example:

Sarah: 'Tom, give him back his pencil.'

Tom: 'OK.'

Teacher: 'What are you doing Tom?'

Tom: 'I am giving him back his pencil.'

34. Even

'Even;' one little word, so many meanings. I start teaching 'even' at intermediate level with the aim that my students will know and use all of the different meanings by upper intermediate. Teach the different uses of 'even' in different lessons.

34.1 Even though and even if

'Even though' and 'even if' are both used to introduce a subordinate clause, which is the opposite of what you expected to happen. For example, 'Even though it is raining, I still want to go to the beach.' Going to the beach when it is raining is not something that people expect to do.

We use 'even though' for things that are real. For example, 'Even though he studied, he didn't pass the exam'. It is therefore used with tenses that express reality such as present and past simple, present perfect and continuous.

'Even if' is used for things that are not real either because they are hypothetical, impossible or haven't happened yet. For example, 'Even if it rains, we will still go to the picnic' or 'Even if we had a car, we would still not arrive on time'. It is therefore used with conditionals, (first, second and third).

How to teach it

Write these sentences on the board:

'Even though I have very little money, we are still going to the cinema.'

'Even if I had very little money, we would still go to the cinema.'

And elicit the difference – the first sentence is real while the second is hypothetical. At this point you may want to look up the translations in a dictionary, because it is very probable that your students have something similar in their own language.

Elicit or explain that 'even though' is a synonym of 'although' and conjoins two ideas that may appear to conflict but are nevertheless real.

'Even if', on the other hand, is only used with conditionals and means something unreal. The above sentence is in second conditional. Elicit the first and third conditional versions and whether they are possible or impossible.

First conditional: 'Even if I have very little money, we will still go to the cinema' (possible).

Third conditional: 'Even if I had had very little money (last week), we would have still gone to the cinema' (impossible).

Controlled speaking practice
Ask your students to write three things:

- o That their sibling or friend can't do.
- o That they can do in their home town but it is better to do somewhere else.
- o That they would never do.

Using these ideas ask them in pairs or as a group to make 'even though' and 'even if' sentences. For example:

Tom: 'I would never rob a bank.'

Teacher: 'Can you make an 'even if' statement from this?'

Tom: Even if I had no money, I would never rob a bank.'

Teacher: And in third conditional?

Tom: Even if I had had no money last year, I would never have robbed a bank.'

Controlled Speaking Practice II
Using 'even if,' construct a chain story in second or third conditional going round the class. For example:

Teacher: 'I don't like hunting…'

Sarah: 'Even if I liked hunting, I wouldn't hunt whales…'

Tom: 'Even if I hunted whales, I would let them go…'

Sarah: 'Even if I let them go, I would…'

And so on. See how many sentences you can make before it doesn't make sense.

34.2 Even (including) and even (comparison)

'Even' has two further meanings; these are 'including,' for example, 'Everyone danced at the party, even my teacher' and as a comparison between two things that are very similar, for example, 'Portugal is even hotter than Spain.' Portugal and Spain have similar climates and so 'even' can be used to make the distinction. However, 'Portugal is even hotter than Norway' doesn't make any sense as the difference is too large.

How to teach it

Write some example sentences and explain the above.

Controlled speaking practice

Ask your students to add 'even' to these sentences.

- o   I passed my exams including Spanish.
- o   Spain is hotter than France.
- o   My current flat is more depressing than my old flat.
- o   They all got a pay rise, including the caretaker.
- o   He has got fatter than his brother.
- o   It's possible nowadays to buy a car online.
- o   She drives better than me.
- o   The new Fiat 500 is faster than the old Fiat 500.
- o   This test is harder than the last.
- o   Surely you can see that he is a great artist.

34.3 Not even

Finally there is 'not even' which means 'not including' – for example 'They don't own any furniture, not even a sofa.'

In this way negative 'even' is placed after the auxiliary verb and 'not even' at the end of the sentence after nouns. Examples: 'He doesn't <u>even</u> wear a tie' and 'she didn't <u>even</u> call me' or 'I don't like chocolate, <u>not even</u> at Easter.'

How to teach it

Write an example of 'even' after auxiliary and 'not even' at the end of a sentence after a noun and elicit the meaning. Highlight the structures.

Controlled speaking practice

Ask your students to change the below with negative 'even' and 'not even'. Where possible elicit both structures. For example, 'They don't even clean their bedrooms' and 'They don't clean, not even their bedrooms.'

- o   He never wears a tie, including at weddings.
- o   None of us passed the exam, me included.
- o   They don't clean, including their bedrooms.
- o   She doesn't own any form of transport, including a bike.
- o   She never does her homework, including the weekends.
- o   We don't like animals, including goldfish.
- o   None of the lightbulbs work, including the one in the bathroom.
- o   She didn't invite anyone to the wedding, including my mother.

Putting it all together: Even and not even

Finally, ask your students to change these sentences with the appropriate positive, comparative or negative 'even'.

- o   Everyone was made redundant including the CEO.
- o   No one was hired including the CEO.
- o   Theme parks are better than the zoo.
- o   An elephant can enter the house, the door is so big.
- o   No one will stop me from wearing that dress, including you Mum.
- o   Salaries are getting smaller.
- o   They never answer their calls, including from the boss.
- o   We eat all our vegetables including broccoli.
- o   He never uses an umbrella, including when there is a storm.
- o   My new desk is smaller than my old desk.
- o   She reads the entire newspaper, including the adverts.
- o   None of us understand the book, including the professor.
- o   Surely your Grandmother can use the machine, it is so easy.

35. Short Answers and Question Tags

35.1 Short Answers

Short Answers are when someone answers with the same auxiliary used in the question. For example, 'Is your sister going to Italy next year? Short answer: 'Yes she is.' This is easy to explain and your students will enjoy the practice.

Controlled speaking practice

Try this drill as a high energy way to finish a lesson. Watch out for questions with 'Do you have' and make sure they answer 'Yes, I do/no, I don't' instead of 'Yes, I have / no, I haven't' For example, 'do you have a car?' 'Yes, I do.'

- Are you French?
- Is your mother French?
- Were you happy yesterday?
- Do you have a dog?
- Did you do something interesting yesterday?

- Do you have a car?
- Have you caught a bus today?
- Did it snow yesterday?
- Is it snowing now?
- Do you have a bike?

- Are you going to have fun this weekend?
- Will you do your homework?
- Are you going to come back on Monday?
- Are you German?
- Am I?

For advanced students

- Should you do your homework?
- Will you do your homework?
- Did you bring a paper and pen to class?
- Did you use them?
- Will you use them next class?

o Would you accept 200 euros if I gave it to you?
o Should you go to your English class on Saturday?
o Would you go to your class on Saturday if the academy were open?
o Would you speak Chinese if you lived in China?

35.2 Question tags

Native speakers add question tags to the end of questions with the same auxiliary verb. If the question is positive then the tag is negative and vice-versa. For example, 'She is going to the cinema with us, <u>isn't she?</u>' or 'He has finished his homework, <u>hasn't he?</u>'

If the question has no auxiliary then you use 'do' or 'did' such as 'She went, <u>didn't she?</u>'

I don't actually teach this grammar point because I have discovered that when learning a language, you must choose your battles wisely. The mental acrobatics a student must go through to select the correct tag (getting the auxiliary, tense and person of the verb right), means that it is simply not worth the trouble.

Tags are not essential to the sentence; they are an add-on and every one can be replaced with the expression 'right?' ('She is going to the cinema, right?').

How to teach it

If you really want to teach it though, or if you have no choice, try this activity.

Write some questions with tags on the board and elicit or explain the meaning. Explain that whatever auxiliary you use, you must repeat it in the tag and if the question is positive then the tag is negative and vice versa.

Controlled speaking practice

Now hand out slips of paper with tags such as, 'Is he?', 'Does she?', 'Didn't they?' 'Should we?' 'Have you? 'Would we?' 'Couldn't she?' 'Won't he?' 'Will they?' And so on. As a group ask your students to invent the corresponding question. For example, 'We shouldn't smoke at the academy, should we?' or 'He has taught English before, hasn't he?'

36. Passive Voice with Get

Normal passive voice runs: object + to be + participle, for example 'The building was painted.' It is used when the object (the thing receiving the action) is more important than the subject (the thing doing the action).

We have already covered the passive in an earlier chapter but there is another form, commonly used among native speakers, and that is to substitute 'to be' for 'get'. For example, instead of 'I was paid' we tend to say 'I got paid. 'Why is this?

Well, we use 'get' when there is no agent (the subject doing the action) because it is either:

Obvious: For example, 'I got promoted' – it is only your company that can promote you, there is no need to explain who did it.

Unknown: For example, 'My computer got stolen' – you have no idea who stole your computer.

Unpleasant: Meaning you want to separate the agent from the action. For example, you may say to your sister, 'Your phone got broken.' In this case you broke your sister's phone, but you don't want to volunteer this information and so putting it into passive makes it *appear* that you had nothing to do with it.

For these reasons 'get' is commonly used with the following:

Work verbs: To pay, to promote, to demote, to fire, to make redundant, to cancel.

Accidents, crimes or something unpleasant verbs: To spill, to hurt, to damage, to destroy, to knock down, to break, to ruin, to wreck, to kill, to lose, to attack, to run over, to infect, to cut off, to steal, to rob, to burn, to wound, to injure, to blow up, to fine, to bite, to vaccinate.

Finally: Get is only used with action verbs and never state verbs. For example, you cannot say 'Nothing gets known' – rather it is, 'Nothing is known.'

How to teach it

Review the passive with a few sentences and check that they remember the meaning and structure.

Now write 'I got paid last week.' Explain that there is another form of passive with 'get.' Using plenty of examples, explain when we use 'get' and why. Emphasise that this form is very common among native speakers; in fact, there are many cases when 'to be' just sounds weird. For example, 'The keys were lost' or 'The milk is being spilt.'

Give students the list of verbs above, but stress that they are used with 'get' only when the conditions apply. For example, it is normal to say, 'The project got cancelled' when it is obvious who cancelled it (such as the management). When it is not obvious you put it into normal passive and include the agent; 'The project was cancelled by Laura.'

Finally, explain that 'get' is never used with state verbs. Remind them of some states, such as 'to understand', 'to know', 'to believe' and 'to like/love/hate.'

Controlled speaking practice

Ask your students to change the following active sentences into passive with 'get.'

- The captain wrecked the ship against the rocks.
- She is spilling the milk.
- He was damaging the car.
- War kills many people.
- They will promote her.
- Someone broke my glasses last Friday.
- The rebels destroyed the town.
- If you do that your mobile someone will steal your mobile.
- The builders accidentally knocked the wall down.
- The motorbike hurt the boy.
- The company is making them redundant.
- The boy ruined his grandfather's shirt.

Freer speaking practice

Pairs' roleplay 'Getting out of trouble': Write the following roleplays on slips of paper and place them in the middle of the table. Student A is the perpetrator of the crime and must speak in passive voice to avoid taking the blame. Student B is the victim and will speak in active voice because they want to find out what happened. For example, with roleplay one:

Tom (the solider): Hello, I'm sorry but your farm house has <u>got destroyed</u>

Sarah (the farmer): How? And who destroyed it?

Tom: Well, it was in the way of an army exercise and it <u>got blown up</u>, sorry.

When they have finished move onto the next roleplay.

Roleplays

1. During an army exercise you and your companions accidentally destroyed a farm house in a rural area. Luckily no one was injured but you must explain it to the farmer.

2. Three days before the wedding you ruin your sister's wedding dress by spilling engine oil on it.

3. You accidentally killed Albert your grandmother's parrot when you let him out of the cage one afternoon while you were cleaning and sucked him up the hoover.

4. You are training to become a tattoo artist and tattooed your friend's arm. Now it has got infected.

5. You accidentally ran over your neighbour's dog.

6. It was your job to pay your company' electricity bill, you didn't and now it has got cut off.

Putting it all together: Passive voice with 'to be' and 'to get'

There are clear cases for when to use 'to be' and when to use 'to get'. In a separate lesson, check your students' understanding by asking them to change the below sentences to passive. Explain why each of their answers are right or wrong.

- The girl has painted the wall ('to be').
- I am writing an email ('to be').
- They have understood the question ('to be').
- The car killed the cat ('to get').
- She will speak to the boy ('to be').
- They were repairing the bike ('to be'/ 'to get' – depending if it is obvious who is repairing the bike).

- The window will break if you keep doing that ('to get').
- The boss could cancel the project ('to get').
- They should promote my brother ('to get').
- They may fire him ('to get').
- I would have done it, if you had asked me ('to be').
- He would have spilt the milk if you hadn't stopped him ('to get').
- I would do it, if you asked me ('to be').

37. To Tell and To Tell Apart

'To tell' means to make a supposition from your sense of sight, hearing, smell and so on. For example with, 'I can tell that she is French', you note that she is French because you have heard her accent. 'To tell' is always used with the auxiliary 'can.'

'To tell apart' is a phrasal verb that means to distinguish between two things. For example, 'I can tell apart strawberry from banana ice cream.' Again it is always used with the auxiliary 'can'.

How to teach it

Start with 'to tell' and write the above example on the board. Elicit or explain the meaning. Speakers of European languages may understand if you explain it as the verb 'to note.' Elicit the structure, the negative 'I can't tell that she is French' and the question, 'Can you tell that she is French?'

Now move on to 'to tell apart' and write the above example. Elicit or explain that it is a very common phrasal verb meaning 'to distinguish between.' Elicit the negative, 'I can't tell apart banana from strawberry ice cream,' and the question 'Can you tell apart banana from strawberry ice cream?'

Controlled speaking practice

Ask your students the following questions. Tell them to invent more questions to ask each other.

If he/she/they:

- Can tell when someone hasn't done their homework.
- Can tell if someone has a good sense of humour before speaking to them.
- Can tell if someone is well-read or not before speaking to them.
- Can tell that he/she has improved their English in the last six months.
- Can tell apart branded from non-brand cornflakes.
- Can tell apart identical twin babies.
- Can tell apart tiredness and boredom in a person.
- Can tell apart an American from a British accent.
- Can tell when someone is angry.

- Can tell when someone is hungry.
- Can tell apart anger from hunger.
- Can tell apart petrol from diesel.
- Can tell when he is beginning to get a cold.
- Can tell apart a good second hand car from a bad one.

Freer speaking practice 'To tell'
Pairs' activity 'What can you tell from the photo?': Print out a selection of photos and paintings depicting interesting characters and scenes and ask your students what they can tell about the people from these photos.

For this activity I suggest reusing the pictures from the Deduction and Possibility lesson. Namely: 'Migrant Mother' and 'Bud Fields' 1935 by Walker Evans, 'The Shell-shocked Soldier' by Don McCullin, 'The Construction of the GE Building at Rockefeller Center' by Charles C. Ebbets by 1932, 'Las Meninas' by Diego Velazquez 1656 and 'American Gothic' by Grant Wood 1930.

38. Likely and likelihood

'Likely' is an adjective used in British English to mean 'probably.'

Its structure runs:

Subject pronoun/noun + to be + likely + infinitive

Example: 'She is likely to come to the party.'

It is often used with the modifiers, 'very', 'quite' and 'not very'.

The negative version is 'unlikely,' for example, 'They are unlikely to go to Italy next year.'

'Likelihood' is a noun and synonym of 'probability'.

Its structure runs:

The + likelihood + of + object pronoun + verb in gerund

Example: 'The likelihood of them accepting the offer is low.'

It is used with the adverbs, 'very high', 'high', 'quite high', 'low', 'very low,' which are placed at the end of the sentence. 'Likelihood' is not as used as 'likely.'

How to teach it

Start with 'likely'; write the above sentence on the board and elicit the meaning and structure. Elicit the negative 'She is not likely to come to the party' or 'She is unlikely to come to the party' and the question, 'Is she likely to come to the party?' Or if you want to know the degree of likeliness, 'How likely is she to come to the party?'

Elicit or explain that the degree of likelihood changes with modifiers. Write a few examples.

Next, move on to likelihood. Write the above sentence on the board and elicit the meaning and structure. Elicit the question, 'What is the likelihood of them accepting the offer?' There is no negative.

Elicit or explain that the degree of likelihood is expressed with the above adverbs. Write these in a cline on the board starting with 'very high.' Explain that likelihood isn't as commonly used as likely.

Controlled speaking practice

Ask your students to think of two 'likelihood' and two 'likely' questions and write them on slips of paper. Mix them up and redistribute them among the class randomly. In pairs, tell your students to ask and answer the questions. Add the below questions to the pile for additional material.

- o   What is the likelihood of me owning a zoo?
- o   How likely is it that a member of the class will join the Olympic team?
- o   How likely is Renaldo to move to Barcelona Football Club?
- o   What is the likelihood that you will live in another country?
- o   Are you more likely to lose your keys or your wallet this year?
- o   What is the likelihood of [insert local football team] winning the league?
- o   Is it likely to snow this month in [insert a city?
- o   What is the likelihood of a tsunami hitting the city?
- o   Is it likely that a lion will escape the local zoo?
- o   Which is more likely: The city will flood this winter or [insert student] will win the lottery?
- o   Are you more likely to buy a motorbike or take flying lessons?

Freer speaking practice

Pairs' roleplay 'At the doctors': Student A is going on a six month trip to the Amazon rainforest and needs advice from Student B, who is a doctor, about the likelihood of problems. For example:

Sarah: What is the likelihood that I will get eaten by an anaconda?

Tom: Unfortunately the likelihood is high, however, it is unlikely that you will be eaten by crocodiles.

Sarah: How likely is it that I will catch malaria?

---

39. To Suppose and To Manage

39.1 To suppose

'To suppose' in present is used to express:

Agreement: 'I suppose so.'

A supposition: 'I suppose she will come to the party.'

An intention: 'I suppose I should call him.'

In all these cases the speaker almost always only use the pronoun 'I' as it is difficult to talk about the agreement, supposition or intention of other people as you don't know what they are thinking. A question is possible with the auxiliary 'do,' such as, 'Do you suppose they will win the election?', but it is not common. It is more common to say 'Do you think...?'

Suppose with passive
The structure of 'suppose' with passive runs:

Subject pronoun/noun + to be + supposed (participle) + infinitive

Example: 'It is supposed to be a good film.'

It is used for supposition (see above) or intention 'She was supposed to work next weekend.'

It is only expressed in present (to mean present or future) or past. You use all personal pronouns: I, you, he, she and so on.

How to teach it

First teach present by writing the above examples and eliciting the meanings. Emphasise that this is mostly used with 'I' as you don't know what other people are thinking or planning. The interrogative is possible but not common. Now move on to passive.

Write the above examples on the board and elicit their meanings and structure. Elicit the negative, 'It isn't supposed to be a good film' and the question, 'Is it supposed to be a good film?' Highlight that the passive only exists in present and past form.

39.2 To manage
'To manage' means to achieve or succeed.

Its structure runs:

Subject pronoun/noun + manage + infinitive

Example: 'She managed to finish the project.'

It is very popular among native speakers as 'achieve' can only be paired with a noun ('He achieved good results') while 'succeed' is used with 'in' plus verb in gerund ('He succeeded in calling her'), making a cumbersome sentence.

How to teach it

Write the above example on the board and elicit the meaning. Elicit or explain that we use 'manage' when the following word is a verb. Explain the limitations of 'achieve' and 'succeed.' As 'to manage' also means 'to direct' some students may find this other meaning hard to accept. Emphasise that it is the verb of choice when expressing achievement and give more examples.

Putting it all together: To suppose and to manage
Controlled speaking practice

Ask your students to write three things they were supposed to do last week, but didn't, and three things they managed to do. Now ask them to write three things they are supposed to do this week and three things they will try to manage to do.

Now, in pairs, tell them to ask and answer questions on the topics.

Freer speaking practice
Pairs' roleplay 'Organising the anniversary': Your Grandparents are celebrating their 50th wedding anniversary and you and your partner must organise it.

As a class brainstorm all of the things you need to organise for the even such as invitations, a DJ, drinks, snacks and so on. Now ask your students to write the tasks on slips of paper and divide them randomly into a 'done' and 'pending' pile. Using these ideas tell your students to ask and answer questions about what they have managed to do and what they are supposed to do (but haven't done yet). For example:

Tom: 'Sarah, have you managed to send the invitations?'

Sarah: (Checks her piles of paper), 'No I haven't managed to do that yet.'

Tom: 'But you were supposed to do that last week, while...(checks paper) I was supposed to call auntie Jill.'

Sarah: 'Have you managed to call her?'

39.3 Supposing
Finally there is the adverb 'supposing' which is paired with a conditional to refer to a hypothetical situation. For example, 'Supposing you were a language teacher for a day, how would you conduct your classes?' For more information, go to the 'Conditionals' chapter.

40. While and Meanwhile

40.1 While

'While' means either that the subject is doing two things at once or two things are happening in the same location. For example, 'Lisa made dinner while she did her homework' (one person is doing two things), or 'The father read a book while the child slept' (two people are doing two things but in the same location). The verb after 'while' is often in gerund, but this doesn't have to be the case. The less formal version of 'while' is 'at the same time.'

Controlled speaking practice

Ask your students to change these sentences with 'while' or 'at the same time.' For example, 'Claudia studied and she waited for a phone call' changes to 'Claudia studied while waiting for a phone call.'

- o   Claudia studied and she waited for a phone call.
- o   Tom walked the dog and thought about an idea.
- o   The painter finished the room and the people unpacked their stuff.
- o   The children sat patiently and their parents loaded the car.
- o   Paula read her emails and she looked after the baby.
- o   The footballer slipped in the mud and the rest of the team tried to stop the ball.
- o   The boy slept and his sister read a comic.
- o   The people protested and the TV company filmed them.
- o   The dog barked and the thief entered the house.
- o   The teacher taught the lesson and the children played.
- o   The technician fixed the TV and his supervisor watched him.
- o   During the party the child cried and the other children danced.

40.2 Meanwhile and in the meantime

'Meanwhile' and 'In the meantime' refers to two events that are happening in two different locations at the same time. For example, 'The policeman called for help, meanwhile the thieves escaped,' or 'I will do the cooking, in the meantime, can you hang out the washing?' There is no difference in meaning between the two words but 'meanwhile' is more commonly used in literature and 'in the meantime' more in speaking.

Controlled speaking practice

Ask your students to change these sentences using 'meanwhile' or 'in the mean-time.' For example, 'I will make the appointment, can you finish the report?' changes to 'I will make the appointment, in the meantime, can you finish the report?'

- o   I will make the appointment, can you finish the report?
- o   She will speak to the clients, can you solve the compute problem?
- o   I will take them to the restaurant and she steals the information.
- o   John chose his wife's birthday present at the same time as his mother-in-law prepared the party.
- o   She will get the popcorn, can you buy the tickets?
- o   He'll write the report, can you find us a meeting-room?
- o   She'll get the films projector, can you review the mistakes in the exam?
- o   John was writing his emails, at the same time his colleagues were having a party.
- o   There was a storm in Barcelona at the same time it was sunny in Madrid.
- o   Sarah read a book at the same time a thief stole the car.
- o   They will take the kids to school, can he call the office?
- o   The children played, at the same time their parents' worked at the factory.

Freer speaking practice
Pairs' roleplay 'Wedding planners': Your students have to organise their sister's wedding within seven days. Using 'while', 'meanwhile' and 'in the meantime' tell them to divide up the chores so everything is done in time. The worksheet for this task can be found in the in the appendix.

---

41. Had better and Would Rather

41.1 Had better
'Had better' is a synonym for 'should.'

Its structure runs:

Subject pronoun/noun + had better + infinitive (no 'to')

Example: 'They had better go to work.'

It is only used in present to mean present and future and is never used in negative or interrogative form.

How to teach it
Write the above example on the board and explain its structure and limitations. Emphasise that it is commonly used among native speakers.

Freer speaking practice
Pairs' roleplay 'We had better...': Give your students the roleplay found in the appendix about reforming a house. Using 'had better' tell them to decide which jobs they can do and which they have to leave for a professional. For example, 'We had better fix the roof before it rains.'

41.2 Would rather
'Would rather' means 'to prefer.'

Its structure runs:

Subject pronoun/noun + would + rather + infinitive (no to)

Example: 'I would rather go to a restaurant than a bar.'

How to teach it
Write the above sentence and elicit the meaning and the question, 'Would you rather go to a restaurant or a bar?' There is no negative.

Controlled speaking practice

Ask your students to write five 'Would you rather...?' questions on slips of paper. Encourage humour and creativity. Mix them up and redistribute them. In pairs tell your students to ask and answer the questions and explain their choices.

Here are some additional questions for the pile:

- Would you rather shut your finger in a door or get a paper cut?
- Would your parents rather live in a lighthouse or a submarine?
- Would you rather eat potatoes or carrots for the rest of your life?
- Would your sister or brother rather lose an ear or a finger in an accident?
- Would you rather be hot or cold right now?
- Would you rather have lots of money or be fluent in English?
- Would you rather own a pig or a sheep?
- Would you rather have dinner with Stalin or Hitler?
- Would you rather share a bath with a turtle or kiss a frog?
- Would your neighbour rather be an elephant or a giraffe?
- Would you rather live in a car or in a shipping container?
- Would your boss rather eat a spider or a cockroach?

42. Ever

Your students will be familiar with 'ever' from the questions 'Have you ever...?' 'Do you ever...?' and 'Would you ever...?'meaning respectively, 'Has it happened one time?', 'Do you usually?' and 'Would you hypothetically?'

'Ever', however, is also coupled with various pronouns to mean 'no matter.' These are:

'Whatever' – No matter what.

'Whenever' – No matter when.

'Whoever' – No matter who.

'Whichever' –No matter which (less than 10 choices).

'Wherever' – No matter where.

'However' –No matter how (not to be confuse with the synonym for 'but').

How to teach it

Write on the board the above definitions along with some example sentences. If they haven't heard of these pronouns before emphasise that (maybe with the exception of 'however') they are very common.

Controlled speaking practice

Dictate the following sentences and ask your students to fill the gaps with the appropriate 'ever'.

Please sit_____you like (wherever).

There is a prize for_____can answer the question first (whoever).

_____he speaks he says something silly (whenever).

I am going to buy it_____expensive it is (however).

_____I buy her, it's always the wrong thing (whatever).

I'll go by bus or train,_____is cheaper (whichever).

If you work through the Internet you can live_____you want (wherever).

In this class you can talk to _____you want (whoever).

_____he has money, he spends it on silly things (whenever).

I'll get to the football match_____difficult it is (however).

_____she does, someone always disapproves (whatever).

We'll see the Will Smith or the Jennifer Lawrence movie at the cinema, _____starts first (whichever).

It is important that_____buys the car has a good credit rating (whoever).

_____restaurant we choose, it has to be cheap because I haven't been paid yet (whichever).

_____we stop for petrol, he buys chocolate (whenever).

Write _____you want, but you're taking responsibility (whatever).

The children can go_____they want, the gate is locked (wherever).

_____much I try, I can't get this report right (however).

Freer speaking practice
Pairs' roleplay 'The teenager': Student A is a teenager who is depressed after failing their exams. Student B is the parent who must try to cheer them up and is ready to do whatever they want. For example:

Sarah: 'I'm sorry you failed your exams Tom. Let's go out to cheer ourselves up. I will go wherever you want. Where do you want to go?'

Tom: 'Wherever, I don't care.'

Sarah: 'What about the cinema? Who would you like to go with you?'

Tom: 'I don't care, whoever.'

Sarah: 'Whoever? Ok, then what about your cousin Jason.'

43. To Become

If you have been teaching English for a while you would have heard something like this 'He became crazy' or 'I am becoming tired.' These sentences are obviously wrong, but how? 'Become' means to change from one thing to another – for example, 'He became a Buddhist' or 'A girl becomes a woman' but it cannot be used for <u>every</u> type of change, which is where students run into difficulties.

43.1 'Become' verbs
There are actually five 'become' verbs, each expressing a particular type of change.

To become
'Become' is paired with either a noun or an adjective. It means gradual change that takes place over a long period of time and is usually permanent, such as:

A change of belief: Buddhist, atheist, liberal, conservative, Christian, Muslim, vegetarian.

Becoming or changing profession: Doctor, teacher, designer, a criminal.

A change in social position: Rich, anorexic, criminal, drug addict, widow, successful, an orphan.

Other permanent changes of personality or physical characteristics: Strong, weak, arrogant, independent, dependent, insomniac, addicted, disillusioned, mean.

To get
To get is paired with an adjective and normally means a fast change of state or emotion that can change back quickly, such as:

A change of state: To get sick, hungry, tired, bored, fit, strong, weak, pregnant, dirty.

A change of emotion: To get angry, unbearable, emotional, nervous, anxious, worried, stressed.

Along a day, you can become several of these things and return to normal.

To turn into
'To turn into' comes before a noun or an adjective and noun. It means a total change of form. For example:

Spring turns into summer, water turns into ice, a baby turns into a child, the frog turns into a prince, night turns into day, water turns into wine.

It also means a complete change of personality or values, such as 'He turned into a radical,' or 'She turned into a bitter person.'

To turn
'To turn' is for colours. For example, 'to turn green with envy' or 'the traffic light turns red.'

It also expresses the completion of an age such as 'My brother turned 30 last year.'

To go
'To go' is paired with an adjective and means an unpleasant and normally permanent change, such as: To go deaf, blind, broke, bankrupt, grey, rotten, mouldy, lame, bald, on strike, out of date.

It is also used for 'crazy,' and all synonyms for 'crazy' such as 'insane', 'mad', 'nuts', 'wacko' etc. In this case the person has not literally lost their mind, but rather has temporarily lost control of their emotions.

If others are provoking 'craziness' in you, you use the phrase 'To drive me crazy'. For example, 'My kids are driving me crazy today.'

To go + colours

Just like 'to turn', 'to go' is also used for colours – for example, 'She went brown in the sun.'

How to teach it

Write on the board an example of a 'become', 'get', 'turn into', 'turn' and 'go' sentence. Highlight the verbs and elicit the meaning with the explanations above. Use plenty of examples to illustrate your points.

Controlled Speaking Practice

Write a five column table on the board headed 'to become', 'to get', 'to turn into,' 'to turn' and 'to go.' Dictate the nouns and adjectives above at random and ask your students to select the correct verb.

Note: There are some cases that two verbs can be used, although the meaning is not the same. For example, 'He became rich' implies that it happened over a long period of time. 'He got rich' on the other hand, implies that it happened overnight.

Freer speaking practice
Pairs' questions 'How have you or people close to you changed over time': Ask your students to use as many 'become' verbs as possible to explain their life changes or how a celebrity historical figure changed over their life.

43.2 To make

'To make' is different from the other 'become' verbs as although it means 'to change' (in emotion) you don't make the change yourself but rather someone or something provokes the reaction in you. For example, 'The dog makes my mother happy;' my mother isn't making herself happy, rather the dog is provoking the reaction in her.

The structure runs:

Object + make + object pronoun + adjective or verb

In this way, a 'make' sentence is the opposite of a 'get' sentence. In a 'get' sentence such as 'I get angry at the film', you are the subject, while the film is the object. In a 'make' sentence it is reversed to 'The film makes me angry'. You are the object, while the thing provoking you (in this case the film) is the subject.

Make is commonly used with: Angry, laugh, cry, smile, sick, worried, emotional, hungry, nervous and upset.

The adjectives 'happy', 'unhappy' and 'proud' can only be used with 'make.' The adjective 'sad' can be used with 'get' but it is better English to use it with 'make.'

How to teach it

Write a couple of 'make' examples on the board and elicit the structure and meaning.

Emphasise that the adjectives 'happy', 'unhappy', 'proud' and most commonly 'sad' are only used with 'make' as in English we believe that we don't make ourselves happy, proud and so on, but rather an outside factor causes the happiness and pride in us.

Freer speaking practice

In pairs get your students to ask and answer the following questions:

It is the simple things in life that make us happy. Do you agree or disagree?

What makes you proud about your country?

When was the last time a news story made you laugh or smile?

What was the last film that made you cry?

---

44. Question Practice

Asking questions is fundamental to conversation, so it amazes me how little time many teachers dedicate to practicing them. Ten minutes of question practice every couple of classes will make a huge difference to your students' English and here is how to do it.

Instead of asking a question, the teacher says the answer and asks their students to work out what the question was. To get the right question the teacher must emphasise the most important part of the sentence with their voice.

For example:

Teacher: 'She runs in *the park*. What is the question?'

Tom: 'Where does she run?'

Without this emphasis, the student could have easily asked, 'What does she do?' which would be grammatically correct but not the question the teacher was searching for.

Below you will find practice for the most common questions that students have problems with such as prepositions at the end of sentences, 'whose' and present perfect continuous. Select statements at random. The expected question is next to the statement, though you can give your students some leeway here. There are only a few of each type and I encourage you to write more.

Basic questions for A1 plus level

Yes, I cleaned the car – *'Did you clean the car?'*

It's on the *table* – *'Where is it?'*

Yes, she likes teaching – *'Does she like teaching?'*

It is red – *'What colour is it?'*

There are *three* cats in the house – *'How many cats are there in the house?'*

I *don't* know how to ski – *'Do you know how to ski?'*

I eat *twice* a day – *'How often do you eat?'*

It's four o'clock – *'What time is it?'*

Yes, she can ride a bike – *'Can she ride a bike?'*

I am a *teacher* – *'What do you do?'*

She is from *Britain* – *'Where is she from?'*

His name is *John* – *'What is his name?'*

They are eight years' old – *'How old are they?'*

Whose

It's *my* pen – *'Whose pen is it?'*

It's *his* car – *'Whose car is it?'*

It *used to be our* house – *'Whose house did it use to be?'*

It *will be* our house next year – *'Whose house will it be?'*

It's *going* to be *their car* when they turn 18 – *'Whose car is it going to be when they turn 18?'*

Weather

The weather is cold and rainy *today* – *'What is the weather like today?'*

It will be sunny and hot *tomorrow* – *'What will the weather be like tomorrow?'*

It was cold and foggy *yesterday* – *'What was the weather like yesterday?'*

It *used to be* cold and rainy here but now it is hotter – *'What did the weather use to be like?'*

Distance

It's 60 km from Cambridge to London – *'How far is it from Cambridge to London?'*

It was 40 km to Oxford – *'How far was it to Oxford?'*

You take the A1 to get to the North – *'How do you get to the North?'*

Brighton is two hours from London – *'How far is Brighton from London?'*

How much, how many

She has *three* brothers – *'How many brothers does she have?'*

He *used to* have *two* dogs – *'How many dogs did he used to have?'*

They eat *a lot of* meat every week – *'How much meat do they eat every week?'*

He used to drink *a lot*, but now he has given up – *'How much did he used to drink?'*

Frequency

I go swimming twice a week – *'How often do you go swimming?'*

She used to work seven days a week – *'How many days a week did she used to work?'*

I will go to the gym three times a week – *'How often will you go to the gym?'*

He plays football once a year – *'How often does he play football?'*

Measurements / degree

My brother is two metres tall – *'How tall is your brother?'*

She weighs about 55kg – *'How much does she weigh?'*

My house is very small – *'How small is your house?'*

It's very hot outside – *'How hot is it outside?'*

She used to weigh 80kg – *'How much did she use to weigh?'*

The heaviest he has weighed is 100kg – *'What is the heaviest he has weighed?'*

It used to cost 50 cents – *'How much did it use to cost?'*

It will cost 100 euros – *'How much will it cost?'*

Take and last

It takes me 15 minutes to make breakfast in the morning – *'How long does it take you to make breakfast in the morning?'*

It took her 20 minutes to get to work – *'How long did it take her to get to work?'*

The meeting should last 20 minutes – *'How long should the meeting last?'*

It used to take him five minutes to get ready in the morning – *'How long did it use to take him to get ready in the morning?'*

The last exercise I did lasted 30 minutes – *'How long did the last exercise you did last?'*

It would take me 20 minutes to get ready if I didn't have children – *'How long would it take you to get ready if you didn't have children?'*

It has taken her two hours to do this work – *'How long has it taken her to do her work?'*

The match lasted 90 minutes – *'How long did the match last?'*

Still, yet, already and anymore

Yes, I have already done the food shopping – *'Have you done the food shopping yet?'*

Yes, he is still painting my flat – *'Is he still painting your flat?'*

No, I haven't sent the letter yet – *'Have you sent the letter yet?'*

No, she is not going out with him anymore – *'Is she still going out with him?'*

Present perfect continuous

I have been working for eight years – *'How long have you been working for?'*

I was studying yesterday – *'What were you doing yesterday?'*

I have known him since I was 12 – *'How long have you known him for?'*

I have been cleaning my flat – *'What have you been doing?'*

She has been swimming all day – *'How long has she been swimming for?'*

They have liked the film since they were children – *'How long have they liked the film for?'*

I have known you for a year – *'How long have you known me for?'*

He was speaking to his brother – *'Who was he speaking to?'*

She has had the car for 10 years – *'How long has she had the car for?'*

We have been playing basketball for five years – *'How long have we been playing basketball for?'*

To be, look, taste, smell and sound like

He is tall with brown hair – *'What does he look like?'*

My house is big and white – *'What does your house look like?'*

She is funny and intelligent – *'What is she like?'*

It smells like Chinese food – *'What does it smell like?'*

His job is stressful but fun – *'What is his job like?'*

He is like *his brother* – *'Who is he like?'*

She looks like *her father* – *'Who does she look like?'*

It sounds like *a car* – *'What does it sound like?'*

It tastes terrible – *'What does it taste like?'*

Prepositions at the end of the sentence

It's made of wood and glass – *'What is it made of?'*

I went to the party *with my sister* – *'Who did you go to the party with?'*

She works with *her mother* – *'Who does she work with?'*

He is taking a photo of *a cat* – *'What is he taking a photo of?'*

She was responsible for the *communications department* – *'What was she responsible for?'*

He is walking *to work* – *'Where is he walking to?'*

The book was written by *Charles Dickens* – *'Who was the book written by?'*

He is in charge of *production* – *'What is he in charge of?'*

She was found guilty of *shoplifting* – *'What was she found guilty of?'*

They were thinking about *France* – *'What were they thinking about?'*

He used to spend his money on *alcohol* – *'What did he use to spend his money on?'*

They will be in charge of *operations* – *'What will they be in charge of?'*

The shares went down by *3%* – *'How much did the shares go down by?'*

You are entitled to five days' holiday – *'How much holiday am I entitled to?'*

She will be promoted to sales manager – *'What will she be promoted to?*

45. Vocabulary

How to teach vocabulary

No matter what vocabulary you're teaching always find out what your students know first. Do this by writing the topic on the board and as a class brainstorming all the vocabulary about that subject. When you're students run out of words, add to their knowledge with the help of the lists below. Try not to teach more than 15 words at a time as more than that can be overwhelming.

How to practice
Questions

Getting your students to create questions for a partner is a great way to practice. For variety always tell them to use a range of question words and grammar points, such as, 'When was the last time...?' 'Did you use to...?' 'How long does it take...?' 'Have you ever...?' and so on. To help, write a list of question words on the board and ask them to make a question from each.

Roleplays

Roleplays are another good source of practice, but do the groundwork first. Write a simple, two line situation on the board and, in pairs, ask your students to brainstorm the vocabulary and questions they need. If your students take owner-ship of the roleplay it is far more likely to work as its success or failure ultimately rests with them.

Problem solving

At the back of the book you will find some problem solving activities. These are also a great way to reinforce vocabulary as students must naturally repeat words several times while they are discussing the problem.

Grammar points

Ideally all vocabulary should be taught with a grammar point and I have in-cluded suggestions in most of the topics below. I typically teach vocabulary first then I introduce a grammar point and incorporate the vocabulary in all the grammar examples. So for example, if my vocabulary point was 'Sport' and my grammar point 'Used to', my example would be 'How often did you use to score goals when you were a teenager?'

Homework

Part of your students' homework should be to memorise the list; yes I know it is boring but you can do all the fun activities in the world and the vocabulary won't stick unless your students invest the time studying it themselves.

Lexical Sets

Below are vocabulary topics. Generally speaking, the easier ones are towards the front and more difficult at the back. For convenience, Business Lessons vocabulary can be found at the back in their own chapter, though of course there is a lot of overlap and normal students will want to know these words too.

45.1 Families

Mother, father, parents, daughter, son, children, grandmother, grandfather, grandparents, brother, sister, siblings, great-grand-parents, only child, aunt, uncle, cousin, second cousin, family-in-law.

Suggested Grammar topic: The Saxon Genitive.

45.2 Clothes

Button, collar, cotton, checked, fashionable, high heels, leather, loose, long / short sleeves, old-fashioned, pocket, patterned, scruffy, smart, sleeveless, spotted, striped, tight, woollen, zip.

Suggested grammar topic: Present continuous 'What are you wearing?'

45.3 Restaurant

The bill, condiment, cutlery, dessert, dish, fork, knife, main-course, meal, menu, set menu, to pay for, salt and pepper, serviette, spoon, starter, waiter, waitress, teaspoon.

Roleplay: 'Ordering in a restaurant and making a complaint.' Ask your students to brainstorm situations.

45.4 Shopping

Aisle, bargain, changing rooms, customer, to look for, to pay for, to put on, to re-fund, receipt, size, shop assistant, to take back, to take off, till, to try on.

Roleplay: 'Taking a faulty item back to a shop.' Ask your students to brain-storm situations.

45.5 Food shopping

Aisle, basket, cart, cashier, checkout, to check out, to discount, a discount, goods, expiry date, to expire, own-brand, range, trolley, value, to be good value for money.

45.6 Basic food and drink

Brainstorm what your students already know and you should end up with a list like: Apples, bananas, beer, bread, cheese, chocolate, coffee, fish, to have break-fast, lunch, dinner and a snack, lentils, meat, milk, orange juice, pasta, potatoes, rice, tea, toast, tomatoes, water, wine.

Suggested grammar point: 'How many, how much, how often.' For example, 'How often do you have orange juice for breakfast?' 'How many apples do you eat a week and how much meat?'

45.7 Directions

Corner, crossroad, exit, to exit, to go past/towards, to keep going straight, on the left, on the right, roundabout, to take a right/left, to turn, traffic lights, zebra crossing.

Problem solving: Print out maps of the students' city. In pairs Student A must pick a secret destination. Starting from an agreed point Student A must guide Student B to the destination using only their directions. If the pair are sitting op-posite each other make sure they agree beforehand on what is left and right.

45.8 Weather

Write a table on the board headed nouns, verbs and adjectives and tell your stu-dents to fill it with the following words. If you only have the noun, elicit the pos-sible verb and adjective and so on.

Cloudy, flood, to flood, foggy, forecast, freezing, hot and cold, ice, rainy, rain, to rain, snowy, snow, to snow, sunny, a storm, thunder and lightning.

Teach: 'What's the weather like today? What was the weather like yesterday? What will the weather be like tomorrow?'

Activity: Print out the weather forecast in different parts of the world and tell your students in pairs to ask and answer questions about today's, yesterday's and tomorrow's forecast.

Weather advanced
Bright, changeable, clear skies, to clear up, drought drizzle, frost, gale, gust of wind, hail, heatwave, hailstorm, hurricane, lightning, mist, showers, tornado.

Suggested grammar topic: Quantifiers 'Not as many,' 'not as much,' 'fewer' and 'less.' For example, 'There are fewer showers in Italy than in Ireland.'

45.9 Landscapes
Bridge, bus stop, castle, cathedral, city centre, factory, fountain, hill, library, market, monument, river, road, police station, port, post office, town hall, market, suburb, street light, stadium, traffic light, train station, tower, village.

Suggested grammar topic: Comparisons 'More, less, fewer.' For example, 'There are more bus stops in the city than the country but there are fewer hills in the city than the country.'

Landscape advanced
Bench, breath-taking, canal, cosmopolitan, crowded, cycle-lane, entertainment football stadium, overcrowding, pavement, pedestrian, poverty, residential area, skyscraper, square, touristy, taxi rank.

45.10 Sport
To beat, to draw/ to tie, a draw/a tie, to catch, coach, to hit, to kick, match, players, to save a goal, to score a goal, to shoot, to throw, teams, to win.

Prepositions of movement: Across, along, into, over, round, towards, through.

Questions activity:

   o   Describe an interesting activity that you have tried.

- o An activity you want to try in the future.
- o An activity you recommend.
- o The most exciting sports event you have ever seen.

Suggested grammar topic: 'Used to' – for example, 'I used to play football when I was a teenager', 'How often did you use to play a match?'

Pairs' roleplay 'Interviewing a sport star': Student A is retired sport star and Student B is the interviewer who must conduct the interview using 'used to'. The sport star must keep their identity secret and their partner must guess. For example, 'I used to play basketball for my country,' 'How many points did you typically used to score in a match and where did you use to train?'

45.11 Travelling
Baggage collection, customs, to go backwards, to fasten your seat belt, flight attendant, to go forwards, homesick, jetlag, journey, passport control, suitcase, scales, to turn around, the day before yesterday, the day after tomorrow, to travel, trip.

Pairs' roleplay 'Going through customs': Student A is the traveller and Student B the customs officer. Several strange items are found in the luggage and the traveller must explain why he/she is innocent.

45.12 Education
To apply for, application, to behave, behaviour, to cheat in an exam, degree, to enrol, enrolment, to fail, fees, to get marks, to mark, to manage vs. to achieve, to pass, pupil, to punish, school report, subjects, to take an exam, to retake, term, to tell off.

Questions activity:

- o What are the positives and negatives of the current education system?
- o If you were the minister of education for your country, which improvements would you make?
- o Maths and science subjects are more useful than the arts. Do you agree or disagree?

45.13 Accidents
To bandage, bandage, to dislocate, to fall over, to graze, nosebleed, to slip, to swell, to throw up, to trip over, to twist.

Problem solving activity: 'Which is worse' found in The Ultimate ESL Book of Speaking Activities available at www.bilinganation.com.

45.14 Bodily actions
To bend down, to cough, to lick, to scream at, to shout at, to sneeze, to snore, to spit, to wheeze, whisper, to wink, to yawn.

45.15 Gestures
To cross your arms, to nod, to point at, to roll your eyes, to shake hands, to shake your head, to wave.

45.16 Senses
To be short-sighted/ long-sighted, eyesight, to hear, hearing, to smell, to sniff, to see, to sense, to be sensitive, to taste, to be tasty, to touch.

Suggested grammar point: Gerund vs infinitive with senses.

45.17 Adjectives as verbs
To cool, to enlarge, to harden, to heat, to lengthen, to loosen, to narrow, to smooth, to sharpen, to soften, to strengthen, to sweeten, to thicken, to thin, to tighten, to warm up, to weaken, to widen, to whiten.

Pairs' activity 'Explain your favourite recipe': For example, 'First soften the potatoes by boiling them and then add them to the soup to thicken it.'

45.18 Food
To bake, to beat, to boil, to dip, to drain, to fry, to grate, to scramble, to slice, to stir, to stew, to steam, to whisk.

Problem solving activity 'Guess my recipe': A student explains a well-known recipe and the others have to guess which dish it is for.

Variation: The student mimes the recipe and the class must comment on what they are doing and then guess the recipe.

Food class II
Aubergines, avocado, beetroot, bitter, bland, cabbage, chewy, chickpeas, creamy, crisp, crunchy, figs, garlic, greasy, herbs, leeks, onion, parsnips, salty spicy, sweet, tasty.

Problem solving activity 'The Dessert Island Food Challenge': The students are stuck on a desert island and must pick five foods from a list of 20 to live on for the next five years. Activity found in The Ultimate ESL Book of Speaking Activities available at www.bilinguanation.com.

45.19 Medicine
To hurt (as in 'pain') and my arm hurts (as in 'to damage your arm'), to twist, to scar, to put in plaster, to bruise, to burn, to operate on, the difference between to heal and to cure, to prescribe, prescription, painkiller, to bleed, to swell, to examine, dose, diagnosis, stitches, to vaccinate, to give and get a vaccine.

Pairs' roleplay 'At the doctors': Student A is the patient with one of the below problems and Student B is the doctor who must give advice.

- o   You twisted your ankle while skipping to work.
- o   Your company is sending you to West Africa for a month.
- o   You crashed into a glass door and cut your leg off at the knee.
- o   You woke up covered in spots. You have a wedding to go to.
- o   You have a strange swelling on your big toe and can't put your shoe on.
- o   You got stung by a jellyfish.

Medicine II
Body parts: Forehead, cheek, palm, thumb, waist, hips, elbow, ankle, spots, to itch, to scratch, a check-up, plasters/band aid, bandage, to amputate, to cut off, to get wounded, to get injured, wounds.

Pairs' roleplay 'Signing up for war:' Student A is a soldier who is about to go to war who must speak to Student B, their captain about their worries about possible injuries.

45.20 Relationships

To ask out, to chat up, to cheat on, chat up line, dating, to date, to dump, to fancy, to fall in and out of love, to flirt, to stand someone up, to split up, to dump, to flirt.

Pairs' roleplay 'The breakup': Two students are in a romantic relationship and want to break up. Talk together about all the silly things you did in your relationship and why you now think enough is enough.

Suggested grammar point: 'Wish and Hope', for example, 'I wish you hadn't flirted with my flatmate', 'I wish you would be more positive,' 'I hope you find someone else.'

45.21 Money

To afford, bank statement, to borrow, bonus, debt, to go bankrupt, to invest, to lend, loan, loss, to owe, to pay back, profit, pocket money, pay-rise, to save up, short term/ long term, shares, to take advantage of.

Pairs' roleplay 'The bank loan': Ask your students to brainstorm ideas for a business. Student A is the entrepreneur who asks for a loan and Student B is the bank manager who assesses their case by asking money-related questions.

Money II

Breadwinner, to be broke, instalments, interest rate, to inherit, inheritance, mortgage, to pay back, pay slip, stocks and shares, to take out a loan.

Group roleplay 'A new business': Three students have decided to set up a real estate business together. But how are they going to market it? Full roleplay The Ultimate ESL Book of Speaking Activities.

45.22 Parenting

Adolescence, babyhood, to bring up, to bottle feed, to breastfeed, birth rate, child-free, to give birth, nappies/diapers, only child, to raise, siblings to spoil, tantrum, toddler.

Questions activity

- o Can being childfree be as satisfying as being a parent? Why/why not?
- o Do only children suffer from not having a sibling? Why/why not?

- What is the hardest stage of bringing up a child?
- Can you spoil a baby?
- What were you like as a child?
- Is it acceptable now in society to be childfree or is there still a stigma?

45.23 Crime

Write a table on the board headed, 'crime', 'verb' and 'criminal.' Elicit the crime and criminal from the verb. For example, with the verb 'To shoplift', the crime is 'shoplifting' and the criminal 'shoplifter.'

To blackmail, blackmail, to bribe, bribery, to burgle, burglary, to get caught, to get away with a crime, to kidnap, manslaughter, to murder, to mug, to pick-pocket, to speed, speeding, to shoplift. The difference between 'to steal' (an object) and 'to rob' (a person or location).

Suggested grammar point: Reported Speech.

Problem solving activity: Put the crimes in the order of most serious for society and the easiest to get away with.

Crime II

The accused, to be charged, with a crime, judge, jury, to rule out, to weigh up evidence, witness, to witness.

Suggested grammar point: Deduction and possibility in past.

Pairs' problem-solving activity: 'What if anything are these people guilty of?' Using deduction and possibility in past, ask your students to speculate what these people must have been feeling, what they could have done, what they can't have done (it was impossible to do).

1. A construction worker on his way to hospital with a seriously injured colleague speeds through a red light accidentally killing a pedestrian.

2. A pensioner who lives alone is burgled three times. On the third time he hits the burglar on the head with a baseball bat, killing him.

3. An unemployed woman with a serious debt problem goes to the supermarket to buy food. When she discovers she doesn't have enough money for everything she shoplifts the rest.

Roleplay: 'The case of John Roberts.' ask your students to image that they are on the jury of this real case. Using deduction and possibility your students must decide what crime Mr Roberts committed. See appendix.

45.24 Media

Broadsheet, to broadcast, to catch up, to decrease, to divert, to give out, to give away, to increase, journalism newsfeed, to publish, to post, paywall, press release, readership, to review, to subscribe, subscriber, to share, tabloid.

Group roleplay 'The failing newspaper': Your students are the directors of a failing national broadsheet newspaper. To survive they have to change your business strategy, but how?

Options:

- o Change from a broadsheet to a tabloid (they are easier to write as they require far fewer words).
- o Make your newspaper online only.
- o Have your readers write reviews and articles for free, but how?
- o Give away your newspaper for free with the hope of attracting more advertising from the larger circulation/
- o Offer gifts to your subscribers: but what?

45.25 TV

Class starter activity 'Think of types of TV shows': Quiz show, soap opera, sports programme, documentary, game show, news broadcast, current affairs programme, detective series, sitcom, screen, stage.

Main vocabulary: Animation, audience, cast, to commission, episode, main character, screenplay, the set, to perform, performance, plot, presenter, script, scriptwriter, series, to show a film, supporting role, to be set in, soundtrack, viewers.

Group roleplay 'Create a new TV show': Channel 6 is commissioning a new TV series with a budget of $100,000. In pairs or teams, tell your students to choose a genre and concept. Full roleplay found in The Ultimate ESL Book of Speaking Activities.

45.26 Technology

To backup, to bookmark, to charge, to crash, desktop, to download, headphones, headset, homepage, to be hooked on, keyboard, laptop, microphone, to upload, to plug in / unplug, a plug, to shut down, to start up, screen, to recover information, search engine, to type.

Questions activity

- A gadget they can't live without and why?
- Is it immoral to download films and music from the internet illegally or is it justifiable?
- Are you more or less sociable with your gadgets?
- Do you know anyone who is hooked on an app/gadget/website, how does it affect their lives?

Pairs' roleplay 'Silicone Valley': Your students have 15 minutes to come up with the next big gadget, application or website and present it to the class in the hope of winning investment. The other pairs have $10,000 to invest and must decide which team will give them the best return for their money. They can split the money between several investments if they wish.

45.27 Appearance

Bald, beard, blonde, brown, black, red and grey hair, clean-shaven, curly, straight, wavy hair, cute, good-looking, handsome, moustache, overweight, slim, short, tall.

Suggested grammar topic: To look like.

Appearance advanced

To be in your early, mid or late 20s, 30s, 40s, bangs, beauty spot, a belly, a brunette, freckles, fringe, muscular, a red-head, skinny, wrinkles

45.28 Personality

Ambitious, bossy, brave, charming, calm, easy-going, funny, giving, jealous, kind, laid-back, mature, moody, reliable, sensitive, sensible, sociable, spoilt.

Suggested grammar topic: To be like.

Personality advanced

Absent-minded, arrogant, cheerful, conscientious, eccentric, forgetful, grumpy, insecure, insincere, loyal, open-minded, optimistic, outgoing, smart, stubborn, thoughtful, talkative, vain, witty, wise.

45.29 Phrasal Verbs: Hobbies

To catch up (get to the same level as everyone else), to go off something (stop liking) to give up, to join in, to put your name down, to take up.

Roleplay 'The summer camp': Student A is a new teenager at summer camp and Student B is the camp supervisor. The teenager must choose from some of the suggested activities below but they don't want to participate. The camp supervisor must convince him or her to try at least one of them.

Variation: 'The retirement community.' A new pensioner has joined the retirement home. The other residents want to encourage him/her to take up a hobby but the new resident is not very enthusiastic.

Activities: Bird watching, chess, Chinese lessons, horse riding, karate, guitar classes, photography.

45.30 Engineering

To drill, drill, to fold / unfold, foldable, to hang, to hammer, hammer, to nail, nails, to put together to put up, to saw, saw, screws, screwdriver, sandpaper, to take apart, to take down.

Problem solving activity: In teams ask your students to think of the best way to: Turn a door into a chair, turn your notebook into a pair of shoes, turn a table into a dog kennel.

Engineering II

To flatten, to loosen, to roll / unroll, to stick / unstick, to smooth, to tighten.

Problem solving activity: In teams ask your student to make a paper bridge from two sheets of paper and sticky-tape and explain how they did it.

45.31 Bathroom
To block/unblock, a burst pipe, cistern, a crack, to drip, a drop, to drain, to flush to leak, to overflow, a plug, to run a bath, shower screen, to smash, plughole, a tap.

45.32 Renting
Deposit, electrician, to fix, handyman, landlord/lady, to mend, plumber, to put together, to rent, the rent, realtor/ estate agent, to take apart, tenant.

Pairs' roleplay 'Renting problems': Student A is a renter with a problem with their apartment and Student B is the landlady who doesn't want to fix it. As a class, brainstorm situations.

45.33 Car
Accelerator, bonnet/hood, boot/trunk, breakdown, to breakdown, to bump into, bumper, clutch, to dent, a dent, gearstick, to jump the lights, to jumpstart, to put into neutral, rear view mirror, to reverse, right-of-way, to start a car, steering wheel, tow truck, to tow, wing mirror, windscreen.

45.34 Roads
A fine, to fine, flyover, to get run over, hard-shoulder, lane, roadside, roundabout, roadworks, to run out of petrol, speed cameras, traffic light, traffic jam, zebra crossing.

Group roleplay 'Roadworks!': Your students are the town planners for the city's roads. They have to save $300,000 from the budget. What can the city do without? Full roleplay found in The Ultimate ESL Book of Speaking Activities.

45.35 Society
Birth rate, death rate, homeless, homelessness, middle-aged, middle-class, posh, upper-class, successful, social-housing, suburb, tramp, working-class.

45.36 Politics
To ban, ballot box, conservatives, election, to encourage, left-wing, to lobby, lobbyist, liberal majority, parliament, political party, prime minister, president, right-wing, to run for president, socialist, to vote for.

45.37 War

To blow up, ceasefire, civil war, coup, to declare, to defeat, a defeat, to loot, to overthrow, to retreat, revolution, siege, surrender, to shell, treaty, to withdraw.

45.38 Environment

Cliff, climate change, energy consumption global warming, greenhouse effect, landmark, to recycle, ozone layer, over-population, to be scarce, a shortage, a spillage, summit tide, the tip of the iceberg, to take for granted, valley.

Questions activity

- Describe your favourite walk.
- If you had to live in another part of the world, where would it be and why?
- What will the world be like when our children reach our age?

Suggested grammar point: Even if / Even though. For example, 'Even though the icebergs are melting we are still using fossil fuels.' 'Even if the sea level rose, we would live in boats.'

Environment advanced

To catch fire, climate change deniers, to clean up, cove, to cut down, to dump rubbish, to be endangered, fossil fuels, oil tanker, polar ice caps, to put out a fire, renewable energy, the rainforest, species, stream, to tip over.

Questions activity

- How has the climate changed in your city since you were a child?
- How will global warming affect your city in the future?
- What type (if any) environmental problem are you most worried about?
- What can we do about it?
- Why do people deny climate change do you think?
- What is your favourite natural space? Can you describe it?

Pair's roleplay 'The political conference': Student A is a politician and Student B a journalist. It is the year 2050 and climate change has affected the country (brainstorm the issues). The journalist must ask about the problems and how the politician intends to fix it.

45.39 Movement

To bend, to bounce, to cross, to lift, to lie down, to raise, to sit up, to stretch, to skip.

Questions activity

- o   Describe an activity without moving.
- o   Give advice on a great exercise routine.
- o   Describe an activity you want to try and why.
- o   Describe an activity you have tried and you don't recommend.

Extra questions:

- o   Are there any sports that women are better at then men?
- o   If you could play just one sport for the rest of your life, what would it be?
- o   If you could replace one sport in the Olympics, what would it be and what would you replace it with?
- o   When is a sport not a sport?

Pairs' game 'Guess my sport': Students must describe one of the sports below without using the related words, moving or naming a person who plays it. The winner is the person who guesses the most sports in five minutes.

- o   **Bowling:** (Related words) Ball, pins, lane.
- o   **Baseball:** Throw, bat, American/America.
- o   **Handball:** Hand, ball, Spain.
- o   **Spinning:** Bike, cycling, gym, exercise.
- o   **Karate**: Hit, kick, punch, pyjamas.
- o   **Tennis:** Racquet, ball, court.

45.40 Prefixes

Mis: Mistake, misunderstand, misspell, misjudge, mislead, misbehave, misinform, misplace misrepresent.

Pre: Predict, premature, preview, precaution, pre-empt.

Fore: Foresee, forecast, forefather, forego, foregone conclusion, forewarn.

Over and under: to overcome, to overreact, to overwhelm, overexcited, over/underpaid, oversleep, overconfident, under/over-sized, under/over-priced, over/underrated, over/undervalued.

Group problem solving activity: Write the root words on slips of paper and ask your students to pair it to the right prefix. For example, for the root word 'behave,' the prefix is 'mis' – 'misbehave.'

45.41 Suffixes

Less: Breathless, careless, defenceless, endless, fearless, lifeless, heartless, help-less, hopeless, homeless, powerless, priceless, useless, senseless, speechless, tasteless.

Ship: Dictatorship, friendship, hardship, internship, leadership, partnership, relationship, scholarship, workmanship.

Ness: Awareness, carelessness, darkness, happiness, illness, loneliness, late-ness, sadness, sickness, senseless, weakness.

Group problem solving activity: Write the root words on slips of paper and ask your students to pair them with the right suffix.

Pairs' roleplay 'The mistake': Your students are a pair of surgeons who may have left an instrument inside a patient. Using all the possible suffixes discuss what to do about the situation. For example, 'We could leave the instrument in there.' 'Don't be so heartless!'

45.42 Out of / in

Out-of-battery, out-of-breath, out-of-control/ in-control, out-of-danger/ in-dan-ger, out-of-date/ in-date, to fall in love/ to fall out of love, out-of-order, out-of-print/ in-print, out-of-reach/ in-reach, out-of-practice, out-of-stock/ in-stock, out of something in a shop, out-of-time, out-of-your-comfort zone.

Pairs' roleplay 'A bad day at work': Student A is a shop assistant at a large department store at Christmas and Student B is a customer. For every question the customer asks, the shop assistant must tell them can't do it using 'out of'.

- o You are out-of-stock on most toys.
- o You are out of most food. You still have milk but it is out-of-date, will that do?
- o Normally you have a delivery service but your truck is out-of-action.
- o They can't order something because they are out-of-time (there is no more time).

Business Lessons Vocabulary

45.43 General business

A branch, business plan, to carry out, a chain, entrepreneur, entrepreneurship, figures, to be fired / sacked, a gap in the market, to invest, loss, to be made redundant, to network, profit, revenue, sales, to sell, to set up a business, staff, to tax, turnover.

Pairs' roleplay 'A meeting with a business analyst': Student A is an entrepreneur and wants funding from a government grant to set up a new company specialising in Segway tours around their city. To receive this money, they must convince Student B, the government's business analyst, that their business is viable. Full roleplay found in The Ultimate ESL Book of Speaking Activities.

Suggested grammar point: 'Likely' and 'likelihood.' For example, 'How likely it is that you will have 1000 customers by the end of the year?' 'What is the likelihood of the Segways getting stolen?'

45.44 Business phrasal verbs

To bring up a subject, to carry on with, to come up with, to draw up a contract, to figure out, to find out about, to give away, to give up, to roll out, to set up, to sort out, to turn out, to take on.

Pairs' roleplay I 'Working from home': Student A is the head of a trade union of a logistics company who must try to convince their boss, Student B, to allow everyone to work from home.

Pairs' roleplay II 'The investor and the CEO': Student A is a major investor in a large department store and Student B is its CEO. The CEO must explain why profits are down this year and how they can improve.

Suggested grammar point: 'Connectors': As long as, provided that, as soon as, unless, while, meanwhile. For example, 'As long as we can come up with new ideas, sales will improve.'

45.45 Marketing

Advertising, advert, banner, billboard, feedback, junk mail, leaflet, logo, market research, to network, to pitch an idea, poster, press release, product launch, public relations, spokesperson, survey, slogan, to target an audience, to take market share, trade fairs, word-of-mouth.

45.46 Company functions
Bonus, catalogue, exchange rate, to negotiate, negotiator, salespeople, payroll, sales quota, showroom, spreadsheet, to trade.

45.47 White-collar crime
To blackmail, blackmail, to bribe, bribery, corruption, to defraud, to embezzle, embezzlement, to get away with a crime, to scam, a scam, to sue.

Group problem solving activity: Put crimes in order of seriousness for society. Which are the easiest to get away with?

Speaking activity: In pairs, talk about current news stories involving these crimes.

45.48 Economy
Austerity, to bailout, a bailout, benefits, inflation, to go bankrupt, employment, to decrease, deflation, on the dole, interest rates, to increase, quantitative easing, recession, to turn out, unemployment.

45.49 Maths
To add up, to break down numbers, decimal number, to divide, to multiply odd/even, to round up, to round down, to take away, to times, to work out, one billion, one trillion.

Group problem solving activity: Tell your students to verbally give each other (easy) sums.

45.50 Charts
Axis, bar chart, to decrease, to decline, diagram, to drop, dotted lines, downward trend, to fall, a fall, to grow, to increase, highest point, line graph, lowest point, pie chart, to plummet, to peak, a peak, scatter graph, steady growth, a trajectory, upward trend.

Problem solving activity: Business students love this class. Print out some up-to-date charts about business and the economy and ask your students to explain them to each other. Ask them also to draw some conclusions from the data. The Economist magazine produces an online chart everyday under the title, 'The Daily Chart.' Reprint it, though with permission.

45.51 Jobs

Background, to fire, full-time, to give notice, to hire, internship, intern, to be made redundant, overtime, part-time, qualification, to resign, to self-employed shift, to suit, to be suitable, to supervise, to take a day off sick.

Pairs' roleplay 'Hiring a reporter': Your students work in a busy newsroom and need to find a new junior reporter. Full roleplay found in The Ultimate ESL Book of Speaking Activities.

Jobs advanced

To cope with, challenging to commute, a commute, to get promoted, to overlook rewarding, role, to swap, to take time off, to take the pressure, to be unbearable, to be willing + infinitive.

Questions activity

- How do you measure success?
- What things do you think an employee needs from their company to be happy?
- Is there a link between money and happiness? If so, how much do you have to earn?
- How has work changed in the last 10 years?
- How will we be working in 10 years' time?

Pairs' roleplay: Student A is looking for a job and Student B is a careers advisor who must help them find their perfect career.

Candidate: Write your profile including your interests, qualifications and experience.

The careers advisor should find out about the candidates:

- Interests.
- Relevant experience.
- Salary expectations.
- Whether they are willing to commute/travel.
- Likes/dislikes.
- Where they want to be in five years' time.
- How much pressure they can cope with.
- Training they have done or are willing to do.

45.52 Formal and informal letters
Dear Sir or Madam, Dear Mrs Jones, to be grateful/thankful, glad, relieved, shocked, to look forward to + gerund, to keep in touch, to lose touch, to put someone in contact with, best wishes/regard, lots of love, yours faithfully/sincerely.

45.53 Collocations
A collocation is the combination of two words which make a phrase.

To call a meeting, to give an example, to go on strike, to go on a diet, to lend a hand, to make sense, to pay attention, to pay a visit, to run a bath, to run a company, to set an example, to take a break, to take an exam, to take into account, to take a look, to take place, to take out a loan, to take a risk.

Pairs' roleplay 'Strike!': Student A is the owner of an English academy and Student B the teacher. Using collocations, debate the new terms of the employment contract.

Boss: The academy is going bankrupt. You have called a meeting because you have to reduce your staff's pay by 50%. To set an example you have also reduced your pay by half.

If they don't accept the pay cut you will have to make 50% of your staff redundant.

Teacher: You are not happy with this proposal (you weren't paid well anyway). What about doing a marketing campaign? You could lend a hand. Why not take a risk and pay for a better location? If your boss reduces pay, you will go on strike.

46. Starters and Finishers

46.1 Starter activities

Students won't be able to speak their best English from the start of the lesson and so the first five to ten minutes should be dedicated to a fun, easy pairs' activity to ease them into it. Here are some ideas:

Spot the Difference: Source some 'spot the difference' pictures from kids' activity books or the Internet and ask your students to spot the difference. This will often elicit some interesting vocabulary.

Root words: Write three root words on the board – for example, 'taste,' 'feel' and 'care' and in teams have a competition to find all the possible words you can make using prefixes/suffixes. For example, 'tasty', 'tasteless', 'tasteful.'

Dead celebrities and historical figures: Write some names of some well-known dead people on the board and tell your students to ask each other as many questions as they can about them. For example, 'Who was she?' 'What did she do?' and so on. For lower levels do this activity with living people.

Compare and contrast: Place two pictures of different environments on the table and ask your students to think of as many ways to compare them as possible. For example,' Mexico is not as cold as Finland,' 'There are fewer storms in Mexico', 'There are not so many tortillas in Finland as in Mexico.'

Explain how to...: Ask your students to explain step-by-step how to do something complicated such as checking your bank balance on the Internet, buying ski equipment or changing a flat tyre.

News stories: Ask your students to recount a news story that interests them.

Have you ever?: Ask a pair to find three things in common using 'Have you ever..?' or 'Do you ever...?'

Money and the city: You have $20 each for a great day in a famous city (the teacher decides where). Ask your students to plan what they will do and how they will spend their money.

Brainstorming: Brainstorm all the ways of getting a cheap holiday, a free lunch, a lift to the capital, free entertainment and so on.

Step by step: Brainstorm all of the steps for going on holiday (from deciding the destination to arriving at the hotel), getting married (from the proposal to the honeymoon) and finding a job (from deciding on the career to your first day in the office). Change the activity depending on the vocabulary topic you are about to study.

46.2 Finisher activities

At the end of the lesson give your students a fun, high-energy finishing activity so that they leave your classroom with a smile on their face. The end is not the time to teach something new, so make sure that the finisher is a review of the content they already know. Here are some ideas:

Days and months: Ask your students to recite the days of the week and months backwards (guaranteed laughs).

The Short Answer drill: Practice short answers (Have you eaten an apple today? <u>Yes I have</u>).

The A-Z of...: Review the vocabulary topic you have just studied by asking your students to give you a word for each letter of the alphabet. For example, with the topic 'Medicine' 'A' could be for 'amputation', 'B' for 'bandage' and so on.

Make vs do: Give them a quick quiz on nouns paired with 'make' vs 'do.'

Plurals quiz: And the same with plurals.

In vs on quiz: The same with 'in' and 'on.'

Get in vs get on quiz: Test them on their knowledge of transport and 'get.'

In, on and at, Making Arrangements quiz: Also for prepositions.

Irregular verbs in past:

Taboo: Get your students to describe something without using the word or any words closely related to it and their partner must guess what it is.

Nations and nationalities: Using a world map ask your students to name the nationalities of the countries. Choose a different continent each time.

47. Games and Speaking Activities

Games are a great way to round off a lesson. Below are my 'go to' activities which are both fun and challenging and will bring laughter to any class.

47.1 Party games adapted for English teaching

These games have been around for years and can be easily adapted to teach English. They can be bought in toyshops or on Amazon. Alternatively you can make variations yourself with card and felt tips.

Taboo: This is a great way to practice that real-life situation when you're in a foreign country, you don't know the word for something but you have to describe what it is.

Divide your students into pairs and give one person a secret set of words to describe to their partner. Underneath each word write four additional words that can't be used in the description. For example, if the word is 'mirror', the extra words would be 'glass', 'reflexion' 'bathroom' and 'yourself.' After a minute, change roles. The winner is the team that manages to get the most words in two minutes.

Level: A2+.

Brainiac: This is a variation on Taboo. Divide your students into pairs and give one person a set of secret words and in the centre of the table place a deck of activity cards on which are written either, 'describe', 'mime' or 'spell it backwards.' This time your students take it in turns to pick a word card and activity card. They must apply the method written on the activity card to explain the word. For example, if the word was 'frying pan' and the activity card was 'mime' then they must mime what they typically do with a frying pan.
Level: A2+.

Snake oil: Students must put random words together to invent products to sell to the other students around the table.

Make two decks; one of random nouns and adjectives and the other of characters composed of professions, people and animals. For example, a supermodel, a spy, a caveman, an international playboy, astronaut, bouncer, the last person on earth, superhero, politician, penguin.

Ask everyone to select a character card at random and show it to the rest of the group. Now deal six word cards to each student. The student must put two random words together to make the best product they can sell to the characters around the table. For example, two words might be 'comfy' and 'sofa', you may be able to sell a comfy sofa to a politician but to a penguin it would be more difficult, and the student must be very persuasive and inventive to make their case.

Each student gets two minutes to sell their product and each character can only buy two products per round. Continue for as many rounds as you wish. The winner is the student who sells the most products.

This is a great game for business classes.

Level: B1.

47.2 Games for A1 students and above
What's in the bag? Place your bag with a random object in it on the table. Using their knowledge of adjectives and nouns your students must guess what it is. You can only say 'yes' or 'no' to their answers. This is a great way to practice questions such as, 'Is it...?' 'Does it have...?' 'How many...?

Lost: Move classroom furniture to one side. Blindfold a student and place a destination marker at one end of the room. Now place obstacles in the way, or better still a long piece of string in a random shape to designate the path. Now the other students must direct their companion to the destination without allowing them to bump into the obstacles or straying from the string path. This is a great way to practice direction vocabulary.

Your house is on fire: Divide your students into pairs. Student A's house is on fire, they are not at home but luckily Student B is and calls them on their mobile. Student A must describe the objects they want rescued and where they are, but they cannot say the name or the function. Once Student B has rescued three objects swap roles. The winning team are the ones who jointly rescue the most objects in five minutes.

This is a great way to practice questions, dimensions, prepositions of place, shapes, colours and materials.

47.3 Games and speaking activities for B1 and above

Interview a stranger: Divide your students into pairs and give each team a different location such as an archaeological site, a wedding show, a Google conference, a young entrepreneur of the year awards, a political conference or a yacht race.

Student A is a journalist and Student B the interviewee (they invent the character). Together they must make the most interesting interview possible with their questions and answers.

To facilitate write the below question prompts on the board:

What do you do? Do you ever? Have you ever? Would you ever? How often? When was the last time? Do you usually? Did you used to? How long have you...? How long does it take...? When were you born? What's it like? What does it look like, sound like, taste like?

Making a story: Tell your students that you are going to invent a story. Tell them to ask you five questions but you can only answer 'yes' or 'no'. For example:

Tom: 'Is it set underwater?'

Teacher: 'Yes.'

Sarah: 'Are there pirates?'

Teacher: 'No.'

In pairs they now must make a story using this information. Give them 10 minutes to complete the task then each pair must recount their story. The winners are the ones with the best tale.

Preposition game: Give your students a preposition and a tense and ask them to make a question using a different question word (who, what, where, when and so on). Do this five times making the tense progressively harder. The winner is the one who comes up with the most interesting or elaborate question. Students will find this a very difficult activity but it's great for practicing prepositions at the end of questions. To make it easier prompt your students with the verbs that go with each preposition.

- o **Of**: Scared, frightened, dream, taste, smell, in charge.
- o **At:** Good, bad, arrive, laugh, shout, look.

- ○ **To:** Get, married, forget, need, try, listen, relate.
- ○ **About:** Talk, speak, worry, think, dream.

47.4 Games and speaking activities for B2 and above

Conditionals chain story: Ask your students to stand up and form a circle. Throw a soft, large ball to your best student and give them the start of a conditional sentence, for example, 'If I lived in China...' Now ask them to complete the sentence – for example, 'If I lived in China, I would speak Chinese.' They then throw the ball to someone else.

The person they throw the ball to must take the end of the last conditional sentence and turn it into a new one. For example, 'If I spoke Chinese, I would work at a Chinese company,' and so on until the ball has been thrown to everyone. Then start another chain story with a new sentence.

Guess my identity with conditionals: Hand out the names of famous and historical figures and ask your student to keep them secret. Ask your strongest student to sit at the front of the class and pretend to be the person. The rest of the students must guess their identity but only by asking questions in the conditional tenses. The student can answer in a real tense if they are right or a conditional if they are wrong. With each answer they must give a small clue. For example:

Sarah: 'If you were married, what kind of woman would you like to be married to?'

Tom: 'Well, I am married and she works with me.'

Sarah: 'If you had kids, what would they be called?'

Tom: 'I don't have kids, but if I did, they would be called John and Lisa.'

Once students have guessed the identity someone else can take the hot seat.

Two truths one lie: At the beginning of the lesson ask your students to write down two facts that are true about them and one that is a lie. Tell them that they will be questioned so the lie must be very convincing. Then towards the end of the lesson ask a student to write their statements on the board. The rest of the class has three minutes to question them to work out which one is the lie.

Hotel from hell: A variation on Taboo but with more laughs. One student is the guest and the other the receptionist. The guest must explain the problem without using the following words.

- You have cut your wrist open on glass and are bleeding to death. **Banned words**: Blood, bleeding, cut, wrist, dead.
- There is a tramp sleeping in your bed. **Banned words:** Tramp, street, man, bed.
- You have set the curtains on fire. **Banned words:** Curtains, fire, fireman.
- There is an axe murderer sleeping in the wardrobe. **Banned words:** Man, axe, murderer, assassin.
- There is a tarantula in the bath. **Banned words:** Spider, bath, tarantula.
- The toilet is blocked with animal hair. **Banned words:** Blocked, toilet, animal, hair.

Homework Resources

Podcasts

I always ask my students to listen to a podcast for homework. This is because a) it provides excellent comprehension practice, b) the student can speak about it during the next class, for speaking practice and c) there is no marking work to do by you. Here are some of my favourites:

Podcasts in English: Provides hundreds of podcasts for English learners for beginner, intermediate and upper-intermediate level. Accent: British. Duration: Five minutes.

Six Minute English BBC: Provides vocabulary-focused podcasts together with a transcription. Accent: British. Level: B1-C1. Duration: Six minutes.

Business English Podcast: Provides topical business podcasts for English learners. Accent: American. Level: B2-C2. Duration: 20 minutes.

TED: Provides thousands of videos about technology, education, politics, science and more. It's a great way for advanced students to practice their comprehension. Accent: International. Level: B2-C2. Duration: Five-20 minutes.

Student resources

It's important to encourage independent study to cut down on your workload and help your students to progress faster. Here are some of the best ESL resource sites.

BBC Learn English: Provides reading material as well as videos, podcasts and activities that students can use to practice their English. Level: A2-B2.

INGVID.com: Provides bite-sized video lessons on most aspects of English grammar. It's a great way to recap a class. Level: Beginner-B2.

Appendix

Common irregular verbs

Am is are	Was, Were	Been
Become	Became	Become
Begin	Began	Begun
Blow	Blew	Blown
Break	Broke	Broken
Bring	Brought	Brought
Build	Built	Built
Buy	Bought	Bought
Catch	Caught	Caught
Choose	Chose	Chosen
Come	Came	Come
Cost	Cost	Cost
Deal with	Dealt with	Dealt with
Do	Did	Did
Drink	Drank	Drunk
Drive	Drove	Driven
Eat	Ate	Eaten
Fall	Fell	Fallen

Feel	Felt	Felt
Fight	Fought	Fought
Find	Found	Found
Fly	Flew	Flown
Forget	Forgot	Forgotten
Get	Got	Got
Give	Gave	Given
Go	Went	Gone
Grow	Grew	Grown
Have	Had	Had
Hear	Heard	Heard
Hold	Held	Held
Hurt	Hurt	Hurt
Keep	Kept	Kept
Know	Knew	Known
Leave	Left	Left
Lend	Lent	Lent
Lose	Lost	Lost
Make	Made	Made
Mean	Meant	Meant

Meet	Met	Met
Pay	Paid	Paid
Put	Put	Put
Quit	Quit	Quit
Read	Read	Read
Ring	Rang	Rung
Rise	Rose	Risen
Run	Ran	Run
See	Saw	Seen
Sell	Sold	Sold
Send	Sent	Sent
Set	Set	Set
Shut	Shut	Shut
Sleep	Slept	Slept
Speak	Spoke	Spoken
Spend	Spent	Spent
Stand	Stood	Stood
Steal	Stole	Stolen
Take	Took	Taken
Teach	Taught	Taught

Tell	Told	Told
Think	Thought	Thought
Throw	Threw	Thrown
Understand	Understood	Understood
Wear	Wore	Worn
Win	Won	Won

Irregular verbs advanced

Bear	Bore	Born
Bite	Bit	Bitten
Bid	Bid	Bid
Bleed	Bled	Bled
Breed	Bred	Bred
Draw	Drew	Drawn
Forbid	Forbade	Forbidden
Forgive	Forgave	Forgiven
Freeze	Froze	Frozen
Hang	Hung	Hung
Hide	Hid	Hidden
Lay	Laid	Laid
Light	Lit	Lit
Mislead	Misled	Misled
Quit	Quit	Quit
Ride	Rode	Ridden
Ring	Rang	Rung
Rise	Rose	Risen
Show	Showed	Shown

Shake	Shook	Shaken
Shine	Shone	Shone
Shoot	Shot	Shot
Slide	Slid	Slid
Spill	Spilt	Spilt
Spoil	Spoilt	Spoilt
Spread	Spread	Spread
Spring	Sprang	Sprung
Swear	Swore	Sworn
Swim	Swam	Swum
Swing	Swung	Swung
Sweep	Swept	Swept
Sow	Sowed	Sown
Wind	Wound	wound
Wring	Wrung	Wrung
Undergo	Underwent	Undergone

Pictures

There is/there are

Comparison

Present continuous

Deduction and possibility

The Case of John Roberts

Ask your class to imagine that they are a jury who have been asked to judge this imaginary case. Using deduction and possibility in past they must decide what crime Mr Roberts is guilty of.

They must return one of the following verdicts:

a) First degree murder: There was a prior plan to kill the person.
b) Second degree murder: No plan but intended to kill.
c) Voluntary manslaughter: Killing someone by accident but intending to harm them.
d) Involuntary manslaughter: Killing someone by accident e.g. traffic accident.
e) Manslaughter in self-defence.

The Facts

A retired solider living on the outskirts of town keeps getting burgled by a group of youths. Every time it happens he calls the police but they never find the criminals. One night the house is burgled again and Mr Roberts shoots dead one of the burglars with his army revolver while he is trying to escape through the back door. The burglar was 20.

1) The burglar was shot in the back.
2) Mr Roberts had been burgled so many times he kept a gun by his bed.
3) Mr Roberts had a history of gun misbehaviour including threatening to shoot a neighbour's dog.
4) Mr Roberts had served in war and had been diagnosed with post-traumatic stress syndrome.
5) Mr Roberts admits that he did mean to shoot his gun, however, he did not mean to kill the burglar.
6) There was no moon that night and it was very dark.
7) The burglar had a long criminal record including robbery and assault.
8) Mr Roberts shows no remorse for what he did.

Yet and already

Reflexives

Had better

You've inherited a house!

You have just inherited a house form your great aunt. You have $10,000 to spend on the renovation. Decide what you must hire other people to do and what you can do yourselves.

- o Fitting new windows: $3000
- o Getting rid of rubbish: $400
- o Fitting a new roof: $2000
- o New drains: $800
- o Fitting new floors: $2000
- o Rebuilding garage: $1000
- o Fitting new bathrooms: $2000
- o Rewiring electricity $1000
- o Fitting a new kitchen: $5000
- o Building a new fireplace: $1000
- o Gardening: $1000
- o Fitting a new front door: $800
- o Painting: $1000
- o Fitting a security alarm $800

While and meanwhile

Wedding Planners

Your sister is getting married in seven days in _____.

You need to arrange the wedding by hiring and making arrangements with the following people:

Divide the tasks between you. Each person must be met in person and you can see up to three people a day.

Name   **Location**

Florist

_____

Cake maker

_____

Priest

_____

Caterers

_____

Limo company

_____

Best Man (check he has written a good speech. If not, you write it.)_____

Wine company

_____

Venue

_____

Maid-of-Honour   Works in_____but lives
in_____

Wedding dress shop

_____

Additional Materials

Worksheet downloads in high resolution
To download all of these activities in colour and high resolution please visit http://www.bilinguanation.com/eslworksheets. Select the activity which you wish to download and type your 8 digit Manual Owner Code **QXBKLM5F** into the box (all uppercase).

Thinking about teaching ESL Online?

Then check out its accompanying book The Ultimate Teaching ESL Online Manual.

With the growing popularity of language learning platforms such as Verbling.com and Italki.com, ESL teaching online is **booming**.

Now, you too can access this market with the tools and techniques provided in **The Ultimate ESL Teaching Online Manual,** and start teaching in your extra hours or as a full-time business –all from the comfort of your own home.

With this book you will have the power to:

o   Teach both **one-on-one** and small group classes online.
o   Teach **vocabulary** with more than 25 pages of downloadable pictures for you to display on your class's shared screen.
o   Teach **grammar** with pictures and activities to practice different language points.

- Keep your students **talking** with speaking activities including roleplays, debates and story-telling, specifically designed for online lessons.
- Add **fun** and **laughter** to your classes with games designed for internet teaching
- Teach language points, **difficult to explain** in a 'non-physical' class (such as pronouns, prepositions of place, conditionals and movement verbs) with purposely designed pictures and worksheets.

Our new ESL Teaching Online Manual gives you the tools and techniques to be able to apply these ideas to internet classes.

The book contains more than **50 pages of pictures**, speaking activities and worksheets, designed to be displayed on your class's shared screen (such as those in Skype and Google Hangouts). ESL Teaching *Online* Manual owners can download these worksheets in full colour from the book's website.

Buy now from Amazon.com for $5.99-11.49 or Amazon.co.uk for £4.99-8.49. Or for more information visit our website www.bilinguanation.com

Looking for great vocabulary material for your lessons?

The Ultimate ESL Vocabulary Manual is a comprehensive and ambitious vocabulary resource for TEFL teachers.

Written over three years, the book provides material for hundreds of fantastic vocabulary classes, categorised by language function, teaching English as it is spoken by natives today.

With this book you will have the power to:

- Help student truly understand, remember and use **phrasal verbs** with a new and proven technique by teaching the deeper meaning of the particle
- Become an accomplished **business English** teacher with a comprehensive collection of verbs, compound nouns and expressions for all work functions including deadlines, launching a product, motivating, problem solving, negotiating and more.
- Impress higher-level students by diving deep into the language with native speaker **expressions** and **ways of speaking**, divided by language function.
- Help your students feel more like themselves when speaking their second language with phrases for **socialising**, expressing opinions and describing their life experience.

Buy now from Amazon.com for $5.99-11.49 and from Amazon.co.uk for $4.99-8.79.

About the Author

Hello there! My name is Andromeda and I am a writer and online English teacher.

I am the author of The Ultimate ESL Teaching Manual, The Ultimate Teaching ESL Online Manual and now the Ultimate ESL Vocabulary Manual.

I am an advocate for teaching English through oral drills and conversation exercises rather than text-books.

Teaching through oral drills is a powerful tool that requires no materials from the tutor, only your voice. In this way, every class is new and exciting with content tailor-made to your students' needs, driven by speaking activities.

When I'm not teaching or writing, I like to spend time with my husband and two kids hiking in the mountains of Scotland.

Thinking of learning Spanish?

Then check out our advanced grammar and vocabulary book 'Spanish for Geniuses.'

With detailed explanations on all grammar including verb tenses, nouns, adjectives, adverbs, pronouns, participles and the subjunctive, box-outs highlighting the differences between English and Spanish grammar and translation lists.

A comprehensive 'how do you say?' section covering phrases to use in all types of conversations including how to talk about feelings and ideas, give and receive advice, organise an event and even tell a joke.

Available now in paperback and ebook form at Amazon for $5.99-$13.99.

Or for more information visit our website www.bilinguanation.com

What people are saying about Spanish for Geniuses on Amazon

Great book for genuine Spanish speaking, by Frosties

I have really enjoyed using this book to refresh on the grammar fundamentals, however the really good thing about it is the simple way it teaches you more typical everyday words and phrases. This is so much more useful than the usual language book formats and gives lots of help with those in between words that help conversation flow more naturally. ★★★★★

60007020R00183